The Anglo-Saxon Achievement

The Anglo-Saxon Achievement

Archaeology & the beginnings of English society

Richard Hodges

Duckworth

First published in 1989 by
Gerald Duckworth & Co. Ltd.
The Old Piano Factory
43 Gloucester Crescent, London NW1

ISBN 0 7156 2130 0

British Library Cataloguing in Publication Data
Hodges, Richard
    The Anglo-Saxon achievement: archaeology & the
    beginnings of English society.
    1. Anglo-Saxon civilization. Archaeological sources
    I. Title
    942.01

    ISBN 0–7156–2130–0

Phototypeset by Input Typesetting Limited, London
and printed by
Ebenezer Baylis & Son Limited, Worcester

Contents

List of illustrations   vi
Preface   ix

1. Archaeology and the Origins of Capitalism   1

2. The Beginnings of English Society   10

3. Inflation, the Church and the Middle Saxon Shuffle   42

4. The Age of Emporia   69

5. The Carolingian Connection   115

6. The First English Industrial Revolution   150

7. The Genesis of a Miracle   186

Index   203

Illustrations

1. Excavation of the Late Saxon levels in Fishergate, Norwich. 5
2. E.T. Leeds at his excavation of an Early Anglo-Saxon village at Cassington (Oxfordshire). 11
3. Map of the Romano-British settlement at Roystone Grange (Derbyshire). 14
4. Plan of the Late Roman villa at Barton Court Farm (Oxfordshire). 18
5. Early Anglo-Saxon timber buildings at Stonea (Cambridgeshire). 19
6. Histograms showing the first-millennium settlements found in the Lincolnshire fen edge. 21
7. Early Anglo-Saxon settlement at Barton Court Farm (Oxfordshire). 27
8. Early Anglo-Saxon cremation urns in the cemetery at Spong Farm (Norfolk). 29
9. Plan and reconstruction of the aisled hall at South Cadbury (Somerset). 33
10. Comparison of Later Roman cottages and Early Anglo-Saxon timber structures. 35
11. Reconstructed Early Anglo-Saxon buildings at West Stow (Suffolk). 37
12. Graph showing the recorded progress of church-building in the kingdoms of seventh-century England as well as documented warfare and pestilence. 45
13. Excavation of the ship in mound 1 at Sutton Hoo (Suffolk) in August 1939. 47
14. Excavation of Intervention 41 at Sutton Hoo (mound 2) in 1987. 48
15. Seventh-century churches located within the ruins of major public buildings in Romano-British towns. 51
16. The Tribal Hidage. 59
17. Reconstruction of the putative timber theatre at Yeavering (Northumberland). 61
18. Schematic development between the fifth and seventh centuries of the Early Anglo-Saxon village at West Stow (Suffolk). 62

19. Diagram showing three stages in the shifting pattern of villages in the seventh century, and the changing relationship between settlements.   63
20. Burial 4 in the seventh-century secondary barrow at Wigber Low (Derbyshire).   65
21. Finds of silver sceattas of the secondary phase (c. 720–755).   75
22. Finds of silver sceattas of the porcupine-standard series attributed to mints in Frisia.   78
23. Finds of the series H secondary sceattas attributed to mint(s) at Hamwic.   79
24. Reconstruction of Hamwic.   81
25. Reconstruction of the Six Dials area of Anglo-Saxon Hamwic.   82
26. Reconstruction of a workshop in Hamwic.   87
27. Principal sites of the Middle Saxon period in eastern Kent.   93
28. Map of the proposed site of the Middle Saxon emporium of London.   95
29. Map showing finds of sceattas in Middle Anglia.   97
30. Map showing finds of sceattas in Mercia.   98
31. Middle Saxon Ipswich.   100
32. Silver penny of King Beonna of East Anglia, c. 760.   101
33. Map showing the proposed location of Eoforwic, Middle Saxon York.   103
34. Reconstruction of the Bedan monastery at Jarrow.   107
35. Brandon Staunch Meadow: excavated remains of post-built timber structures.   109
36. The sequence of excavated plans found at Raunds (Northamptonshire).   111
37. Interpretation of the phases of the remains of the Old Minster, Winchester.   125
38. The chancel and crypt at Repton (Derbyshire).   127
39. Ninth-century panel showing a pair of figures from Breedon-on-the-Hill (Leicestershire).   130
40. Excavated remains of the ninth-century stone hall at Northampton.   131
41. Reconstruction of a hand-driven mortar-mixer found beside the stone hall at Northampton.   133
42. Ninth-century silver strap-end from excavations at Portchester Castle (Hampshire).   137
43. Reconstruction of the ninth-century minster settlement at North Elmham (Norfolk).   138
44. Plan and reconstruction of the Middle Saxon water-mill excavated at Tamworth (Staffordshire).   140
45. The Fuller Brooch.   145
46. Late Saxon London.   157
47. Map showing the sources of London's tenth-century pottery.   158

48. Assemblage of tenth-century pottery from recent excavations
    in London.   159
49. Evolution of Anglo-Saxon Norwich.   163
50. Map showing mints operating in King Edgar's reign.   165
51. Anglo-Saxon charters and writs arranged by decades.   167
52. Reconstructions of the Late Saxon fortified manor and
    subsequent Early Norman castle at Goltho (Lincolnshire).   169
53. View of the excavations inside St. Martin's, Wharram Percy
    (North Yorkshire).   171
54. Raunds, Northamptonshire: development of a tenth- and
    eleventh-century graveyard.   173
55. Tenth-century stirrup from the river Witham (Lincolnshire).   175
56. King Edgar adoring Christ: the New Minster Charter, BM
    Cotton Vespasian A.viii, folio 2v.   197

*

I am grateful to the following for supplying and giving permission to
reproduce illustrations: Brian Ayres and the Norfolk Archaeological
Unit, Mark Brisbane and Southampton City Museums, Bob Carr and
the Suffolk Archaeological Unit, Professor Martin Carver and the
Sutton Hoo Trust, Dr John Collis, Professor Barry Cunliffe, Dr
Catherine Hills, John Hurst and the Medieval Settlement Research
Group, Dr Arthur MacGregor and the Ashmolean Museum, Dr P.M.
Metcalf, John Mitchell, Dr Tim Potter, Mike Shaw and the
Northampton Development Corporation, Dr Alan Vince and the
Museum of London, Keith Wade and the Suffolk Archaeological Unit.
I am also indebted to English Heritage for permission to reproduce
Fig. 56, and to the Norfolk Archaeological Unit for permission to
reproduce Fig. 43.

Preface

> What virtue can there be in studying the muddled history of an offshore
> island, whose supposed achievements have turned out to be illusory?
> (G.R. Elton)[1]

In this book I aim to illustrate Anglo-Saxon history from a new
perspective which may offer valuable insights into the way the island
race developed. The wealth of new archaeological data from recent
projects in England, as well as on the Continent, favours such an
approach. Many of these projects may provide outstanding contri-
butions to European history. Yet too often the labours of skilful
archaeologists are reduced to incidental episodes worthy only of the
margins of Sellar and Yeatman's comic masterpiece *1066 and All
That*. Worse still, these labours are transformed into what Eric R.
Wolf has described as a developmental history: 'a moral success story,
a race in time in which each runner of the race passes on the torch of
liberty to the next relay.' Wolf goes on to claim that 'history is thus
converted into a tale about the furtherance of virtue, about how the
virtuous win out over the bad guys'.[2] People who are denied history,
he argues, have made as powerful a contribution to the modern world
as the historical figures familiar to us. Archaeologists should be
emboldened by Wolf's thesis, as most archaeological data are
concerned with the small farms and simple town dwellings once occupied by those 'denied history'.

I owe the central theme of this book, however, to Alan Macfarlane's
controversial work, and to the opportunity to participate in a seminar
at Cambridge on 'The European Miracle'. Modern historians and
anthropologists, I learnt, are re-examining the contexts of the Industrial Revolution and the rise of capitalism. Nowhere is this more
evident than in Macfarlane's essay on the individual in later medieval
and early modern times.[3] Essentially Macfarlane challenged the
commonly held view that the English peasantry in those times
suffered a drudgery that was as socially and economically restrictive

1. G.R. Elton, *The History of England* (Cambridge, 1984), 13.
2. Eric R. Wolf, *Europe and the People without History* (Berkeley, 1982), 5.
3. Alan MacFarlane, *The Origins of English Individualism* (Oxford, 1978).

as that endured by many modern peasantries. He believed it was more socially advanced, and that it shared a strong sense of personal identity.

Not everyone, it should be stressed, is sympathetic to Macfarlane's thesis. Some contend that he replaced one myth with another. Most are unhappy about the sharp distinction drawn between the English and their Continental neighbours. Yet one point is shared by Macfarlane and his critics. Both have a very traditional perspective of Anglo-Saxon history. In their appraisals of first-millennium origins they revert to a form of history alien to their normal critical styles. They seldom acknowledge that in this crucial period, as the English nation was being shaped, the historical sources to which they relate best are either rare or absent. Most notably, only a scant documentary record survives in Anglo-Saxon times for the farmers who constitute the forebears of the late medieval peasantry. Almost all of the surviving documentation concerns the Anglo-Saxon elite.

Yet it would be no exaggeration to claim that the medieval and modern experience owes something to the emergence of the nation-state in Anglo-Saxon times. It makes sense to pursue the genesis of our culture back to the age of King Alfred, and even to the Anglo-Saxon migrations. Here archaeological stratigraphy can be as significant as any form of Anglo-Saxon documentation in illuminating this quasi-prehistoric age. Of course, only a fool would scorn the written sources. Together the two bodies of data offer an often patchy, but potentially invaluable, perspective.

In this book I have avoided summarising the archaeological or historical data. Furthermore I have avoided any explicit statement about the inherent archaeological methodology, since I have set out my views on this matter elsewhere.[4] This, therefore, is neither an archaeology book nor a history book using archaeology to illuminate its margins. Rather it is a view of the history of the period based on my interpretation and observations of the archaeological and historical data. It is patently a sketch which, in common with all accounts of the period, stands in need of more evidence. I cannot pretend, for example, that my analysis of the political history of Anglo-Saxon England is anything but rudimentary and at times verging on the naïve. I hope, however, that it will help archaeologists and historians to pilot their way through new encounters as the archaeological record becomes more substantive, as it inevitably will.

While writing, I have often reflected upon my good fortune to have attended as a student the stimulating lectures of Peter Addyman and Martin Biddle on Anglo-Saxon archaeology, and of Paul Harvey and

4. Richard Hodges, 'Method and theory in medieval archaeology', *Archeologia Medievale* VIII (1982), 7–38; *Primitive and Peasant Markets* (Oxford, 1988).

Colin Platt on the archaeology and history of post-Conquest England. Since then Colin Renfrew has encouraged my pursuit of the themes developed here in an inimitable and profoundly fascinating way. As in my previous studies of the first millennium, I owe an enormous debt to Klavs Randsborg for his original and wide-ranging insights. More recently, I have benefited from valuable discussions with the following: Philip Andrews and Mark Brisbane, currently working at Southampton; Richard Gem, on Anglo-Saxon architecture; Andrew Boddington, Glenn Foard and others of the Raunds team; Alan Vince, on the Middle Saxon history of London; Keith Wade and Bob Carr, directors of the excavations at Ipswich and Brandon respectively; Mark Blackburn and Philip Grierson, on Anglo-Saxon coinage; and David Hill, with his highly idiosyncratic views on everything, including Anglo-Saxon England. I am also indebted to John A. Hall and Michael Mann for the chance to attend the seminar on the European Miracle at Emmanuel College, Cambridge in September 1985; to the ESRC for a personal research grant which afforded me leave between November 1986 and April 1987 to explore many of the themes arising from the San Vincenzo Project; and to the Danish Research Council for electing me to a Visiting Professorship at Copenhagen, between December 1987 and May 1988, where I was able to finish the last of three drafts.

Strange as it may seem, much of the book has grown out of the San Vincenzo Project in Italy. I am especially grateful to Peter Hayes, John Mitchell, John Patterson and Chris Wickham, my principal colleagues in this enterprise, for turning my attention in new directions. Finally, I thank Nicoletta and Riccardo Francovich for their incomparable hospitality and memorable discussions in the most affable of European settings.

In the matter of preparing the book, I am indebted to Deborah Blake and Colin Haycraft for their patience and sound advice as I worked through the three drafts. Barry Vincent has skilfully prepared the line drawings.

Lastly, I am eternally grateful to my wife, Debbie, and our two small children, Charlotte and William, for creating the happy atmosphere in which this protracted venture has been nurtured.

University of Sheffield   R.H.

To Charlotte & William

1

Archaeology and the Origins of Capitalism

At the risk of being taxed with an impenitent liberalism, I say. . .that in order to mount the multiple thresholds of history, all doors seem to be good. None of us knows all of them. At first the historian opens onto the past the door he is most familiar with. But if he wants to see as far as pos sible, necessarily he will knock on one door, then another. Each time a new vista will open to him, and he is not worthy of the name historian if he does not juxtapose some of them: cultural and social vistas, cultural and political, social and economic, economic and political.

(Fernand Braudel)[1]

Archaeology opens a new vista on to the Anglo-Saxons. The image conjured up seems at first remote. Yet there is a sense that the modern nation stems from a lineage dating back to these distant times. Popular historians, from Churchill to Michael Wood, have paid attention to the first-millennium roots of the English.[2] Unlike many European nations, the English owe almost nothing in recent centuries to revolutions. A more or less unbroken line connects the age of Bede with the Industrial Revolution, and thence with us. Only 1066, wittily caricatured in the comic history of Sellar and Yeatman,[3] interrupted the flow of history. Nevertheless this epic story is treated in two different ways. The history of post-Conquest England is the subject of rigorous scrutiny and debate, while historians of the Anglo-Saxons have tinkered with the details but barely altered the framework. The crucial question of how the English identity was forged is generally answered simply by charting the Germanic migrations and the tribal histories that followed.

The dichotomy between pre- and post-Conquest analysis has become sharper in recent years as historians of later medieval England have claimed that their period was the making of the modern age. They point to a complex society which takes shape, to some extent, with the Normans and Plantagenets. They emphasise family relations, village stratification, commodity circulation and economic issues affecting the

1. Fernand Braudel, *On History* (Chicago, 1980), 1.
2. Winston Churchill, *A History of the English-Speaking Peoples* (London, 1950); Michael Wood, *In Search of the Dark Ages* (London, 1982).
3. W.C. Sellar & R.J. Yeatman, *1066 and All That* (London, 1930).

majority. The most controversial example of this kind of history is Alan Macfarlane's *Origins of English Individualism*.[4]

Macfarlane challenged a long-held thesis about the contribution of the English to modern capitalism. He argued that the apparent changes in basic social and economic structure between 1400 and 1700 did not take place at all, but are an illusion created largely by the surviving documents. England in 1400 was far more advanced than is generally allowed. The concept of private, absolute property was already fully developed; the household was not the basic social and economic unit but had been replaced already by the individual; a money economy was widely established, and there was a large class of full-time wage-labourers. The drive towards accumulation and profit, Macfarlane believed, was well entrenched in later medieval England. Kinship groups had been dissolved, so that the individual was not wholly subordinated to large family structures. People were geographically and socially mobile.

Macfarlane traced the roots of this condition to the thirteenth century – 'the present limits of my competence' – contending that the thirteenth-century peasant was not a peasant in the sense familiar to anthropologists. The traditional definition of the peasant is someone wedded to the land: someone engaged in neither an agricultural nor a commodity market. A peasant society traditionally produces to fulfil fiscal obligations to a seigneurial class and to consume what remains. Little or nothing is produced for surplus exchange. By contrast, the social relations underpinning the Industrial Revolution existed centuries before the Stuarts. In short, a social identity existed that distinguished the English from their Continental neighbours and thereby facilitated the smooth transition to the capitalist world.

If we took this thesis literally it would be tempting to attribute the origins of capitalism to the thirteenth century or even earlier. As Macfarlane briefly shows, Marx, among others, had at least considered this. But for Marx the capitalist mode of production had three inter-related characteristics. First, capitalists keep control of the means of production; secondly, labourers are denied independent access to the means of production and so must sell their labour to the capitalists; thirdly, the maximisation of surplus produced by the labourers, while the means of production is owned by the capitalists, leads to ceaseless accumulation, accompanied by changes in methods of production. This accumulation, in Marx's opinion, was made possible and actual by the monetisation of the economy. It began with the separation of town and country and was based upon a necessary division of classes. But Marx in fact was opposed to the notion of mercantile capitalism and dismissed any measure of proto-capitalism. (And, we may suspect, this

4. Alan Macfarlane, *The Origins of English Individualism* (Oxford, 1978).

is how he would have interpreted Macfarlane's thesis.) Capitalism – to be capitalism in his sense – must be capitalism-in-production.[5]

But Macfarlane hinted that the medieval personality of England owed much to even earlier generations. Indeed he searched for its origins as far back as 1066, though he did not probe further. 1066, of course, is not simply a date: it is shorthand for the divide between the Dark and Middle Ages and marks the point beyond which peasants cannot be identified from written sources.[6]

Macfarlane's book has generated a great deal of criticism. David Cannadine, for instance, dismissed it derisively as a 'Thatcherite, Little England interpretation of Britain's past. . .ignoring most of the available evidence'.[7] Many historians favour the general approach but are unconvinced that England was very different from her Continental neighbours in later medieval times.[8] Richard Smith, on the other hand, agrees that 'a major task awaiting students of society. . .is to increase our understanding of the long-term dialectic of economic individualism and political and philosophical collectivism that exists as a recurring theme in England both past and present'.[9] J.C.A. Pocock made a similar point, adding that Macfarlane 'is now free to embark on the study of Cymric, Anglo-Saxon and Norse villages during the half-millennium or so before 1200 – when churlish individualism may well have flourished as richly as in later ages'.[10]

In this book I seek to investigate the makings of the English identity in the half-millennium before 1200 or, to be precise, before the Norman Conquest. The origins – or, perhaps more accurately, the genesis – of England's distinctive medieval personality, I contend, must be sought in the first, not the second, millennium.

A crucial aspect of the enquiry is the formation of the English state. We must investigate the demise of Roman Britain, the Anglo-Saxon

5. In describing capitalism I have been influenced by Eric R. Wolf, *Europe and the People without History* (Berkeley, 1982), 77–9.

6. Macfarlane, op. cit. (n. 4); Paul Harvey, *The Peasant Land Market in Medieval England* (Oxford, 1984), 356 also interprets Macfarlane as I have done.

7. David Cannadine, 'British history: past, present and future', *Past and Present* 116 (1987), 168–91 at 89 and n. 57.

8. Some important criticisms are made by Lloyd Bonfield, 'Normative rules and property transmission: reflections on the link between marriage and inheritance in early modern England', in L. Bonfield, R. Smith & K. Wrightson (eds.), *The World We Have Gained* (Oxford, 1986), 154–76, at 176. Bonfield, like many historians, believes Macfarlane exaggerates those differences with the Continent. Bonfield favours John Hajnal's view described in 'Two kinds of pre-industrial household formation system', in R. Wall (ed.), *Family Forms in Historic Europe* (London, 1983), 65–104, that England shares many similarities in these matters with regional parts of western Europe.

9. Richard M. Smith, ' "Modernisation" and the corporate medieval village community in England: some sceptical reflections', in A.H.R. Baker & D. Gregory (eds.), *Explanation in Historical Geography* (Cambridge, 1984), 140–79, at 178–9.

10. J. Pocock, review of Alan Macfarlane's *The Origins of English Individualism*, in *History and Theory* 19 (1980), 100–5, at 104.

invasions and the impact of the missionaries. But it is not enough to accept the later written descriptions of these momentous events. They are too partisan, too quixotic and, in certain cases, plainly misleading. This does not mean, as Patrick Sims-Williams supposes,[11] that the detailed record of the age is entirely lost. In the absence of village records, which are the stuff of later medieval history, we can make far more use of archaeology to bring this largely prehistoric age to life. Just as a new wave of historians is questioning the validity of their (written) sources, so archaeologists are beginning to understand theirs.

Modern archaeological fieldwork directs our attention to the widening European orbit within which Anglo-Saxon history took shape. It helps us appreciate the international context of the age of Arthur; it compels us to assess St Augustine and the introduction of Christianity to the English in a pan-European perspective; and it adds a crucial new dimension to the evolution of English kingship. In his European setting Alfred, while dealing with the Danish Vikings in the late ninth century, assumes a critical part in the making of the English. Archaeological evidence, in fact, enables us (to paraphrase Marc Bloch) to put the right questions to the episodic written sources which constitute our witnesses.

History and archaeology

'Heroic history', wrote Marshall Sahlins, 'proceeds more like "Fennimore Cooper Indians" – to use Elman Service's characterization: each man, as they walk single file along the trail, careful to step in the footprints of the one ahead, so as to leave the impression of One Giant Indian.'[12] Sahlins argues that heroic history involves individuals who, as he puts it (citing a Maori chief), live the life of a whole tribe.[13] This is not Great Man Theory; it is acknowledging that the role of the individual in pre-state societies can be immensely significant. In this way we account for the impression left by King Arthur, St Augustine, Bede, King Offa, Alcuin, King Alfred, Bishop Aethelwold and even King Canute. Each, by mastering his community, has bequeathed a trail which conjures a sense of perpetual progress. It would be easy to conclude, as Macfarlane perhaps intended, that the trail culminates in thirteenth-century England, whence it appears to lead directly to the Industrial Revolution and the age of capitalism.

Naturally the trail is not so straightforward. Not all heroic history involved tribes who were prepared to follow their leaders. The Middle

11. Patrick Sims-Williams, 'The settlement of England in Bede and the *Chronicle*', *Anglo-Saxon England* 12 (1983), 1–41.
12. Marshall Sahlins, *Islands of History* (Chicago, 1985), 36–7.
13. ibid., 35.

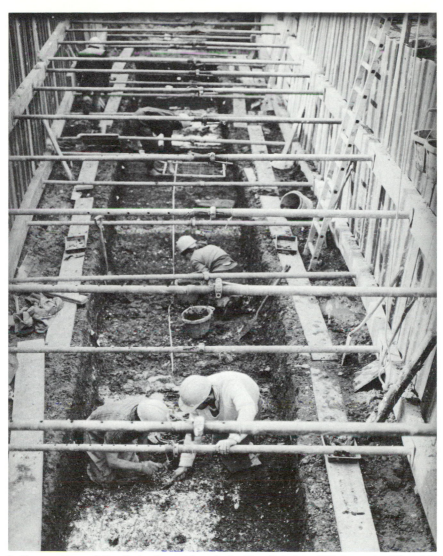

1. Excavation of the Late Saxon levels in the district of Fishergate, Norwich (courtesy of Brian Ayres and the Norfolk Archaeological Unit).

Saxon epic *Beowulf* neatly contrasts the heroic king with the other self-possessed characters. These cause disruption and dismay, while the king (to put it simply) concentrates on living his life for his tribesmen. Hence, although a trail across the ages exists (fifth-century tribal England produces a largely coherent state five centuries later), it would be foolish to ignore the other, often disruptive, aspects of Anglo-Saxon history.

The pattern of progress is charted unconvincingly in most recent histories. The individuals who figure in the documentary sources lack substance: we are told what the sources wished us to be told. More often, histories of Anglo-Saxon England concentrate on what Fernand Braudel colourfully describes as surface disturbances, crests of foam that the tides of time carry on their backs. *L'histoire événementielle*, as Braudel defines it, begins to be comprehensible only when it is set in the context of two other rhythms of past time. The first, according to him, might best be imagined as the waves bearing the foam – the rhythm of social process. The second (to extend the metaphor) is the sea itself – the *longue durée* – man's relationship with his environment. Human history, in Braudel's view, is guided by the unpredictable conjunction of these rhythms of time.[14] Viewed thus, the Indians and the trail on which they are journeying are mere strands in the history of which they are a part. Climate, the geographical setting, the unfolding social configurations and the economic relations created as a result transform the caricatures into human actors.

Braudel's Olympian vision of history inevitably depends upon the sources. He was a master of early modern history. From the thirteenth century onwards, as Macfarlane acknowledges, detailed records, from state to manorial level, make it feasible to reconstruct the rhythms of time. But for the first millennium the written sources are primarily chronicles, biographies, letters and poems. Few wills and charters survive before about 950, and virtually no records of village life. The historian is at an obvious disadvantage. With these personal sources only at his disposal, it is not surprising that the result commonly amounts to what Colin Renfrew has termed the 'Dark Age myth', which he defines as follows:[15]

(a) Attempt by new power groups to establish legitimacy in historical terms with the creation of genealogies either (i) seeking to find a link with the 'autochthonous' former state or (ii) relating the deeds by which the 'invaders' achieved power by force of arms.

(b) Tendency among early chroniclers to personalise historical explanation, so that change is assigned to individual deeds, battles, and invasions, and often to attribute the decline to hostile powers outside the state territories.

(c) Some confusion in legend and story beween the Golden Age of the early vanished civilisation and the Heroic Age of its immediate aftermath.

(d) Paucity of archaeological evidence after collapse compared with that for preceding period (arising from loss of literacy and abandonment or diminution of urban centres).

14. Fernand Braudel, *The Mediterranean and the Mediterranean World in the Age of Philip II* (London, 1972), 21.
15. Colin Renfrew, 'Systems collapse as social transformation: catastrophe and anastrophe in early state societies', in C. Renfrew & K.L. Cooke (eds.), *Transformations* (London, 1979), 484.

(e) Tendency among historians to accept as evidence traditional narratives first set down in writing some centuries after the collapse.

(f) Slow development of Dark Age archaeology, hampered both by the preceding item and by focus on the larger and more obvious central place sites of the vanished state.

The myth itself is a feature of Anglo-Saxon history. Anglo-Saxon authors, such as Bede or the compilers of the Anglo-Saxon Chronicle, began the process. As Renfrew points out, it was in their political interest to project history in this form. Modern historians, to be fair, are well aware of this.[16] None the less the literal acceptance of the Anglo-Saxon invasions as a crucial factor in the making of a new society after the Romans, the axial part played by the Church, and the Christian virtues of later Saxon kingship (to name just three issues) are still the stuff of modern interpretations. These issues were embellished by the Victorians. On the one hand, they admired classical civilisation and abominated the barbarian invasions: classical culture became in many ways a symbol of the British Empire. On the other, they admired the British and Anglo-Saxon heroes who introduced and defended Christianity. Men of empire and missionaries were needed to work in Victoria's pagan territories.[17] Nineteenth-century historians therefore lauded King Arthur, in whom the legacy of Christian Rome was invested. Likewise King Alfred, defender of the realm – the First Lion of the English, as William Manchester calls him in his notable biography of the 'Last Lion', Winston Churchill[18] – was the subject of statues, portraits and popular stories. These simple portraits do not appeal to twentieth-century historians. Yet to some extent, in less exaggerated form, they have remained the stuff of modern interpretations as well. Roman Britain is therefore commonly regarded as the benchmark of civilisation, while the Anglo-Saxon age marks the onset of barbarism.[19]

Of course the myth takes no account of the intricate social relations that made the Anglo-Saxons an enduring society, in marked contrast to Roman Britain. Furthermore the myth diverts our attention from the confrontation of ideal and reality which forms an integral part of the history of all societies. In fact it is a thread woven through most of the major written sources of the age.

The central argument of this book is constructed upon new archaeological data employed to reveal reality as well as the character of the

16. e.g. Sims-Williams, op. cit. (n. 11).

17. Janet L. Nelson, 'Myths of the Dark Ages', in L. Smith (ed.), *The Making of Britain: The Dark Ages* (London, 1984), 145–58.

18. William Manchester, *The Last Lion: Winston Spencer Churchill. Visions of Glory 1874–1932* (London, 1983), esp. 3–18.

19. Michael J. Rowlands, 'The concept of Europe in prehistory', *Man* 22 (1987), 558–9 at 559.

Dark Age myth. It goes without saying, however, that archaeological data are a controversial source of evidence. In a recent text-book on the Anglo-Saxons, James Campbell trenchantly asserts that 'it is an illusion that archaeology can tell you what happened, it cannot; by its nature it cannot do more than provide an imperfect echo of what happened'.[20] This is not an uncommon standpoint. In fairness to historians, they should not be criticised for the failure of archaeologists to do more than echo historical studies. Archaeology often remains the driest dust that blows – a fact which a generation ago worried no less distinguished an archaeologist than Sir Mortimer Wheeler.

Campbell, to judge from the influential book he edited, *The Anglo-Saxons*, has a rather antiquarian view of archaeology. Archaeological sites and objects appear as embellishments throughout his text.[21] Such a use of archaeology was prevalent in the first sixty years of the century, referred to by Renfrew as the 'long sleep'.[22] Modern archaeology, Renfrew believes, came about with 'the great awakening' of the late sixties and seventies, when the subject became inter-disciplinary in outlook. Scientific analysis, rather than antiquarianism, is the stock of archaeology today.

This new archaeology in many ways suits the needs of modern historians. Man's relationship with his environment is a prominent theme of modern archaeology. The rhythms of this relationship are an important contribution to Anglo-Saxon history. In regions as diverse as the Sandlings of Suffolk or the Lincolnshire Fens, archaeology is more than an imperfect historical echo. As we shall see, it offers a way of bringing these otherwise poorly documented areas within the scope of mainstream history. Similarly social and economic processes figure largely in archaeology studies today. Regional field-work programmes reveal the changing landscape. At the same time large-scale excavations show how different sites in the settlement hierarchy are integral to the landscape. The hierarchy itself, of course, is revealing. So too are its components: the history of production (industrial and technical, agrarian, human), the history of trade, the history of consumption at different points in the settlement hierarchy, and cultural history through time at different points in the hierarchy. No written sources offer such detail.

The great awakening, however, amounts to more than this. In common with historians of the celebrated Annales school, of which Braudel was a great advocate, archaeologists have broadened the scope of their intellectual enquiries. Concepts and models have been borrowed from anthropology, geography and sociology. These offer

20. James Campbell (ed.), *The Anglo-Saxons* (Oxford, 1982), 37.

21. ibid.

22. Colin Renfrew, 'Explanation revisited', in C. Renfrew, M. Rowlands & B. Segraves-Whallon (eds.), *Theory and Explanation in Archaeology* (London, 1982), 6–7.

new vistas, even though in the end they may prove no more attractive as hypotheses than those previously favoured. What matters is to re-examine the period by opening new doors. This should enable us to consider the existing sources afresh, thereby enriching the discipline.

The great awakening also involves a widening of horizons. In a study of the English it is tempting for English historians to become insular. Such a view is at odds with the sweep of history. For the past hundred years nationalism, paradoxically, has had fixed barriers, at the same time as international commercial relations have flourished. This strange contradiction has caused some people to believe that far-flung commercial and political relations have existed only in modern times. Nothing is further from the truth. Palaeolithic and Mesolithic hunters wandered extensively across the European landmass. Sinuous exchange networks united the first Neolithic farming communities. Iron Age society likewise included highly mobile groups and individuals.[23] The Romans created an empire that embraced people far beyond its frontiers who were clearly captivated by its material wonders. Roman manufactured goods not only reached the wildest parts of the British province but also Russia, Sri Lanka and central Africa. The Christian missionaries of Anglo-Saxon times offer a well-documented illustration of England's European connections.[24] At the same time many Anglo-Saxon objects occur on the Continent, while some beads have been found as far away as Dar es Salaam.[25] In short, England's insularity was for the most part relative.

This book, therefore, seeks to throw further light on Macfarlane's thesis by cross-examining traditional sources from a new angle. I cannot claim to pinpoint precisely the origins of capitalism, or the beginnings of English individualism. Nevertheless archaeology allows us to chart the genesis of English individualism and the social division of labour. It allows us also to detect the preconditions for capitalism, attributed by Marx himself in *Grundrisse* to the High Middle Ages, and to ascribe them instead to the curious synthesis of ancient and medieval societies of the first millennium.[26] Above all, these rough notes are intended to show that the singular propensities which caught Macfarlane's imagination were present in English society from its beginnings.

23. See, for example, M.J. Rowlands, ' "Europe in Prehistory": A unique form of primitive capitalism?', *Culture and History* 1 (1987), 63–78.

24. Wilhelm Levison, *England and the Continent in the Eighth Century* (Oxford, 1948).

25. Joan R. Harding, 'Two Frankish beads from Tanganyika', *Medieval Archaeology* 4 (1960), 126–7.

26. Karl Marx, *Pre-capitalist Economic Formations* (London, 1964), 110–20.

2

The Beginnings of English Society

> I confess that the more I examine this question, the more completely I
> am convinced that the received accounts of our migrations, our subsequent
> fortunes, and ultimate settlement, are devoid of historical truth in every
> detail.   (J.M. Kemble)[1]

Kemble's view of the Anglo-Saxon invasions, written more than a
century ago, appears particularly perspicacious now. But for most of
this century a contrary thesis has held sway. Two eminent Oxford
archaeologists, E.T. Leeds and J.N.L. Myres, followed by their many
students, embellished Bede's laconic eighth-century description of the
invasion of Britain by Angles, Saxons and Jutes. Using the grave
goods found in the many hundreds of fifth- to seventh-century
cemeteries belonging to this period, they have constructed a detailed
picture of the Anglo-Saxon settlement.[2] The invasion hypothesis
following the cataclysmic end of Roman Britain, like the Norman
Conquest of 1066, has become a traditional chronological horizon,
punctuating the long history of Britain. Yet, as with all invasions and
migrations, we must distinguish between myth and reality. Moreover
it must be noted that in the galaxy of myths describing the origins of
nations few can be stranger than England's: with the extinction of
Roman civilisation came barbarian warriors, from whom the Anglo-
Saxons are descended.

Kemble, it seems, was sensitive to the oversimplification of later
Roman and Early Anglo-Saxon history. So too was Leeds, who brought
some scientific rigour to the study of the period. His outstanding
achievement was to initiate an interest in the settlements associated
with Anglo-Saxon cemeteries. At Cassington, Oxfordshire, he undertook the first excavations of an Early Anglo-Saxon village.[3] Unfortunately his skills as an excavator were limited (Fig. 2). Only the many

---

1. J.M. Kemble, *Saxons in England* (Oxford, 1849) 1, 16; see also R.A. Wiley, 'Anglo-
Saxon Kemble. The life and works of John Mitchell Kemble 1807–1857', in D. Brown
et al. (eds.), *Anglo-Saxon Studies in Archaeology and History* (Oxford, 1979), 165–273.
2. E.T. Leeds, *The Archaeology of the Anglo-Saxon Settlements* (Oxford, 1913); J.N.L.
Myres, *The English Settlements* (Oxford, 1986).
3. E.T. Leeds, 'A Saxon village near Sutton Courtenay, Berkshire (third report)',
Archaeologia 92 (1947), 79–93.

2. E.T. Leeds taking notes on his excavations of an Early Anglo-Saxon village at Cassington (Oxfordshire) (courtesy of the Ashmolean Museum).

sunken huts at Cassington (probably working-sheds and store-rooms) were discovered, while the post-holes relating to timber halls were ignored. As a result the excavations seemed to confirm a picture of barbaric living consistent with the written sources.

In recent years the pendulum of opinion has swung in the opposite direction for three reasons. First, the invasion hypothesis in prehistory has come under critical scrutiny. Indeed most prehistorians now doubt that there were invasions or migrations in the early Neolithic and early Bronze Age. Their reasoning, drawing upon a miscellany of anthropological parallels, has not been lost on Anglo-Saxonists.[4] Secondly, the quality of excavations has improved enormously in

4. C.J. Arnold, *Roman Britain to Saxon England* (London, 1984); usefully reviewed by Philip Dixon in *Landscape History* 6 (1984), 21–5.

recent decades, enabling Roman archaeologists to chart the final ephemeral phases of Roman settlements, and permitting the discovery, excavation and interpretation of Anglo-Saxon sites that consist of little more than post-holes relating to the superimposed plans of timber halls. Such sites offer a graphic impression of the age which deviates sharply from the fashionable, cataclysmic thesis. Had Leeds witnessed such excavations, he might have questioned the invasion hypothesis. Thirdly, even if he remained unconvinced by skilfully excavated sites of the period, he would probably not have ignored the recent studies of historians David Dumville and Patrick Sims-Williams.[5] They have cast doubt on the details of the settlement described at a later date, notably by Gildas and Bede: these texts, so we now learn, tell us more of their authors and their view of the world than of the history they describe. Both historians urge archaeologists (and linguists) to construct hypotheses which might be used to cross-examine the texts. Sims-Williams concludes, however, citing Kemble in 1849: 'I look upon the genuine details of the German conquests in England as irrevocably lost to us.'[6]

At present I agree with Kemble. The archaeology is too patchy to offer a picture of the changing configurations of the myriad regions of sub-Roman Britain. In the first place, while we are well-informed about the decline of Roman towns, forts and villas, too few peasant farmsteads have been excavated. The process of transition from Romano-British peasant to Anglo-Saxon ceorl remains unclear. Likewise too few Anglo-Saxon villages have been discovered, and only a handful are related to cemeteries. Even the ubiquitous cemetery data have to be treated with caution. Most of the thousands of graves were excavated in the age of Kemble, and modern techniques reveal how much more is to be learned by painstaking stratigraphic fieldwork. Even so, the archaeology may offer new vistas of the age (to repeat Braudel's contention, quoted above), and it is inconceivable that we could ignore it in any consideration of the roots of English individualism. On the contrary, the archaeological evidence, as we shall see, points to the decline of the Roman province and the emergence of the English tribes as among the most formative phases in the history of English culture.

The end of Roman Britain

Fifty years ago O.G.S. Crawford questioned the English 'debt to Rome', and decided that there was none,[7] identifying a clean break between

5. e.g. Patrick Sims-Williams, 'The settlement of England in Bede and the *Chronicle*', *Anglo-Saxon England* 12 (1983), 1–41.

6. ibid., 41.

7. O.G.S. Crawford, 'Our debt to Rome?', *Antiquity* 2 (1928), 173–88.

the Roman and the Anglo-Saxon past. Recently Kathleen Biddick has used her studies of later prehistoric, Romano-British and Anglo-Saxon animal-bone assemblages to argue the reverse. The faunal collections, she contends, suggest a continuum of pastoral farming from later prehistory until the seventh or eighth century. Prehistoric territorial organisation, she believes, remained unaltered by the Romans and was only transformed in Middle Saxon times.[8] There is room, however, for a third thesis about the lasting impact of Roman imperialism on Britain.

The Romans obviously introduced aspects of their Mediterranean culture to Britain. Towns, forts and villas in which the British elite were cultivated by a pan-European culture undeniably contributed to the eclipse of Iron Age political organisation. Of greater significance, however, were the changes in agricultural practice. Intensive systems had existed in central southern England and parts of East Anglia on the eve of Claudius' invasion in AD 43. By the mid-second century, as surveys in Essex, Nottinghamshire, the Lincolnshire Fens, the Peak District (Fig. 3) and the Yorkshire Wolds now show, virtually every part of the province was covered by a mesh of fields, within which were located a multitude of new farms.[9] As in all the provinces of the Empire, the Romans were raising revenues through the creation of surplus agricultural products, minerals and, of course, taxation. State bureaucracy and markets had replaced tribal economics.

The history of the peasant population is still hardly known. Yet, as we shall see, it is an important aspect of the Early Anglo-Saxon period. In particular, how were these people persuaded to colonise new ground, and to build new villages, farms and the miles of field walls, banks and hedges? In comparison with the scale of agricultural transformation, the construction of towns and villas was a minor achievement. The sudden expansion in the population of Britain made this transformation possible to some extent. As P.J. Fowler has pointed out, 'the Romano-British population was certainly much larger than that conventionally estimated from Domesday Book...clearly undermining one of the assumptions of English history, viz. that the popu-

8. Kathleen Biddick, 'Field edge, forest edge: early medieval social change and resource allocation', in K. Biddick (ed.), *Archaeological Approaches to Medieval Europe* (Kalamazoo, 1984), 105–18, at 106.

9. For Essex see W.J. Rodwell & K.A. Rodwell, *Rivenhall: investigations of a villa, church, and village* (London, 1986) (though see also the review by M. Millett, 'The question of continuity: Rivenhall reviewed', *Archaeological Journal* 144 (1987), 434–37; Lincolnshire: P.P. Hayes, 'Roman to Saxon in the south Lincolnshire Fens', *Antiquity* 62 (1988), 371–7; for Nottinghamshire: Derrick Riley, *Early Landscape from the Air* (Sheffield, 1980); see also Richard Hodges & Martin Wildgoose, 'Roman or native in the White Peak?' *Derbyshire Archaeological Journal* 101 (1981), 42–57; Colin Hayfield, *An Archaeological Survey of the Parish of Wharram Percy: the evolution of the Roman landscape* (Oxford, 1987).

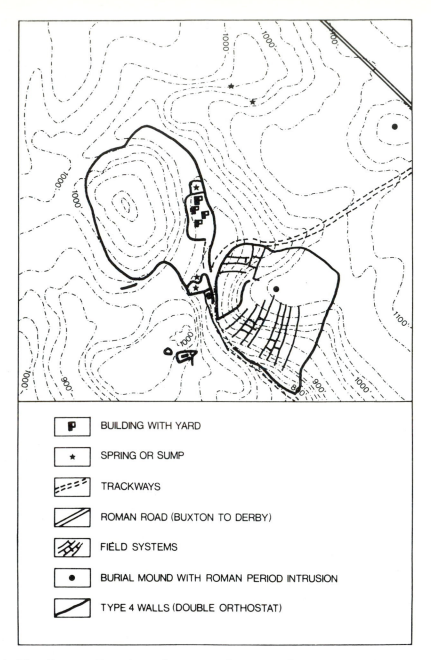

P	BUILDING WITH YARD
★	SPRING OR SUMP
⌐===⌐	TRACKWAYS
⟋	ROMAN ROAD (BUXTON TO DERBY)
⧸⧸⧸	FIELD SYSTEMS
●	BURIAL MOUND WITH ROMAN PERIOD INTRUSION
⟋	TYPE 4 WALLS (DOUBLE ORTHOSTAT)

3. The Romano-British settlement at Roystone Grange (Derbyshire). The settlement is typical of the upland White Peak communities, with a western enclosure for in-field winter grazing, an eastern enclosure for growing arable crops, and access to extensive pasture for summer grazing (drawn by Barry Vincent after Richard Hodges and Martin Wildgoose).

lation in 1086 was greater than at any previous time'.[10] Fowler estimates a second- to third-century population of three million or more – that is, about three times larger than the population of the Late Iron Age or at 1086. The difference between the population at its zenith in Roman times and, say, 1086 is most apparent in marginal areas. Villages existed, for example, throughout the Peak District by AD 200, whereas the region was largely uninhabited in later prehistory and comparatively uninhabited in Norman times.[11]

In general, however, the few excavations of peasant cottages show that they were adequately equipped with material goods. Pottery and other objects suggest a greater affluence than was available to their counterparts in the Mediterranean. This impression (and it is no more) may explain how the drudgery of intensification was mitigated. The opportunity of sharing in the Roman imperial market offered material incentives unknown in prehistoric Britain. A critical threshold in this expansion, however, was certain to be reached when the imperial market system became over-extended or suffered from recession, or when the incentives to produce were no longer perceived as attractive.

In common with tribesmen beyond the imperial frontiers, tribesmen in Britain – one of Rome's most distant provinces – were bound to suffer economic reversals before, and on a greater scale than, those close to the heart of the Empire. The critical threshold in the imperial economy was reached in the third century. The crisis that has galvanised the attention of historians of ancient Italy had a more immediate impact upon the far-flung provinces, and especially on those whose economic expectations had been created by the boom of the early Empire. Recent fieldwork in the Pennines and Fens, for example, confirms the early decline of the farms in these margins. Many sites were abandoned in the later third or early fourth century. Everywhere the rural settlement structure was altered. As in Italy, some peasants probably migrated from their homes, seeking new opportunities; in the Fens, for example, a new estate centre has been identified at Stonea near March.[12] Others may have migrated to the towns. According to E.H. Thompson, some displaced British peasants may have disturbed the Roman peace in the late fourth century, much as their Gallic counterparts did a century before.[13] But the vast majority disappeared in much the same way as they had come: strange as it may seem to us, they adapted their reproductive strategies to suit the

10. P.J. Fowler, 'The countryside in Roman Britain: a study in failure or a failure in study', *Landscape History* 5 (1983), 5–9, at 8–9; see also Peter Salway, *Roman Britain* (Oxford, 1981), 544; and Michael Fulford, 'Demonstrating Britannia's economic dependence in the first and second centuries', in T.F.C. Blagg & A.C. King (eds.), *Military and Civilian in Roman Britain* (Oxford, 1984), 129–42, at 131.

11. Hodges & Wildgoose, op. cit. (n. 9).

12. (Tim Potter), 'Stonea', *Current Archaeology* 81 (1982), 298–301.

13. E.A. Thompson, 'Britain AD 406–410', *Britannia* 8 (1977), 308–18.

economic circumstances. Quite how they did this remains a mystery. Only a scientific analysis of appropriate cemetery populations will illuminate this vexing historical issue.[14]

The third-century crisis is often overlooked by traditional historians of Roman Britain, partly because of the apotheosis of the villa tradition in southern Britain in the early fourth century. Sprawling new country houses, reminiscent in their grandeur of England's eighteenth-century aristocracy, superseded villas which had hitherto been modest by European standards. Great country houses like Chedworth (Gloucester) and Gatcombe (Somerset) for two or three generations were remarkable reactions to the economic and political crises. These members of the elite may have profited to some extent from the reorganisation of the Empire after Rome and Constantinople were divided in 330. They may have prospered as Rome became less efficient at collecting taxes and peace prevailed within the province. The archaeology clearly reveals the short-lived introduction of new trade connections and the formation of a Rhine-Seine-Thames commercial and cultural triangle, which in some respects prefigures an economic zone of the seventh and eighth centuries (see p. 72). Corn from Wessex, for instance, was probably sent to the Rhenish frontier troops, while German pottery, glass and millstones were imported into Britain.[15] The cultural implications of this commerce will be considered below.

Nevertheless such places should not deflect attention from Britain as a whole. Despite the prosperity of the great houses, the country was changing. The towns were contracting in size, and their great municipal monuments were falling into ruin. Even towns in the heart of southern England, like Bath, Cirencester and Silchester, were experiencing the first phase of an inexorable urban decline.[16]

In the second half of the fourth century, and especially in the last two decades of Roman administration, the province fell into astonishing decline. Villas and towns collapsed in ruin. Maintenance of villa estates seems to have ceased, while the urban landscape was slipping into complete dereliction. Some rudimentary repairs and tentative reconstructions were made to town and country houses, as was discovered by Warwick and Kirsty Rodwell at Rivenhall (Essex) and by Barry Cunliffe in late-fourth-century Bath.[17] But these show

14. P. Garnsey & R. Saller, *The Roman Empire: economy, society and culture* (London, 1987), 126–47.

15. Michael Fulford, 'Pottery production and trade at the end of Roman Britain', in P.J. Casey (ed.), *The End of Roman Britain* (Oxford, 1979) 120–32.

16. Arnold, op. cit. (n. 4), 84–120.

17. Rodwell & Rodwell, op. cit. (n. 9); Barry Cunliffe, *Roman Bath Rediscovered* (London, 1971), 91–8. Documentary evidence to support this interpretation of Britannia's decline is outlined in Philip Bartholomew, 'Fourth-century Saxons', *Britannia* 15 (1984), 169–85, esp. 179–80.

that the construction industry had been replaced by do-it-yourself expediency. Likewise manufacturing industries, such as pottery and iron, simply ceased to function. The New Forest potteries and the Wealden iron-works were abandoned. Household industries, and even domestic production, replaced the factories which for three hundred years had been an essential ingredient of the Roman economy. These changing configurations are the context for the adoption of Christianity by the elite, for the conspicuous revival of many Celtic cults, for a prominent use of Germanic ornamental styles and for the menacing raids by North Sea pirates, Picts, Scots and Irish.

The question of continuity in towns like Bath and Winchester or villas like Barton Court Farm (Oxfordshire) (Fig. 4), Rivenhall (Essex) or Stonea (Cambridgeshire) is no longer contentious. Excellent excavations at these and many other places demonstrate that, while the size of the community diminished and its facilities all but disappeared, some semblance of inhabitation nevertheless existed up to, and often well beyond, the imperial withdrawal. Perhaps the most striking feature of this decline is that it was allowed to happen at all. The archaeology plainly documents the degradation of the state apparatus. In contrast to Gaul a century later, or indeed to Italy during the sixth century, not only were the margins of the province allowed to decline, but also its core area in southern England. (Commodity production, for instance, continued sporadically in parts of Gaul and Italy throughout the Dark Ages, providing threads linking antiquity to the Middle Ages.) In Britain, under the last days of Roman jurisdiction, the essential elements of imperialism were virtually snuffed out. The Angles, Saxons and Jutes, therefore, would have encountered a province that in most respects had returned to pre-Roman conditions.

In this period, it should be remembered, Rome itself suffered a series of reverses before enjoying a brief revival in the first half of the fifth century. Recent archaeological research illustrates how Byzantine commerce gave new life to the coastal regions of Italy, Provence, Spain and North Africa.[18] As a result, it is tempting to associate the migrations of the Goths, Huns, Vandals and others with the recession of the Empire's economy north of the Alps and its moment of fresh expansion in the Mediterranean basin.

But, with widespread dereliction in Britain, there was no incentive for the surviving Roman provinces to build commercial or cultural links with the island. The British squatters who are often pictured in these ruined places, which were once the homes of the elite, are an image transmitted by a *Readers' Digest* style of history. In fact it must be supposed that these squatters were the post-colonial elite of late

---

18. Richard Hodges & David Whitehouse, *Mohammed, Charlemagne & the Origins of Europe* (London, 1983), ch. 2.

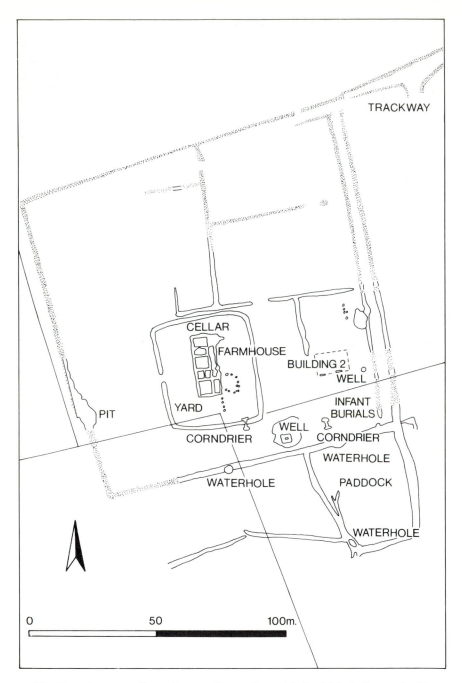

TRACKWAY

CELLAR

FARMHOUSE

BUILDING 2

WELL

PIT

YARD

INFANT
BURIALS

CORNDRIER

WELL

CORNDRIER

WATERHOLE

WATERHOLE

PADDOCK

WATERHOLE

0   50   100m.

4. The Late Roman villa at Barton Court Farm (Oxfordshire) (drawn by Barry
Vincent after David Miles and the Oxfordshire Archaeological Unit).

5. The Early Anglo-Saxon timber buildings found beside the ruined Romano-British villa at Stonea (Cambridgeshire) (courtesy of Tim Potter and the British Museum).

fourth- and fifth-century Britain. Clinging to their traditional seats of administration and power, they must be contrasted with the peasants who quit the claylands, the fen-edge and the hill-country. Quite how the colonial political structure dissolved is not known in any detail, but enough textual evidence survives to reveal the complete fragmentation of government into regional and sub-regional units. Despite lively theological debate by some of the British elite, recalled by Bede, the archaeology leaves us in no doubt that the administration and the economy took a primitive prehistoric form. A patchwork of small territories, well-documented by the seventh century, had begun to form, perhaps even before the legionaries departed.

Unlike the rest of the Empire when it experienced this fate between the later fifth and seventh century, Britain degenerated to a uniform (as opposed to a sporadic) state of aboriginal power. In the words of E.A. Thompson, 'knowledge of the outside world and knowledge of the past had been wiped out of men's minds'.[19] No amount of special

19. E.A. Thompson, *Saint Germanus of Auxerre and the End of Roman Britain*, (Woodbridge, 1984), 115.

pleading can deny the remarkable poverty of the material record and indeed the quite spectacular demise of an epoch. In our terms it was a catastrophe, transacted over several generations.

How could this happen? Francis Haverfield, Camden Professor of Ancient History at Oxford, provided a cogent explanation in 1905: 'Romano-British life was on a small scale. It was, I think, normal in quality and indeed not very dissimilar from that of many parts of Gaul. But it was in any case defective in quantity. We find towns in Britain, as elsewhere, and farms or country-houses. But the towns are small and somewhat few, and the country-houses indicate comfort more often than wealth . . . We have before us a civilisation which, like a man whose constitution is sound rather than strong, might perish quickly from a violent shock.'[20] Was it a small province with poor investment in its infrastructure, yet so Romanised that it was helpless when the government quit? The material culture certainly supports this view. The inability after the late fourth century to repair villas properly or to manufacture wheel-thrown pottery points to a high level of specialisation. Yet, as Richard Reece has pointed out, we should not let the decline mask the fact that a colonial age was being superseded in the mid to later fourth century by a post-colonial age, which he, at any rate, considers to have persisted throughout the Early Anglo-Saxon period.[21] Of course it is those who outlived the demise of the province who are important to the making of England. In this connection we need to emphasise the obvious: Britain was not a desiccated marginal landscape such as the pre-Sahara, where desertion on a similar scale was occurring at this time. Niches existed in most parts of this temperate landscape which were quite sufficient for sustaining mixed-farming methods.

It appears that the pattern of settlement no longer embraced the high-risk landscapes, but was reduced to niches in river valleys (e.g. Thames and Trent), on coastal plains (e.g. Sussex) and within the well-cultivated environs of traditional seats of government, close to towns like Canterbury, Dorchester-on-Thames, London, St Albans, Winchester, Wroxeter and York. A central feature in the strategy for survival must have been the largely reduced numbers inhabiting the province. In common with most regions of the western Empire, Britain seems to have experienced a massive depopulation after about AD 300, mirroring in some ways the huge rise in population in the second and third centuries. This often surprises scholars in the twentieth century, but the field-survey evidence is crystal clear on this point. In regions such as the Lincolnshire Fens the rise and fall of the Roman

20. Francis Haverfield, 'The Romanization of Roman Britain', *Proceedings of the British Academy* 2 (1905), 185–218.

21. Richard Reece, 'Town and country: the end of Roman Britain', *World Archaeology* 12 (1980), 76–92; Bartholomew, op. cit. (n. 17), 179–80.

SOUTH LINCOLNSHIRE FEN EDGE

SETTLEMENT & ENVIRONMENTAL ZONES

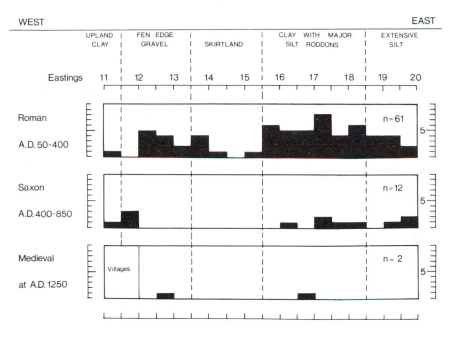

6. Histograms showing the number of first-millennium settlements found in field survey in the Lincolnshire fen edge (drawn by Barry Vincent after Peter Hayes and the Lincolnshire Archaeological Trust).

community is satisfactorily demonstrated (Fig. 6).[22] We must presume (the data are not yet available) that reproductive strategies were adapted to the economic conditions of the sub-Roman age. Restrictions on marriage within kin imposed by the Church in the fourth century may have affected the elite populations in towns and villas, as Jack Goody has shown.[23] He notes in particular that the Church stood to inherit estates as a result of regulating marriage, with fewer marriages and the probability of late childless marriages.

But these restrictions are unlikely to have been imposed on peasant households. In the circumstances these people may have adopted alternative strategies. One was to marry later, in the early twenties rather than the teens, thereby shortening the potential period of repro-

22. Hayes, op. cit. (n. 9); I am indebted to Peter Hayes for many discussions about this issue.

23. Jack Goody, *The Development of the Family and Marriage in Europe* (Cambridge, 1983), chs. 5 & 6.

duction. Another may have involved differential attitudes to the weaning and upbringing of male and female children. Shorter weaning periods for female infants, for example, made them vulnerable.[24]

Strategies of these kinds, however, had cultural implications which I shall explore later. In particular, males might outnumber females and, with late marriage (if it happened) in more and more thinly distributed populations, we might expect smaller kin groups or some change in the family unit. A preponderance of males might lead to further social instability, while late marriage made the handing down of (social and technical) traditions across generations more difficult as adult life-spans tended to terminate in the thirties. Such strategies, it has to be emphasised, are mere speculation – but demographic decline did occur and has not been explained adequately. Given such circumstances, it is not difficult to imagine the British community losing its grasp of craft production, for instance, and becoming in many respects prehistoric.

In sum, the debt to Rome cannot be ignored. Undoubtedly the Romans transformed Celtic society, and the strange poverty of the late fourth and early fifth centuries is testimony to the impact of the Empire. Yet, as we shall see, there is increasing archaeological evidence to support Richard Reece's contention that later Roman Britain and Early Anglo-Saxon England comprise a period which can be distinguished from those before and after. Such issues, of course, will remain the substance of historical debate for years to come. But as less emphasis is attached to the Anglo-Saxon invasions – as another invasion hypothesis is discarded – we must appreciate that, in the annals of British history, the invasion of Claudius in AD 43 stands out as an indisputable watershed.

A prehistoric episode

Gildas, more than any other figure, deters the historian from describing the fifth and sixth centuries as prehistoric.[25] Much rests on this priest's credibility. Bede, and later the author(s) of the *Anglo-Saxon Chronicle*, owed much to Gildas. His *On the Fall of Britain* was written in about 550 – a time, as we shall see, remote from the events of the ninth century. The facts, as he records them, seem to be as follows. After the Roman withdrawal the Britons appealed to the Roman commander-in-chief, Aetius, for support against the barbarians. No help materialised. Instead, so Gildas tells us, his forebears indulged in luxurious debauchery. In this period (the first half of the fifth century) Saxons were imported to defend eastern Britain

24. Garnsey & Saller, op. cit. (n. 14).
25. Patrick Sims-Williams, 'Gildas and the Anglo-Saxons', *Cambridge Medieval and Celtic Studies* 6 (1983), 1–30.

from further attacks. These forces, however, rebelled and created havoc. There followed a period of comparative peace, when the Saxons apparently went home, before the rise of the British chief Ambrosius Aurelianus. Ambrosius – perhaps the Arthur of later history and myth – fought a series of battles against the invaders, culminating in a mighty confrontation at Mount Badon, which modern interpreters of Gildas date to about AD 500. Ambrosius' legacy was a peace which persisted until Gildas' time.

Gildas' account lacks detail; it is punctuated instead with sin and anticipated providential retribution. It is difficult to assess, except by cross-checking against later texts. Hence Bede's writings, Procopius' laconic observations made in sixth-century Constantinople and the ninth-century *Anglo-Saxon Chronicle* have been deployed to construct a model of Early Anglo-Saxon history.

The model, familiar from modern textbooks, describes the pioneering history of the first settlers who, step by step, like the migrants to the New World in modern times, established new homesteads and extended the frontiers of their community. The story bears the hallmarks of a community at a much later date searching for its origins, translating an often confused oral tradition onto parchment to legitimise the political status quo. Gildas himself was responding to the increasingly perplexing character of his age, as his near-contemporaries Gregory of Tours and Cassiodorus were also doing, in Gaul and Italy respectively. As a source he may be accurate, though he is often vague and prejudiced.

Yet Gildas, it must be remembered, was writing about three to four generations after the supposed advent of the Saxons in the mid-fifth century, and at least two generations later than the world of Ambrosius Aurelianus. He was writing when Frankish Christianity was gaining a firm hold on the sub-Roman territories of Gaul; when the Merovingians were forming alliances with certain Anglo-Saxon courts; and when Anglo-Saxon society was beginning to experience important social and economic changes. In particular the increasingly conspicuous paganism of Anglo-Saxon society must have dismayed him. It was a threat to the residual Christian communities in Britain and gave rise to aggressive conflict in the middle and later decades of the sixth century. In such circumstances his rhetoric is intelligible. Gildas in the midst of change, we may speculate, saw himself as the inheritor of an increasingly isolated and archaic tradition.

If we bear in mind Sims-Williams' views, discussed above (p. 12), the written sources do not provide the means to reconstruct the events of the fifth and sixth centuries. Archaeology instead offers a rather different conspectus.

Excavations and surveys along the North Sea littoral demonstrate beyond reasonable doubt the steady growth of complex societies since early Roman times. Until recently the focus of attention was directed towards the instability of the period, and in particular on deserted villages like Wijster (in the Netherlands) and Feddersen Wierde (in North Germany).[26] These places, however, now appear to belong to the reorganisation of these societies as central power was enforced in increasingly developed forms. Lotte Hedeager, for example, has convincingly charted the evolution of kingship and concomitant tributary systems as early as the third and fourth centuries, in which the 'old tribal structure based on ties of kinship and alliance transformed gradually into permanently class-divided states'.[27] In fact the formation of these kingdoms may have been stimulated to some extent by the decline of the Roman Empire and by the third-century recession, which inevitably created severe economic difficulties in these regions. Abundant archaeological evidence indicates that Rhine-based traders had played an important part in the social and economic evolution of these territories. A ready alternative to trading was raiding, for the acquisition of resources necessary to sustain the political system. In some ways the Saxon Shore forts constructed in the late third century along the coasts of Flanders, Gaul and Britain remain a vivid expression of the scale of the Germans' socio-economic problem.

At the same time, with the division of the Empire in the Mediterranean and the rise of Byzantium, there are signs of the emergence of a North Sea culture zone embracing not only the Rhineland and the North Sea coastal littoral but also Britain. The most familiar expression of this is the chip-carved jewellery of Late Roman times.[28] This distinctive Germanic style is best known on decorated strap-ends, which commonly blend zoomorphic images of a central and north European antiquity with essentially classical forms. Not long ago these chip-carved strap-ends were interpreted as vestiges of a fashion in clothing that might be associated with ethnicity: the type fossils of displaced Germans serving as mercenaries in the Late Roman army, or else part of the costume of German communities deployed as buffers to prevent further depredations by barbarians. The thirst for an ethnic trait with which to characterise the Anglo-Saxons has prevented many

26. I am indebted to Klavs Randsborg for enlightening me on this issue; his paper 'Subsistence and settlement in Northern Temperate Europe in the first millennium AD', in G. Barker & C. Gamble (eds.), *Beyond Domestication in Prehistoric Europe* (London, 1985), 233–65, offers preliminary insights of his far-reaching research on this subject; see also Klavs Randsborg, 'Ranks, rights and resources: an archaeological perspective from Denmark', in C. Renfrew & S. Shennan (eds.), *Ranking, Resource and Exchange* (Cambridge, 1982), 132–9.

27. Lotte Hedeager, 'Empire, frontier and the barbarian hinterland: Rome and northern Europe from AD 1–400', in M. Rowlands, M. Larsen & K. Kristiansen (eds.), *Centre and Periphery in the Ancient World*, (Cambridge, 1987), 125–40 at 137.

28. For a useful review of the history of strap-end studies in this period, see Catherine Hills, 'The archaeology of Anglo-Saxon England in the pagan period: a review', *Anglo-Saxon England* 8 (1979), 297–329.

archaeologists from considering how such artefacts were made and distributed, and why they took the form they did. Nowadays it is generally agreed that these strap-ends reflect the change of identity of those in the northern frontier zones on the eve of Rome's collapse. Along with the adoption of Christian cults and the revival of Celtic deities, the prominence of German ornamentation must be regarded as a sign of the growing fragmentation of the Empire, as it was broken down into manageable regions.

Britain, however, was hardly a prosperous alternative to North Germany and Jutland. The old Roman province was certainly no longer an entity as such. If the seventh-century fiscal survey known as the Tribal Hidage is taken as a guide (see p. 64), at least thirty, and probably many more, tribal units now filled the breach left by the Roman administration. Britain, in short, had become a patchwork of small territories. We can easily imagine the small-scale political jostling between these peer groups, none more prominent than the next, locked into post-imperial dereliction. What incentive was there for the Angles, Saxons and Jutes – remembered elegiacally by Bede – to come to Britain when many other north and central European tribesmen were migrating southwards to seek a place in the temporary economic revival of the Mediterranean basin? Gildas, of course, may be scrupulously accurate when he records the incidence of shiploads of mercenaries enlisted to help the aspiring leaders of some peer groups. However, the invasion hypothesis in its full-blown form seems improbable, since it was to be several centuries before Anglo-Saxon England came to resemble the highly complex proto-state existing in Denmark at this time. In such circumstances the archaeology merits close scrutiny and an open mind.

Two aspects of the archaeology have been assumed to relate to the pioneers of the invasion period. First, as Myres observed long ago, the pattern of early fifth-century cemeteries largely conforms to the decaying geography of Roman Britain. That is, the cemeteries were situated close to defunct towns, and alongside the road system, as they had been in the fourth century.[29] However, from the late fifth to the early seventh century the distribution of cemeteries shows a new pattern. Cemeteries were generally situated away from Roman land-marks, suggesting that they were markers in new territorial units. This break with the Romano-British pattern has also been identified in the sphere of settlement archaeology. The desultory fifth-century occupation of many large and small Roman towns, ranging in size from Winchester to Heybridge (Essex), ended in about 500 when the last timber buildings within the decaying ruins were deserted. Similarly, many delapidated villas, such as Rivenhall (Essex) and Barton

29. J.N.L. Myres, *Anglo-Saxon Pottery and the Settlement of England* (Oxford, 1969).

Court Farm (Oxfordshire) (Fig. 7), were finally abandoned towards the end of the fifth century.[30]

Some Late Roman settlements, of course, span the entire period. The village excavated at Mucking (Essex) and a small nucleus inside the old Saxon Shore fort at Portchester Castle (Hampshire) are examples of non-villa communities that were occupied continuously from the fourth to the seventh century.[31] Mucking is a particularly interesting site. Located on the north shore of the Thames, it was the scene of near-continuous occupation from the later Iron Age through to the eighth century. Numerous sunken huts of Germanic type have been dated from the end of the fourth century. Mostly they cannot be related to either halls or ditched enclosures that are typical of the Dutch, German and Danish villages. The ensemble of huts bears some resemblance to the temporary coastal villages, often associated with trading, which are found in southern Scandinavia in the Migration, Viking and medieval periods.[32] The village before the construction of halls in the later fifth and sixth centuries is quite unlike either contemporary Continental or Anglo-Saxon settlements. It is worth noting too that distinctive deep-furrowed, carinated funerary wares of the fifth century occur not only in the cemetery but also in the silty accumulations within several huts.

Some new sites were also founded in the earlier half of the fifth century and remained in use throughout the next two or three centuries. The Early Anglo-Saxon village at West Stow (Suffolk) is a particularly important example of this class of settlement. West Stow was one of several villages which replaced Roman farms in the Lark Valley soon after the imperial administration had left Britain. In much the same way the villages of Catholme (Staffordshire) and Raunds (Northamptonshire) were founded at about this time.[33] In sum, a new so-called Anglo-Saxon settlement pattern began in the early to

30. Arnold, op. cit. (n. 4), ch. 2; P.J. Drury & N.P. Wickenden, 'An Early Saxon settlement within the Romano-British small town at Heybridge, Essex', *Medieval Archaeology* 26 (1982), 1–40; Rodwell & Rodwell, op. cit. (n. 9); Millett, op. cit. (n. 9).

31. On Mucking see Margaret U. Jones, 'Saxon Mucking – a post-excavation note', in S.C. Hawkes, D. Brown & J. Campbell (eds.), *Anglo-Saxon Studies in Archaeology and History* 1 (Oxford, 1979), 21–38; for Portchester Castle see Barry Cunliffe, *Excavations at Portchester Castle*, vol. 2: *The Saxon* (London, 1976).

32. Note the huts recently excavated in the Migration Period (?) emporium at Lundeborg on Funen: Per O. Thomsen, 'Lundeborg 1. Havn og handelsplad fra 3 og 4 arhundrede efter Kr.', *Arbog for Svendborg and Omegns Museum* (1986), 12–52, and those from the Viking Period emporium at Löddekopinge in Scania: Tom Ohlsson, 'The Löddekopinge investigation I', *Meddelanden fran Lunds Universitets Historiska Museum* 1 (1975–76), 59–161.

33. Stanley West, 'West Stow: the Anglo-Saxon village', *East Anglian Archaeology* (Ipswich, 1985); Graham Cadman, 'Raunds 1977–1983: an excavation summary', *Medieval Archaeology* 27 (1983), 107–22; S. Losco-Bradley & Hazel Wheeler, 'Anglo-Saxon settlement in the Trent Valley', in M. Faull (ed.), *Studies in Late Anglo-Saxon Settlement* (Oxford, 1984), 101–14.

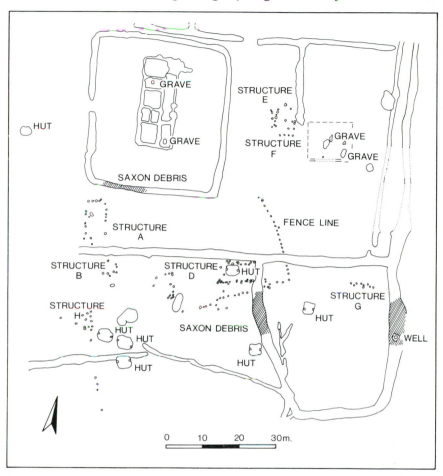

7. Early Anglo-Saxon settlement alongside the Romano-British villa at Barton Court Farm (Oxfordshire) (drawn by Barry Vincent, after David Miles and the Oxfordshire Archaeological Unit).

mid-fifth century, and had generally superseded the last phase of Roman settlements by the end of the century.

The second feature said to illustrate the archaeology of the migrants is the cemeteries. In practice most cemeteries cannot be dated with precision. Only by taking various categories of grave-goods together and constructing model assemblages is it possible to construct broad chronological sequences that permit us to form a picture of funerary behaviour. Arnold made a study of southern English cemeteries using this method, as did Dickinson for the Thames valley.[34] Their results show that the majority of graves belong to the sixth or early seventh century, fifth-century graves being far fewer in number. This pattern has been identified, though not so rigorously quantified, also in other parts of England.

Earlier fifth-century burials in these cemeteries are distinguished by brooch and pottery types that bear strong continental motifs and ornamentation. Pottery funerary vessels with deep furrowed decoration, pronounced carination and sometimes pedestal bases are characteristic of this period. However, late in the fifth century, a commoner style of ornamentation is widely adopted, bearing strong affinities to north Germany and south Scandinavia. This includes the disjointed animal ornamentation of Salin's style I which is found on square-headed brooches, and the wide-ranging Germanic stamp-decoration occurring on a variety of globular funerary pots.

The 'first-generation' fifth-century graves occur in small numbers in a dispersed pattern in those cemeteries which were used for most of the Early Anglo-Saxon age. Arnold, for instance, draws attention to their isolated existence at Collingbourne Ducis and Petersfinger (Wiltshire), as well as at Lyminge (Kent).[35] At the Buckland cemetery, Dover, Vera Evison has made much the same observations. Like the neat rows beside tenth-century parish churches opening a chapter of parish graveyard burial (see p. 172), 'first-generation' burials appear to be scattered as if in expectation, as heads of families, that others will be joining them. It is tempting to interpret these burials as pioneers, especially perhaps to account for their Germanic grave-goods.[36] Yet the parallel with the founding of tenth-century cemeteries around parish churches, or the evolution of row-grave cemeteries in later fifth- and sixth-century Gaul, merits more than passing consideration (see below, p. 30).

The creation of a new settlement pattern and the 'first-generation' graves may be the archaeological expression of the invasions and migrations described by Gildas and Bede. Yet the evidence is far from conclusive. The new settlements may reflect an adaptation to different social and economic resources as the legacy of the Empire diminished. Similarly the first-generation burials might be interpreted in an alternative way. The new cemeteries and their funerary rite mark a new direction in popular ideology. The disposal of grave-goods denotes the inception of conspicuous destruction of moveable wealth, markedly at odds with the consumption of wealth while living, or with the collec-

34. C.J. Arnold, 'Wealth and social structure: a matter of life and death', and T. Dickinson, 'The present state of Anglo-Saxon cemetery studies', both in P. Rahtz, T. Dickinson & L. Watts (eds.), *Anglo-Saxon Cemeteries 1979* (Oxford, 1980), 81–142 & 11–34 respectively.

35. Arnold, ibid., 122–33, esp. 132–3.

36. Vera I. Evison, *Dover: Buckland Anglo-Saxon cemetery* (London, 1987).

8. Early Anglo-Saxon cremation urns in the cemetery at Spong Farm (Norfolk) (courtesy of Catherine Hills and the Norfolk Archaeological Unit).

tive destruction of wealth at temples. The tradition was popular in later Roman Europe, especially in Germanic areas beyond the limes, which attained new significance from the late fifth century in most parts of western Europe.

Once again, to appreciate the context of these changes to resource management and the funerary rite we must take advantage of the wide-angle vision available to the archaeologist. We must consider the European circumstances in the later fifth century.

Between about 400 and 475 the west Mediterranean experienced a brief economic revival. But in the last quarter of the century, while the Ostrogoths acquired control of Italy, the Mediterranean took on a new and less hopeful economic complexion. The Byzantine boom seems to have slowed down, and the repercussions soon had an impact on inland districts beyond the sea-towns of the west Mediterranean. Inland villas and farms in Italy, for example, reflect the impact of the new economic down-turn.[37] In France the implications were bound to be far more serious.

37. Hodges & Whitehouse, op. cit. (n. 18), ch. 2.

It may be no coincidence that at exactly this moment the Frankish kings adopted a new course of action. Far from the Mediterranean, Childeric (d. 481) became a Christian, and his son Clovis set out soon after to conquer new territories reaching towards Italy, the heartland of Christianity. Most significantly, Frankish funeral customs seem to have altered substantially while Clovis was king. Edward James has written most convincingly about this, linking the inception of the ubiquitous row-grave cemeteries of the Merovingian (Gallo-Roman) kingdoms with the spread of Frankish lordship.[38] The argument is worth restating briefly for, as he notes in parenthesis, it has important implications for Early Anglo-Saxon England. James believes that the Frankish burial rite involving inhumation of fully-dressed individuals accompanied by weapons and other equipment is an uncommon feature of the early Frankish aristocracy between the late fourth century and the age of Clovis. Traditionally, the diffusion of the custom has been associated with the Frankish invasion of northern and central France by Clovis. James, however, suggests that the aristocracy, having adopted Christianity, were buried in traditional fashion within churches. Their followers and dependants, by contrast, were now buried in row-grave cemeteries, which had hitherto been reserved for the the their lords. In James's words, 'the row-grave cemetery. . .is therefore to be associated with the spread of Frankish lordship over Northern Gaul and not with the spread of the Franks themselves as a colonising people. In many cases the cemeteries may represent communities of men dependent upon a Frankish aristocracy – his warriors and his free and unfree dependants – but there is nothing to suggest that those who imitated their lord's mortuary customs were necessarily Franks.'[39] Moreover, it might be added, the customs themselves reflect a significant development in attitudes to wealth, as well as (it may be assumed) to inheritance strategies.

It may be no coincidence that many new villages were being founded at this time.[40] Pollen diagrams from the Rhine delta area, as well as from the middle Rhineland, depict an ecological change. Scrubland vegetation that had regenerated after the third-century crisis was being cleared. The era of Clovis (481–551) also witnessed the expan-

---

38. Edward James, 'Cemeteries and the problem of Frankish settlement in Gaul', in P. Sawyer (ed.), *Names, Words and Graves: early medieval settlement* (Leeds, 1979), 55–90.

39. Edward James, 'Merovingian cemetery studies, and some implications for Anglo-Saxon England', in P. Rahtz, T. Dickinson & L. Watts (eds.), *Anglo-Saxon Cemeteries 1979* (Oxford, 1980), 39.

40. Klavs Randsborg pointed this out to me; he briefly examines vegetational history in his paper on 'Subsistence and settlement in northern Temperate Europe', op. cit. (n. 16); Walter Janssen, 'Römische und frühmittelalterliche Landserschliessung im Vergleich', in W. Janssen & D. Lohrmann (eds.), *Villa-Curtis-Grangia* (Bonn, 1983), 81–122.

sion of commercial connections around the North Sea that were to have enduring implications. Between about 400 and 500 the primitive nature of the British economy cannot have offered much to the Franks. Incentives to develop cross-Channel commerce, for example, must have been few. But with the new Mediterranean recession the Frankish aristocracy responded by initiating a new resource strategy as well as developing a long-established ideology that had its roots in the Germanic past. It is no coincidence therefore that archaeological evidence indicates the revival of trade connections at this time between the Frankish kingdoms and other territories around the North Sea. In particular Ulf Nasman has charted the flow of Frankish goods to southern Scandinavia from this time. Hayo Vierck similarly has used the distribution of bracteates around the North Sea to illustrate the beginnings of strong maritime connections.[41] It is significant therefore that Ian Wood has recently made a case for 'Britain (perhaps best interpreted as Kent) having been brought within the political sphere of Clovis'.[42] The suggestion is based on a fresh interpretation of a clause in the *Pactus Legis Salicae*, probably compiled during Clovis' reign, which outlines the procedure for retrieving a slave who has been stolen across the sea. Wood tentatively interprets this as some indication of formal arrangements between the Franks and certain English. Such arrangements, he speculates, may have existed intermittently or continuously until the reign of King Ethelbert of Kent in the 560s, when the cross-Channel relationship was upgraded by his marriage to a Parisian princess.

Could great changes in Gaul have triggered comparable changes in Kent, ultimately influencing the culture of other parts of England? Were some of the many sub-Roman tribes drawn into contact with the increasing numbers of voyagers across the North Sea? Was the isolation of sub-Roman Britain brought to an end in the age of Clovis? If so, given the political complexity of the old province, and bearing in mind its material poverty, it is not difficult to envisage the tensions such contacts might have created and, in some cases, the avid adoption of alien ideas and goods.

Kent certainly acquired prestige goods from overseas at this time.

41. Ulf Nasman, 'Vendel period glass from Eketorp II, Oland', *Acta Archaeologia* 55 (1984), 55–116; Hayo Vierck, 'Zum Fernverkehr über See im 6 Jahrhundert angesichts angelsächsischer Fibelsätze in Thuringen', in K. Hauck, *Goldbrakteaten aus Sievern* (Munich, 1970), 355–95; Egil Bakka, 'Scandinavian-type gold bracteates in Kentish and Continental grave finds', in V.I. Evison (ed.), *Angles, Saxons and Jutes. Essays presented to J.N.L. Myres* (Oxford, 1981), 11–38. On the wider chronological implications of these Scandinavian styles see John Hines, *The Scandinavian Character of Anglian England in the pre-Viking Period* (Oxford, 1984) and a review of that book by M.G. Welch in *Norwegian Archaeological Review* 18 (1985), 136–8.

42. Ian Wood, 'The end of Roman Britain: continental evidence and parallels', in M. Lapidge & D. Dumville (eds.), *Gildas: new approaches* (Woodbridge, 1984), 23–4.

The excavations of the Buckland cemetery at Dover illustrate the first incidence of Frankish glass beakers. Many more beakers of this type have been found in Kent, as in southern Scandinavia. Similarly Danish gold bracteates belonging to the late fifth and sixth centuries occur in a number of graves in the region but are rare elsewhere in Britain. It is worth recalling that the *Anglo-Saxon Chronicle* attributes the founding of the South Saxon and West Saxon royal houses to this time. According to the *Chronicle*, Aelle landed in Sussex and Cerdic invaded Hampshire. Whether these events occurred or not will always be debated.[43] But the sub-Roman culture in these parts now assumed a new character. Distinctive Anglo-Saxon grave goods such as those at Collingbourne Ducis (Wiltshire) and Droxford (Hampshire) are often attributed to the new wave of warriors. In this connection C.J. Arnold has drawn attention to the unpublished work of an American physical anthropologist, C.M. Stuckert, who claims that 'the majority of the bodies (in Hampshire) adorned with Germanic style grave-goods. . .were of native stock, not migrant Germanic'.[44] This tantalising evidence needs to be fully substantiated. None the less, as Arnold shows, the picture of waves of invaders overwhelming the sub-Roman communities is likely to be misleading. Instead it must be assumed that the *Anglo-Saxon Chronicle* was confusing a complex history in which certain existing households, possibly with overseas help, began to assert their political prowess.

The winds of change affected not only the 'English'. Beyond the forest of Sellwood, separating Somerset and western Britain from the embryonic English territories, an equally distinctive cultural profile was being forged. Arthur's Britain, as Leslie Alcock has called it, is readily distinguished from southern and eastern England.[45] Nucleated hillfort communities, contacts with the Mediterranean and large regional or sub-regional cemeteries mark this area as quite different in many cultural respects from its neighbours to the east.

The hillforts, in contrast to the old Roman administrative centres like St Albans or Winchester, reveal a powerfully centralised elite able to mobilise labour to repair hundreds of metres of fortifications. South Cadbury camp, the scene of Alcock's memorable excavations, provides the clearest picture of Arthurian Britain. The refurbished Iron Age defences reveal an exercise of military command quite unlike that found in south-eastern England. Equally the ability to acquire type A (African Red Slip ware) dishes (from modern Tunisia) and east Mediterranean amphorae reflects not only the wide range of Byzantine merchants but also the standing of these tribal leaders. Unlike the

---

43. Sims-Williams, op. cit. (n. 5).
44. Arnold, op. cit. (n. 4), 130.
45. Leslie Alcock, 'Cadbury-Camelot: a fifteen-year perspective', *Proceedings of the British Academy* 68 (1982), 355–88.

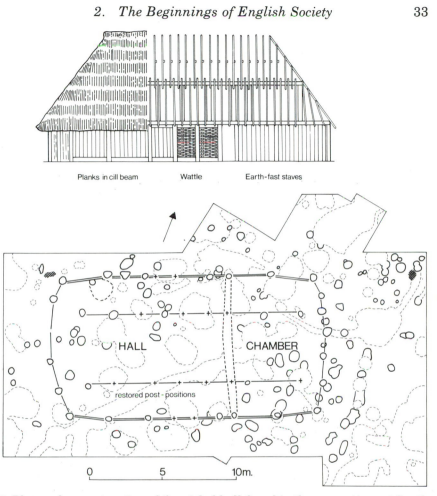

Planks in cill beam Wattle Earth-fast staves

HALL CHAMBER

restored post-positions

0 5 10m.

9. Plan and reconstruction of the aisled hall found in the excavations at South Cadbury (Somerset) and attributed to the Arthurian re-occupation of the iron-age hillfort (drawn by Barry Vincent, after Leslie Alcock).

tribesmen in Kent, however, or even Wiltshire, those in Somerset deployed their imported goods in ceremonies in their homesteads rather than in funerary rites. Sherds of these dishes and amphorae occurred at South Cadbury, for example, while the large Christian cemetery at nearby Cannington by contrast was bereft of grave goods. The cultures within the two halves of sub-Roman Britain could not have been more different.

The Arthurian age, therefore, may mark the moment when these two cultures clashed. Frankish influence may have incited not only a wider political awareness among the 'English' tribes, but also wars of expansion for slaves and for goods to trade with the Franks. Mount

Badon, the great battle between these two cultures recalled by Gildas, was apparently the high point of Arthurian resistance. It brought an end to a prehistoric interlude in which sub-Roman groups, conscious of a colonial past and their Christian connections, were encouraged to match themselves against tribesmen who found affinities to other North Sea tribes adapting to the ultimate demise of classical antiquity. This was the final episode in the history of Roman Britain, which stretched back beyond the invasion of Julius Caesar to the time when Roman traders first exchanged small quantities of prestige goods with Celtic tribal chiefs. Shortly afterwards, as Gildas sadly recounts and the archaeology of sites like South Cadbury broadly confirms, the Christian, sub-Roman communities were conquered by the ascendant Anglo-Saxon tribes. In sum, at the end of this episode, in the age of Arthur and Clovis, Aelle and Cerdic, the archaeology points to the beginnings of English society.

The beginnings of English society

The precise political configurations of England in the age of Clovis cannot be reconstructed with any certainty, though there is good reason to believe that many territories existed at this time (see above p. 25). Indeed no evidence of conspicuous political leadership exists much before the mid-sixth century. In contrast to the fortified hilltops of western Britain, Early Anglo-Saxon England is notable for the egalitarian quality of its modest farmsteads.

In fact the absence of any apparent differences or ranking of Early Anglo-Saxon settlements is a striking feature of the period. Most of the excavated settlements consist of three or four farms. The extensive excavations at West Stow (Suffolk) revealed the intermittent rebuilding of the farms on almost the same spot. Unlike Romano-British villages, however, the dwellings were not enclosed by either ditches or fences. At West Stow the enclosures around each of the farms were made in the seventh century (see p. 61). But in other respects these farms resemble Romano-British homesteads. Philip Dixon first drew attention to the similarity between Anglo-Saxon and Romano-British buildings.[46] The farms in the excavated village at Catholme (Staffordshire) have a similar plan, for example, to that of a Romano-British homestead excavated at nearby Dunston's Clump (Nottinghamshire).[47] As several archaeologists have now agreed,

46. Philip Dixon, 'How Saxon is the Saxon house?' in P.J. Drury (ed.), *Structural Reconstruction* (Oxford, 1982), 275–88; see also S. James, A. Marshall & M. Millett, 'An early medieval building tradition', *Archaeological Journal* 141 (1984), 182–215.
47. S. Losco-Bradley & H.M. Wheeler, 'Anglo-Saxon settlement in the Trent valley', in M. Faull (ed.), *Studies in Late Anglo-Saxon Settlement* (Oxford, 1984), 101–14, esp. 111.

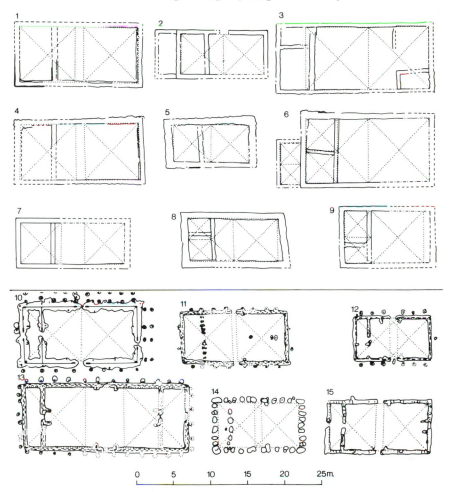

10. Comparison of Later Roman cottages (1–9) and Early Anglo-Saxon timber structures (10–15) showing continued use of a building tradition. (1) Gatcombe 5; (2) Bradley Hill, period 2; (3) Hibaldstow; (4) Cirencester; (5) and (6) Catsgore 2.3 and 3.2; (7) Gatcombe 6; (8) Catsgore 2.1; (9) Bradley Hill 2; (10) Yeavering C3; (11) Cowdery's Down C8; (12) Cowdery's Down C9; (13) Cowdery's Down C12; (14) Cowdery's Down A20; (15) Chalton AZ1 (drawn by Barry Vincent, after S. James, A. Marshall and M. Millett).

Early Anglo-Saxon vernacular architecture appears to uphold an insular tradition which stems back to the later first or second century (Fig. 10).[48] Long-houses, the traditional Germanic dwellings of this

48. James, Marshall & Millett, op. cit. (n. 46); Martin G. Welch, 'Rural settlement patterns in the Early and Middle Anglo-Saxon period', *Landscape History* 7 (1985), 15–16.

age, which embody not only a means of ecological and economic adaptation, as has often been stressed, but also the social units of complex
tributary societies, seem not to occur in England.

The continuity of this insular tradition raises a vital question about
the eclipse of Roman institutions and the beginnings of English
society. The household, according to David Herlihy, does not often
figure in censuses and surveys of classical antiquity.[49] Servile labour
and clusters of families attached to great estates were apparently
usual. Households, he argues, only occur as broadly equivalent units
in the foundation of new settlements or colonies. Veterans, for
example, worked their farms primarily with the aid of their families.
But Herlihy appears to have been unaware of the multitude of Roman
homesteads throughout the Empire, unrecorded at the time and yet
the most distinctive feature of archaeological field surveys. Such homesteads were especially important where the Roman estate system was
poorly developed, especially in central and northern England. The
continuity of the Romano-British plan into Anglo-Saxon times lends
some encouragement to speculation that the household structure
formed under the Roman aegis outlived the colony's demise. It
suggests that the eighth-century family structure by which Bede, for
example, assesses the size of estates and regions of England was not
rooted in the migration period (as he implies) but in the unusual
cultural cauldron of the Roman age. Pre-Roman Celtic household units
which reappeared in post-Roman Wales, for example, did not reappear
in fifth-century England. In short, the vernacular architecture of the
Early Anglo-Saxon farm may be an expression of a peasant family/
household unit which withstood the long depopulation of the countryside, the decline of the state and the demise of classical antiquity.

The evidence from West Stow and other excavated villages shows
that the economy was structured principally to meet domestic needs.
At West Stow a mixture of livestock was kept by the community, and
there was a marked increase in the number of pigs. The farmers
practised mixed cereal agriculture, although spelt had been replaced
in the local diet by breadwheats and rye. Stanley West's survey of the
Lark Valley, in which West Stow is situated, shows that as early as
AD 500 the area was divided into territories not dissimilar in shape
or size from later parishes.[50] At Barton Court Farm, while the villa
fell into ruin changes in the landscape were less drastic. 'As in the
Roman period, seeds and beetles point to a presence of local grassland.
Arable farming evidently continued as six-row barley was found in

49. David Herlihy, 'Households in the Early Middle Ages: symmetry and sainthood', in
R.McC. Netting, R.R. Wilk & E.J. Arnold (eds.), *Households: comparative and historical
studies of the domestic group* (Berkeley, 1984), 383–406, and *Medieval Households*
(Boston, 1986).

50. West, op. cit. (n. 33), 167–70.

11. Reconstructed Early Anglo-Saxon buildings at West Stow (Suffolk) (courtesy of the Suffolk Archaeological Unit).

the Saxon well, though the wet-ground weed species common in the Roman period were now absent. Presumably the low-lying ground at Thrupp was no longer cultivated ... Flax, however, continued to be cultivated, possibly on the terrace slope ... Around the settlement beetles associated with refuse and manure show a marked decline, creating an impression of less intensive settlement than in the late Roman period.'[51] As in West Stow, the evidence illustrates that fifth-century England may have been primitive by Roman standards but was far from primeval.

Artefacts confirm the picture. A few craftsmen were able to expend a great deal of time producing ceremonial objects which were distributed over restricted areas. But the quantity and variety of artefacts was limited by the domestic mode of production in which the objects were made. Traces of potting activities, for example, were found in the West Stow excavations. These produced richly ornamented funerary wares used to hold cremations, and, in addition, probably poorer hand-made domestic wares for a small region (present-day north-west Suffolk).[52] The various symbols on these pots were probably

51. David Miles, *Archaeology at Barton Court Farm, Abingdon, Oxfordshire* (London, 1986), 52.
52. J.N.L. Myres, *A Corpus of Anglo-Saxon Pottery* (Cambridge, 1977) is the best text on this matter; note, however, B. Green, W. Milligan & S. West, 'The Illington/Lackford workshop', in V.I. Evison (ed.), *Angles, Saxons and Jutes* (Oxford, 1981), 187–226, one of several studies illustrating the regional dispersal of such wares.

devised by the potters, and perhaps helped to identify a tribal or smaller social unit, although to interpret either the potter or the recipient of his wares as an ethnic Anglian, as Myres has done, is to assume a good deal. On the other hand, the farmers and potter(s) at West Stow shared a distinctive culture that grew more strident in its range of symbols as, with the passing of generations, the migrations probably came to represent a common past rather than an exact memory.

The beginnings of social stratification must be sought within these household farming units and the kinds of territorialism identified in the Lark Valley. Further archaeological research of such sites promises to be of considerable importance. At present, however, the origins of English society are most readily traced in the funerary archaeology.

About 25,000 graves belonging to the Early Anglo-Saxon period have been excavated (although the counting of cremation urns as individuals distorts the number slightly). The numerous cemeteries, like the row-grave cemeteries in the Frankish territories, are the most distinctive feature of this age. But the heroic manner of the mortuary rituals is essentially at odds with the egalitarian farming communities described above.

In recent years several scholars have attempted to use grave-goods to determine whether some form of ranking existed in these cemeteries.[53] This type of analysis has been ferociously criticised in other fields of archaeology, but in this case any picture of social ranking must take the settlement data into account. In short, we need not assume that the way these people were represented in death necessarily corresponded with their circumstances in life. Two of these studies on ranking are worth summarising here. First, C.J. Arnold has noted that the range of grave goods is very limited in the fourth- to fifth-century cemeteries. The pattern alters little during the late fifth and early sixth centuries. Two marked trends, however, become clear by the mid-sixth. First, the range of grave goods becomes noticeably greater. Secondly, by the second half of the sixth century the grave goods associated with women have higher values than those associated with men. The difficulty of dating these grave-goods should not be overlooked. None the less the funerary rite appears to take a new direction in the first half of the sixth century.

Using the range of grave goods from many old excavations, Arnold suggests that four tiers of ranking existed within some mid- to later sixth-century cemeteries. Recently Vera Evison has been able to

53. Arnold, op. cit. (n. 34); J.F. Shephard, 'The social identity of the individual in isolated barrows and barrow cemeteries in Anglo-Saxon England', in B.C. Burnham & J. Kingsbury (eds.), *Space, Hierarchy and Society* (Oxford, 1979), 47–80; see also Leslie Alcock, 'Quantity or quality: the Anglian graves of Bernicia', in V.I. Evison (ed.), *Angles, Saxons and Jutes* (Oxford, 1981), 168–86.

improve upon Arnold's method of ranking graves using a modern
excavation of an Anglo-Saxon cemetery at Buckland, Dover.[54] She
arrives at broadly the same conclusions as Arnold, but her method is
worth describing here as it is corroborated by the spatial arrangements
of the cemetery, as well as by the details of the graves. She divides
the male graves into four types: those which have a sword, those with
a spear but no sword, those with goods but no weapons, and those
without objects. She classifies the women's graves in much the same
way: 'the rich graves with brooches matching the sword graves,
followed later by the rich graves without brooches matching spear
graves . . . The medium rich and poor female graves must match the
rest of the spear and weaponless graves in status. The poor female
graves might represent poor relations in the free class, but not slaves,
for most contain keys, and these may be taken to indicate the
possession of precious articles normally locked up and not committed
to the grave.' Finally, she notes, 'with [two] possible exceptions, no
slaves were buried in this cemetery. As most of the slave
population. . .was no doubt British, a completely separate cemetery
must have been in contemporary use.'[55] As no separate cemeteries
have yet been identified, it suggests that those ranking lowest in
the cemetery may be of slave status. If so, the status of the other
classifications needs to be reconsidered. Clearly slaves belong to a
social category which is poorly understood before the arrival of the
Church when new scales of ranking were probably introduced.

For our purposes perhaps the most interesting of these tiers is the
rich group, prefiguring the great seventh-century burials like that
contained in the Sutton Hoo ship mound. Burials in this category
commonly occur in low mounds, or are set within enclosures and
furnished with a range of imported Frankish goods. Vera Evison interprets these high-ranking burials as those of an eorl or noble.[56] If a
parallel can be drawn between grave furniture and social ranking, it
offers us some insight into the origins of the English minor aristocracy,
and it illustrates their use of warrior equipment and imported goods
to establish their esteem within the evolving spectrum of ranking
systems in Early Anglo-Saxon England. Yet the differences in the
ranking systems between Kent and Wessex revealed by seventh-
century laws warn the archaeologist at this stage against drawing
specific conclusions about the social hierarchy in Early Anglo-Saxon
England. It is worth noting, though, that in Kent where there existed
plentiful access to imported goods the distinction between a ceorl and
eorl was much narrower than in Wessex. Significantly, in Wessex,
where the limited sixth-century access to imported goods, for example,

54. Evison, op. cit. (n. 36), 146–50.
55. ibid. 149.
56. ibid.

may have been off-set by conquering and colonising new territory, a considerable distinction separated these social levels.

The apparent status of women in these cemeteries in the context of several recent observations about sex differentiation in the first millennium is especially interesting.[57] Fewer women appear to have been present in later Roman cemeteries, such as those excavated at Cirencester and Lankhills, outside Winchester. It has yet to be resolved whether women were generally rarer in society or just absent in these urban contexts. By AD 600, however, the discrepancy appears to have been rectified. Males and females in roughly equal numbers occur in Anglo-Saxon cemeteries. Moreover preliminary studies of their pathology suggest that they were living longer and growing taller than in Roman times.[58] Finally, it is notable that many of these women, especially those in Kent, were attired at death in Frankish vestments. Here it is worth recalling that Ethelberht, king of Kent, married Bertha, a Merovingian princess from Paris, in about 560, thereby accepting Frankish hegemony over his territory. Can these other rich female graves be related to the assimilation of Frankish culture, or even to a flow of Frankish brides to England? Sadly the evidence does not exist for an answer to such questions. Yet the role of England a century after the arrival of the Church is better documented and may help to throw light on sixth-century society.

David Herlihy has argued recently that by the seventh and eighth centuries women were being collected into the households of the wealthy for sexual as well as servile purposes.[59] This resource polgyny was condemned by Bede and Boniface in the eighth century (see p. 110). By Bede's time, of course, women were considered important in reproductive strategies, as households attempted to secure inheritance through male lines. Such a strategy was at odds with the bilateral lineage systems or partible inheritance favoured by Celtic tradition. Primogeniture, already familiar to Christian Frankish society, was certain to distinguish English society from the sub-Roman British.

It is a bold step to interpret the status of women from their grave goods as an index of primogeniture. But it is not inconceivable that this reproductive strategy, in existence by the later seventh century, pre-dated the Christian missions and owes its origins to Clovis' time when the exchange of gifts and cross-Channel alliances were first initiated. In such circumstances women (to quote Levi-Strauss) were

57. Arnold, op. cit. (n. 4).
58. Andrew Nelson, *A study of stature, sex and age ratios and average age at death from the Romano-British to the Late Anglo-Saxon period* (unpublished M.A. thesis, University of Sheffield, 1985).
59. Herlihy, op. cit. (n. 49), 65.

perhaps 'the supreme gift among those that can only be obtained by reciprocal gifts'.[60]

One final aspect of Early Anglo-Saxon society merits further consideration: the conspicuous use of goods in the funerary rite, whereby these objects are withdrawn from circulation. Anthropologists have linked this mode of withdrawing goods to gift-giving and, in particular, to the alienation of moveable wealth. The theory of gift-giving owes much to the work of Marcel Mauss and Claude Levi-Strauss, who defined it as the process by which an inalienable thing or person is exchanged between two reciprocally dependent transactors.[61] In some respects the aim of the gift economy goes against the grain of contemporary capitalist thinking. The intention is to accumulate social or personal credit through the action of giving gifts. This is what C.A. Gregory has defined as 'gifts-to-men'.[62] Credit provides the giver with status which may be maintained thereafter if the transactor controls the flow of gifts circulating in the community and thus prevents any suitable repayment of the gift. Soon, as long as the flow of gifts in circulation can be controlled, power and credit become virtually synonymous.

Gregory has described a second type of gift-giving mechanism which he calls 'gifts-to-gods'. Gifts-to gods are made at ceremonies in which goods are withdrawn from circulation by destroying them in ritual hoards or burials.[63] Gifts removed ritually in this manner place social emphasis on the acquisition of goods in order to win credit from the gods. To perpetuate status in society, it therefore becomes necessary to control the supply of gifts as well as the rituals, creating checks and balances to keep earthly and celestial creditors in place. In such ways, so the Eskimo saying goes, gifts make slaves, as whips make dogs.

The influence of Frankish funerary customs, along with the acquisition of Frankish manufactured goods ranging from glasses and pots to clothing, may have had a critical impact upon the many tribal groupings in later fifth-century Britain. Exchange, as Marx observed, is a major agent of individualisation.[64] It is not difficult to envisage the social competition engendered within each tribal grouping, as well as the intensification of competition between peer groups. Step by step, once they found release from the aboriginal conditions of the fifth century, simple hierarchies began to be re-established. At the same time, to judge from the evidence of several field surveys, the

60. Claude Levi-Strauss, *The Elementary Structures of Kinship* (Boston, 1969), 65.
61. Marcel Mauss, *Essai sur le don* (Paris, 1925).
62. C.A. Gregory, *Gifts and Commodities* (London, 1982).
63. C.A. Gregory, 'Gifts to men and gifts to god: gift exchange and capital accumulation in contemporary Papua', *Man* 15 (1980), 626–52.
64. Karl Marx, *Pre-capitalist Economic Formations* (London, 1964), 96.

number of settlements in regions as diverse as Northamptonshire and Lincolnshire were beginning to increase. In these volatile and unusual circumstances, it is easy to imagine how the search began for some grammar whereby these peoples might express themselves, and how this was rapidly diffused to the many tribes jostling to obtain greater resources. The likeliest grammar, as later dynasties well appreciated, was embodied in some shared ethnic past. Thus it is not difficult to imagine how a few thrusting chiefs, who were either descended from fifth-century immigrant mercenaries or simply wished to project a distinguished past, associated themselves with an oral tradition that was much more relevant than any vestige of Roman colonisation. In this connection, the cultural implications of small-scale trading links across the North Sea, beginning in the late fifth century, should not be ignored. North Sea contacts, rather than those with the Mediterranean, had triggered great changes in sub-Roman Britain. Abstract though these origins are, this explanation may account for the emergence of a conspicuous cultural profile in the mid-sixth century, at a time of social tension, at least four generations removed from the migrations. With the creation of kingship on the eve of the first Christian missions to England, it was a short step to making myths about charismatic forebears who made the perilous voyage to Britain to gain the authority to enforce tribesmen to create public works and perform military duties.

*

Gildas, in fact, was writing at about the time of the marriage of Ethelberht, king of Kent, to Bertha, the Parisian princess. By then the western British enclaves were threatened with extinction by their Anglo-Saxon neighbours. As Gildas recalled, the ascendancy of the English owed something to a few migrants a century or more before. Archaeology does not help us to define the number of these migrants or their status, but it confirms that Kemble was right to be suspicious about the migration. Nevertheless, with more archaeological investigations the ebb and flow of Britain's relations with the Continent from the fourth century onwards appears increasingly to be a critical variable in the creation of an English culture. In all likelihood, contact was haphazard and highly individualised before the late sixth century. With the arrival of the Church the relationship suddenly altered and savage minds were domesticated.

3

Inflation, the Church and the
Middle Saxon Shuffle

Writing . . . encourages special forms of linguistic activity associated with
developments in particular kinds of problem-raising and problem-solving,
in which the list, the formula and the table played a seminal part. If we
wish to speak of the 'savage mind', these were some of the instruments
of its domestication.   (Jack Goody)[1]

With the advent of writing, which was widely reintroduced by St
Augustine's mission to Kent in 597, England starts to bear (in Levi-
Strauss's phrase) the scars of events. The domestication of the savage
mind brought with it, among other things, the concept of historical
time and, with that, new attitudes to resources. Previously, between
the departure of the Romans and Augustine's arrival, the heathen
religions of England, as far as we can tell, had maintained what
Edmund Leach describes as primitive time punctuated by a magical
time in which rituals worshipping the present and perhaps the past
were of pre-eminent importance.[2] Thus in an elegy for the passing of
the old order, the Christian author of *Beowulf* sums up the heathen
values described in the story and simultaneously illuminates an age in
which the poem was maintained by oral rather than written tradition:

Each of us must experience an end to life in this world, let him who can
achieve glory before he dies, that will be best for the lifeless warrior
afterwards.[3]

The Church, by contrast, held that life on earth was a preparation
for paradise in the next world. Human life, Bede tells us, can be
likened to the flight of a sparrow through the king's hall, 'coming in

1. Jack Goody, *The Domestication of the Savage Mind* (Cambridge, 1977), 162.
2. Edmund Leach, 'Two essays concerning the symbolic representation of time', in E.
Leach (ed.), *Rethinking Anthropology* (London, 1961), 124–36; see also Anthony
Giddens, *A Contemporary Critique of Historical Materialism* (London, 1981), 130–5 on
the general issues of time; Kenneth Harrison considers the historical implications for
the Anglo-Saxons in *The Framework of Anglo-Saxon History to AD 900* (Cambridge,
1976).
3. *Beowulf*, trans. D. Wright (Harmondsworth, 1957), lines 1386–9.

from the darkness and returning to it'.[4] In such ways the Church shook the concepts of time-present and time-future, inviting man to invest in paradise now, to pay his fare for the future. Subsidiary to this ideological conflict with the heathens was a no less significant attitude to time-budgeting. Events were now chronicled. Time was regulated by Christian ceremonies in such a way as to connect events once more across Europe.[5] A cyclical calendar doubtless existed before, but the Latin calendar fervently disputed at the Synod of Whitby in 664 brought England within a much larger time-zone.

Bede's history of the Anglo-Saxon Church makes it clear how in the course of three generations territory by territory succumbed to the portfolio of ideas brought by the missionaries. Yet their arrival, like that of the Romans 550 years before, occurred at a special time. As we have seen, an English identity was being formed as a reaction, as much as anything, to the aboriginal cultural and economic conditions which prevailed after the Roman withdrawal. But in the search for the genesis of English individualism it should be noted that by the seventh century all the tribal societies around the North Sea basin were eager for change. Already the political and economic status of Rome had become a distant memory, leaving the Church as the only link with a classical past. In this chapter, therefore, I shall examine the impact made by the early Church on England. Once again it will be apparent that the interplay between insularity and the reception of Continental concepts was to be singularly important in creating a notion of Englishness.

The impact of the Church

The most conspicuous expression of the new religion is the churches themselves. According to Richard Morris,[6] about ninety churches are recorded from the seventh century, and a good many more probably went unrecorded. These belong to three periods within the seventh century, which serve as a rough chronological framework for several other aspects of the age. About ten belong to the first two decades of the century (which I shall term period A), ten more to the following years up to about 670 (period B), and about half to c. 670–700 (period C). The numbers must be treated with some care since the calibre of the sources is hardly good. Nevertheless the pattern reveals the gradual extension of Christianity to the population. Once again it can

4. Bede, *A History of the English Church and People*, trans. L. Sherley-Price (Harmondsworth, 1955), 127.

5. Cf. John A. Hall, *Powers and Liberties* (Oxford, 1985), quoting Thomas Hobbes. I shall consider this matter again in Chapter Seven.

6. Richard Morris, *The Church in British Archaeology* (London, 1983), 35–8.

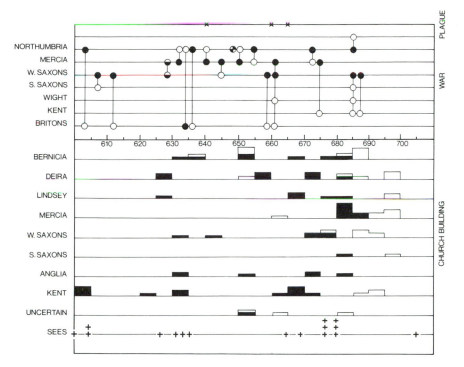

12. Graph showing the recorded progress of church-building in the kingdoms of seventh-century England as well as documented warfare and pestilence in this period. Warfare: solid circles represent aggressor, open circles represent victim. Church-building: solid blocks represent foundations of churches, open blocks represent the first references to the existence of churches (drawn by Barry Vincent, after C.J. Arnold).

be depicted as ripples spreading out from the point of impact in Kent, marginal territories being slow to convert to the new religion. But the character of the conversion seems to have altered significantly during the course of the century. The architectural form of seventh-century churches may be an instructive index of the changing character of the English clergy.

According to Eric Fernie, the early basilican churches belong to a south European setting. Fernie believes that 'parallels with Kent can be found in Ravenna, in the Alps and in Tunisia. Italy, via Sicily and the Po valley, is the obvious common element in these three areas'.[7] A Mediterranean concept, in other words, was being introduced in period A. But by the 670s (the beginning of period C) Frankish models may have been in the minds of a new generation of church-builders.

7. Eric Fernie, *The Architecture of the Anglo-Saxons* (London, 1983), 46.

The first minster (the Old Minster) in Winchester, for example, is quite unlike the Kentish missionary buildings and, in Fernie's opinion, shares common characteristics with St German in Speyer.[8]

A second vivid expression of the impact of the Church is to be found in the burial customs of this period. The tradition of accompanying the dead with grave goods persisted to a varying degree. Hence the Kentish and East Anglian communities, exposed first to continental and missionary influences, were probably discarding this tradition by the 630s and 640s (period B), while the *Pecsaetan*, for example, of the Peak District or the western outliers of the newly conquered West Saxon community in Dorset maintained the tradition until comparatively late in the seventh century (period C). Graves lacking accoutrements or furnishings, post-dating the climax burials, occur in a number of well-established cemeteries. It is as though the old tradition had died but the spirit of the place persisted for a generation or so. At the same time new cemeteries were created (invariably at monasteries), some beginning, it seems, with climax graves and then continuing with inhumations lacking accoutrements. The early eighth-century sceattas (silver pennies) from cemeteries like Garton-on-the-Wolds (West Yorkshire) illustrate this sequence, albeit some generations later.[9]

The most spectacular climax of traditional burial customs occurs at Sutton Hoo and the barrows of similar date at Broomfield and Taplow. There is some reason to suppose that the arrival of the Church may have generated this extraordinary inflation in the existing funerary system, especially in south-east England, which was thereafter transmitted to other territories. Certainly brooches made with imported gold and garnets, skilfully fashioned by Anglo-Saxon craftsmen, influenced by Frankish styles and Christian iconography, are hallmarks of this age. The Church, it seems, condoned the great funerary ceremonies and, more pertinently, became involved, if Bede is accurate on the matter, with the inheritance issues that figured prominently on these occasions. In other words the pagan idol planted in the fictional missionary Eorpwald's tomb at Melpham in Angus Wilson's *Anglo-Saxon Attitudes* is not so far-fetched. The Church was associated with pagan sumptuary rites, as the pectoral cross from St Cuthbert's grave to some extent

8. ibid.; see also Birthe Kjolbye-Biddle, 'The seventh-century minster at Winchester interpreted', in L.A.S. Butler & R.K. Morris (eds.), *The Anglo-Saxon Church* (London, 1986), 196–209.

9. D.M. Metcalf, 'Monetary circulation in southern England in the first half of the eighth century', in D. Hill & D.M. Metcalf (eds.), *Sceattas in England and on the Continent* (Oxford, 1984), 27–69.

13. The excavation of the ship in mound 1 at Sutton Hoo (Suffolk) in August 1939 (courtesy of the British Museum).

14. Excavation of Intervention 41 at Sutton Hoo (mound 2) in 1987 (courtesy of the Sutton Hoo Research Trust).

betrays.[10] The most spectacular illustration of this inflation has been excavated at Sutton Hoo, the site which sparked Wilson's interest in the concept. Besides a boatful of treasure, it now appears that the funerals were accompanied by the ritual sacrifice of other persons who were thrown, often awkwardly, into shallow graves surrounding the barrows. The extravagance of these rituals is closely paralleled by the contemporary Valsgarde-Vendel barrows in central Sweden, and has persuaded many archaeologists to seek a dynastic connection between the two areas.[11] It would be foolish to deny the probability of some shared affinity between these kingdoms, especially as the scale of commerce within the North Sea interaction zone was beginning to

10. Angus Wilson, *Anglo-Saxon Attitudes* (London, 1956); for the full account of St Cuthbert's tomb see C.F. Battiscombe, *The Relics of St Cuthbert* (Oxford, 1956). It is worth noting Martin Carver's point, made in a lecture at Sheffield University, that the Christian objects at Sutton Hoo may represent just one of a number of gifts made to the deceased as opposed to his earthly possessions. There is some evidence to suggest that the ship-burial contains sets of prestige goods, possibly donated by those who attended the funeral. The material expression of the deceased's Christianity, in other words, can at least be questioned. In the great literature arising from the Sutton Hoo excavations clearly this aspect owes a good deal to our twentieth-century familiarity with Bede's account of the Wuffingas.

11. Martin Carver, 'Anglo-Saxon objectives at Sutton Hoo, 1985', *Anglo-Saxon England* 15 (1987), 139–52.

grow at precisely this time, necessitating new means of control. Yet the inflation in the ritual owes a great deal to the intrusion of Christian time and Christian connections which, as I shall try to show later in this chapter, accentuated the need to emphasise a mythic past in order to control the future of measured resources.

The third expression of the impact of the Church upon the embryonic Anglo-Saxon tribes is to be found in ancient Roman centres. These were largely abandoned – ruinous and overgrown fossils of the 'age of giants' (to quote the Anglo-Saxon poem *The Ruin*). Yet a number of recent investigations testify to the existence of early churches within Roman monumental buildings at such places as Exeter, Leicester, London, Verulamium and York (Fig. 15).[12] In addition, excavations over the past thirty years in Canterbury have identified many small clusters of early seventh-century buildings within the deserted town, presumably associated with the Kentish court and Augustine's mission.[13] A similar pattern has been recognised at Winchester, where the Old Minster was founded in about 650 by Cenwalh; and, to judge from the excavations at Brook Street nearby, at least one small elite community continued to occupy the ruins of the Roman town. Hardly surprisingly, some archaeologists believe that some old Roman towns had been continuously occupied since the Roman withdrawal, and were administrative centres of the new tribes when the missionaries arrived.[14]

Following an idea proposed by Carl-Richard Brühl for comparable centres in the Frankish kingdoms, Martin Biddle interprets the cluster of buildings at Brook Street, Winchester – several graves with grave-goods and a striking quantity of vessel glass – as a residential complex/enclosure of thegn-status. This interpretation and its wider implications have been forcefully challenged by Barbara Yorke in a study of how the missions used the abandoned Roman centres in England.[15] In her opinion the documentary evidence does not sustain Biddle's hypothesis. She believes that the long-established Continental tradition of locating bishoprics in old Roman towns may have led the Church to consider the foundation of the West Saxon bishopric in Winchester. But no evidence exists to show that there was a royal

12. Warwick Rodwell, 'Churches in the landscape: aspects of topography and planning', in M.L. Faull (ed.), *Studies in Late Anglo-Saxon Settlement* (Oxford, 1984), 1–23; Richard Morris, op. cit. (n. 6), chs 2 & 3.

13. T. Tatton-Brown & N. Macpherson Grant, 'Anglo-Saxon Canterbury. Topography and pottery', *Current Archaeology* 98 (1985), 89–93.

14. Martin Biddle, 'The study of Winchester: archaeology and history in a British town, 1961–83', *Proceedings of the British Academy* 69 (1983), 93–135 at 116–17; see also D.A. Brooks, 'A review of the evidence for continuity in British towns in the fifth and sixth centuries', *Oxford Journal of Archaeology* 5 (1986), 77–102.

15. B.A.E. Yorke, 'The foundation of the Old Minster and the status of Winchester in the seventh and eighth centuries', *Proceedings of the Hampshire Field Club* 38 (1982), 75–84.

centre here. Quite the contrary, she argues: the small cluster of buildings excavated in Brook Street is consistent with a modest ecclesiastical foundation nearby. Small royal centres, she asserts, may have
existed within the ruins of Canterbury and London in about 600, but
there is no evidence to suggest that Winchester shared the same status
as these places.

Brühl's thesis has been substantially supported by archaeological
and historical evidence on the Continent. Recent excavations, for
example, show that Frankish and Lombard towns contracted to small
communities, but that aristocratic, ecclesiastical and ancillary
craftsmen continued nevertheless to occupy the ruins. By the sixth
century many were no longer competitive market places supporting
large communities of artisans and merchants, though they were still
central places as far as regional administration was concerned.[16]
Hence it is hardly surprising, as Yorke notes, to discover southern
European bishops seeking centres with which they had some
sympathy. Nor is it surprising that they chose to plant their principal
churches in old Roman towns, since building materials were abun-
dantly available. Archaeology, however, provides no indisputable
evidence that towns like Winchester were occupied during the century
or so between the 480s and 580s. On the contrary, only the cemeteries
distributed within their surrounding territories provide these places
with a tenuous link with the past. Such evidence can be interpreted
in any way possible. In fact it is more useful to examine why the
Continental towns continued to be centres of settlement through this
period to see whether this sheds light on circumstances in England.
Two reasons may appropriately be mentioned here. First, the towns
of Late Roman Gaul and Italy were seats of political power in territories many times larger than the English towns. The scale of these
early post-Roman kingdoms made it necessary for the elite to maintain
classical communication systems, as well as control of the traditional
foci of communication in the key towns. Secondly, in contrast to
Britain, there was not a total collapse of all commodity production in
Gaul or Italy. Mass-produced pottery and glass, for example, were
manufactured by traditional methods in many old centres, including
towns. In marked contrast to Britain, the classical fabric did not
utterly disappear in the Continental provinces.

The location of the Church outside the old towns is rather more
intriguing. Janet L. Nelson contends that 'the churches of Angles and
Saxons grew up in the interstices of local aristocratic lordship. That
was why ecclesiastical property was so vulnerable, why kings treated
it no differently from other powerful laymen, and why the charter,

16. Bryan Ward-Perkins, *From Classical Antiquity to the Middle Ages: urban public
building in Northern and Central Italy AD 300–850* (Oxford, 1984).

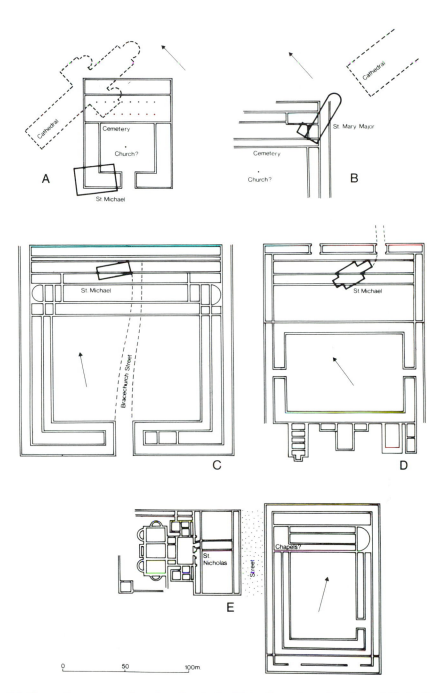

15. Seventh-century churches located within the ruins of major public buildings in Romano-British towns: (A) York, (B) Exeter, (C) London, (D) Verulamium, (E) Leicester (drawn by Barry Vincent, after Warwick Rodwell).

the land-book, intended by churchmen to protect church property, could become in England, in the hands of the lay aristocracy, an instrument to guarantee the rights of noble kindred.'[17] Invariably the Church was granted lands far from the centres of the English kingdoms. Cuthbert was given great tracts of land in northern Northumbria, while Guthlac established a powerful monastery at Crowland, far from Mercia in the Lincolnshire Fens.

A pertinent illustration of this is the foundation of the monastery at Abingdon (Berkshire). In the 670s the monastery was granted twenty hides of land by Cissa, an under-king of Wessex. A little later, King Ine of Wessex encouraged the construction of the abbey and made further endowments to it. Abingdon may well have been envisaged as a buffer estate, not unlike the monastic lands established by King Alfred alongside the frontier with the Danelaw.[18] In this instance the monastery at Abingdon was situated between Mercia and the heartland of Wessex. Apart from being an illustration of Nelson's point, the estate is interesting for another reason. Recent research suggests that the 'land of the Barton Court Farm villa estate was included in the first grant of twenty hides to the new Christian foundation'. As a result, David Miles, the excavator of the Barton Court Farm villa, speculates that the Roman estate may have passed down from the fourth to the seventh century as a coherent operational unit. This is not a new idea. H.P.R. Finberg tried to show that the villa estate of Withington (Gloucestershire) survived more or less intact during this period to become a medieval farm.[19] At Barton Court Farm, however, a small body of archaeological evidence exists to show that the sub-Roman settlement was occupied until the mid-seventh century and then abandoned. Miles questions whether the desertion coincides with the monastic settlement or is part of a more widespread phenomenon. The latter, for reasons outlined below, may carry more weight. Yet it appears highly probable that the Church and perhaps the English kings had some appreciation of the geography of the historic houses of the Roman age. Since the villas managed good land, we should not be surprised by 'continuity' of this kind. It shows, nevertheless, that for the Church at least the aura of the classical past was not simply confined to England's derelict towns.

17. Janet L. Nelson, ' "A King across the sea": Alfred in Continental perspective', *Transactions of the Royal Historical Society* 36 (1986), 45–68, at 66.

18. David Miles, *Archaeology at Barton Court Farm, Abingdon, Oxfordshire* (London, 1986), 52.

19. H.P.R. Finberg, *Roman and Saxon Withington, a study in continuity* (Leicester, 1955). For a fuller discussion of these issues in the light of modern research see Tom Williamson, 'Parish boundaries and early fields: continuity and discontinuity', *Journal of Historical Geography* 12 (1986), 241–8; 'Settlement chronology and regional landscapes: the evidence from the claylands of East Anglia and Essex', in Della Hooke (ed.), *Anglo-Saxon Settlements* (Oxford, 1988), 153–75.

With the advent of the missions not only the Church but the English kings were attracted by the spirit of the classical past. Palaces were built in Canterbury, London and York, and from these some English kings began to express themselves in charters and laws initially (in period A) using Mediterranean formulae.[20] Yet this revival of classicism should not be exaggerated. The Church may have liked these derelict, weed-infested places,[21] but Anglo-Saxon kings did not take to them naturally. The kings were still closely tied to their communities, compelled by the primitive political economy to regulate affairs at local level. This invariably meant that those palaces in ruined Roman centres were simply on a circuit of residences maintained by a peripatetic leadership. Until archaeologists have investigated at least one circuit, debate will continue on the question. But the secular elite can be spotlighted from another angle. Their attitudes to prestige goods and their management of resources generally reveal not only the momentum of individualism in English society, but also how receptive they were to some important teachings of the Church.

The supply of gifts

The age of St Augustine (period A) marks a time of inflation in the circulation of primitive valuables. The climax graves, as I described them above, are spectacularly rich in their endowments to the dead. The disposal of wealth, it was argued in Chapter Two, relates to a gifts-to-gods strategy linked to inheritance strategies. Put simply, these well-furnished graves show that tension over inheritance persuaded the likely inheritor to promote lavishly the status of the deceased. But it was not simply an English fashion. It was equally common in Austrasia, Neustria and even Lombardy. As in England, in these territories a phase of climax graves preceded the desertion of the cemeteries in the later seventh century.[22] The widespread pattern in the funerary rite of the seventh century is not a coincidence.

Professor Middleton in Angus Wilson's *Anglo-Saxon Attitudes* disarmingly states: 'I know nothing whatsoever about Dark Age Trade, or at any rate no more than befits a gentleman.'[23] Treating England as an insular entity in this age, as I hope I have already illustrated, may befit a gentleman but it is poor history. The world of late antiquity was a bubbling crucible into which the Anglo-Saxons

20. Patrick Wormald, *'Lex Scripta* and *Verbum Regis*: legislation and Germanic kingship', in P. Sawyer & I. Wood (eds.), *Early Medieval Kingship* (Leeds, 1977), 105–38.
21. Biddle, op. cit. (n. 14); R. Macphail, 'Soil and botanical studies of the Dark Earth', in M. Jones & G.W. Dimbleby (eds.), *The Environment and Man* (Oxford, 1981), 309–31.
22. e.g. J. Slofstra, H.H. van Regteren Altena, N. Roymans and F. Theuws, *Het Kempenprojekt; een regionaal- archeologisch onderzoeksprogramma* (Amsterdam, 1982), 114–24.
23. Wilson, op. cit. (n. 10), 37.

were drawn. England, as we have seen (p. 29) was affected by the disintegration of the western Roman Empire. The Frankish king Clovis' territorial aspirations, in responding to these circumstances, may have encompassed southern England, as I noted in Chapter Two. Other notable consequences included the beginnings of the North Sea interaction zone and a chain of inter-territorial trade partnerships which connected the Lombardic, Alamannic, Burgundian, Austrasian and Neustrian courts.[24] The Kentish and East Anglian courts were probably tied intermittently into these chains of gift-giving, which extended southwards to northern Italy as well as up to southern Scandinavia. But the transalpine route by which the flow of Mediterranean goods ultimately reached the English appears to have declined in importance in the later sixth century. Turmoil within the old Ostrogothic courts, the rise of the Lombards and wars with the Byzantines stationed in southern Italy almost certainly led to a cessation in the flow of prestige goods. In about 600, a new route stemming from Provence appears to have supplanted it briefly. This linked southern Gallic communities directly with the last generation of East Mediterranean traders to penetrate western markets. Their goods were channelled northwards through the Rhone valley – a route which flourished for possibly two generations. By about 630, however, the heyday of Provence as an entrepôt had passed – Byzantine trade in the West Mediterranean had declined enormously and by the middle of the century was virtually snuffed out. With this the economic symbiosis which had generated western Europe for nearly a millennium was at an end.

Henri Pirenne rightly pointed out that the North Sea basin now became the focus of an economic interaction zone featuring those communities bordering it.[25] The nucleus of territories, which since Clovis' time had been closely bound together by trade connections, now joined together to enlarge upon their commercial ties. Naturally, although the thrust of these changes was generated with the Merovingian heartlands, it nevertheless affected the English. Not only did the supply of gifts and wealth in circulation within the Anglo-Saxon territories increase, but so did attitudes to resources generally.

It may be no coincidence that the classic Anglo-Saxon funerary rite began in the period when Clovis orchestrated wide-ranging social and economic changes in northern Gaul. Likewise, with the formal alliance between the Neustrians and Kentish kingdoms resulting from the marriage of Bertha to Ethelbert in the 560s, if not a little before, we must envisage a new phase not only in cross-channel connections but also of gift-giving. New sources of primitive valuables gave the

24. Richard Hodges, *Dark Age Economics* (London, 1982), 31–9.
25. Richard Hodges & David Whitehouse, *Mohammed, Charlemagne and the Origins of Europe* (London, 1983), ch. 4.

Kentish king, for example, an attractive opportunity to develop his status within his own Anglo-Saxon orbit. This was an occasion, to quote Karl Marx, when exchange might prompt 'individualisation'.[26] But inflation in the gifts-to-gods rite, generated by the evolution of individualisation, the continued existence of a patchwork of territories, each with competing elites, and the growing volume of goods was bound to necessitate political changes.

The foundation of Quentovic by the Neustrian king during this period may be one expression of the increased importance attached to long-distance trade and the need to control exchange at frontiers to prevent prestige goods from falling into the hands of the aristocracy.[27] Quentovic was founded near Montreuil-sur-Mer not far from the English Channel. Its history, together with the first tentative archaeological investigations, shows strong connections with southern England. Initially it was probably a simple (type A) emporium resembling a fairground where traders set sail for Kent.[28] It was also probably a place at which the imports collected by the traders might be registered and taxed.

The archaeology of the early seventh-century Kentish cemeteries bears witness to the changing rhythm of cross-Channel contacts at this time. Imported pottery bottles, imported glasses, Frankish textiles, Frankish gold coins and many other prestige objects of Continental origin occur commonly in the graves of at least the upper two of the three identified strata of society. Such is the volume of imports that some point of disembarkation in Kent, perhaps resembling Quentovic, must have been established. Possible sites are Fordwich close to Canterbury and Sarre beside the Wantsum Channel, where a large cemetery has been excavated which includes several men accompanied by merchant's balances (see p. 92 for a further discussion).[29] Both may have functioned as temporary fairgrounds where successive Kentish kings controlled alien merchants, thereby preventing the re-routing of prestigious imports to others in the community.

Kent, however, was not the only kingdom forging contacts with the Franks across the North Sea. Recent excavations in Ipswich have revealed evidence of an emporium that was used intermittently by alien traders in this formative period.[30] Imported Frankish pottery found at Ipswich appears to be the refuse of traders rather than

26. Karl Marx, *Pre-capitalist Economic Formations* (London, 1964), 96.

27. Jan Dhondt, 'Les problèmes de Quentovic', *Studi in Onore di Amintore Fanfani* (Milan, 1962), 185–248. I am grateful to David Barrett and David Hill, the discoverers of Quentovic, for some useful discussions about this site as well as the opportunity to inspect material from their investigations.

28. Hodges, op. cit. (n. 24), 50–2.

29. Tim Tatton-Brown, 'The Anglo-Saxon towns of Kent', in Della Hooke (ed.), *Anglo-Saxon Settlements* (Oxford, 1988), 213–32.

30. ibid.

trading transactions as such. Much of the pottery was made in kilns in the Low Countries and the Rhineland. In an age best known for the Sutton Hoo ship burial, the East Anglians therefore were carving out a European profile. Redwald, the most renowned East Anglian king, is often said to be the person buried at Sutton Hoo. During his long reign from the 590s to about 624, he almost certainly dealt not only with Christian missionaries, but also with those Franks who made the day-long crossing to Ipswich. Certainly the archaeological discoveries in Ipswich contradict the view that the Austrasians approached the East Anglians because they were 'an out-of-the-way dynasty', as Professor Wallace-Hadrill once described them.[31]

A constancy in the supply of prestige objects, nevertheless, may have induced spiralling inflation in gift-giving and funerary rites which, paradoxical as it may appear to us, may have been fuelled rather than tempered by the advent of the Church. The Church, after all, was familiar with stratified societies in Gaul and Italy. As Bede illustrates, it sought out the emergent elite in Anglo-Saxon England who, as it happened, had hitherto been closely associated with tribal rituals. This served the purpose of the Church in obtaining support and resources, and it inevitably conferred some status upon the elite. It was a strategy to be repeated in eighth-century Frisia by English monks; in tenth-century Denmark by German missionaries, and even in recent times in New Guinea where the existing establishment allied itself with the Church in the expectation of changing the ideological foundations of society to its advantage.[32] Yet just as the Church focussed upon individualising its support in the Anglo-Saxon courts, so enclosed burial plots become a commoner feature of the cemeteries as certain families in each community keenly sought to emphasise their identity even in death.

In about 630, with the decline of the Provençal trade-route, the supply of Mediterranean valuables, particularly gold, diminished in north-west Europe. This left the Merovingian and Anglo-Saxon kings who had been dependent on these valuables at a cross-roads. They could either try to stay as they were, perhaps seeking other sources of wealth, or they could seek alternative strategies for acquiring it. Significantly the Merovingians and, perhaps as a result, the Anglo-Saxons opted for the second solution.

Land management was a major plank in the new strategy. By accepting gifts from the living, as well as benefices from the deceased, the Church appears to have been prepared to give support to the rights

31. J.M. Wallace-Hadrill, *Early Germanic Kingship in England and on the Continent* (Oxford, 1971), 70.

32. C.A. Gregory, 'Gifts to men and gifts to gods: gift exchange and capital accumulation in contemporary Papua', *Man* 15 (1980), 647–48; see also the same author's *Gifts and Commodities* (London, 1982).

of an individual to inherit from his father. In principle an inheritance strategy could be sustained without the destruction of moveable wealth. Instead the Church took these goods as the broker's price.[33] Simultaneously it must have guided a shift in emphasis away from the moveable wealth upon which most notions in Germanic society were constructed towards the Roman concept of land-holding. Land was not just territory that might be equated with power when its communities were assembled as armies, but the repository of agrarian commodities. Land had symbolic, military and productive value. The switch in emphasis from moveable to landed wealth occurred over many centuries, but its beginnings in the seventh century, as we shall see in the last part of this chapter, heralded many new attitudes.

Exchange in these circumstances took a different form. First, it appears that individuals have a blood-feud value which, if Professor Grierson's interpretation of the mid-seventh-century Crondall hoard from Hampshire is correct, was actually observed in coin, as opposed to being an abstract measure of personal standing in society.[34] Anglo-Saxon gold coins minted in Wessex, Kent and the territory of the East Saxons may indicate the appearance of a ranked society modelled to some degree upon Continental patterns. It may be no coincidence that the final phase of traditional Early Anglo-Saxon cemeteries in these territories occurred during this time (period B). Secondly, a generation later (period C) these territories were drawn into a major increase in the scale of commerce around the North Sea, fostered by silver coins which were fractions of the gold bullion, based on Germanic rather than classical weights.[35] In sum, the momentum of economic and thus social evolution appears to have been more or less sustained in southern England, despite the recession in the supply of gifts.

Away from direct contact with alien merchants, some inland territories maintained existing funerary traditions for a further generation or two until the decline in the circulation of prestige goods perhaps reached a critical state. The need for adaptation, it can be surmised, came fastest and hardest to land-locked tribes like the Mercians. It may be no coincidence that their kings, Penda (632–54) and later Wulfhere (658–74), were markedly bellicose during this brief transitional period (period B).[36] Through raiding and conquest, new resources could be found to augment the declining volume of prestige goods, thus maintaining the status of the elite. It is perhaps significant, however, that, in Wendy Davies's opinion, the Tribal Hidage,

33. Jack Goody, *The Development of the Family and Marriage in Europe* (Cambridge, 1983), 103ff.

34. Philip Grierson considers this question in his paper: 'The origins of money', *Research in Economic Anthropology* (1978), 1–35.

35. Hodges, op. cit. (n. 24), 110–11.

36. This point is made by Richard Morris, op. cit. (n. 6), 46–8 while discussing the patronage of seventh-century churches.

the first great survey of English territorial holdings, belongs to the reign of King Wulfhere of Mercia (Fig. 16).[37] If her analysis is correct, by the 670s even the land-locked Mercians had become cognisant of the need for new forms of resource control to manage a social order that had evolved considerably in less than a century.

The settlement shuffle

'Why,' asked Professor Wallace-Hadrill, 'did Aethelberht [king of Kent] and his continental contemporaries devote the bulk of their legislation to detailed and lengthy tariffs of compensation for personal injury and loss or damage of personal property?'[38] These may seem difficult matters for the archaeologist to investigate with confidence. Nevertheless archaeology is shedding fresh light on attitudes to property and in particular the different sizes and classes of sites and their sub-divisions. In this way, as traditional tribal codes were foresworn, the individualism of the English can be charted with some confidence.

By 600 the egalitarian settlement structure described in Chapter Two was finally at an end. The Church itself was a new element in the system, as were the small but politically important settlements now located in derelict Roman towns (see above, p. 50). Early type A emporia like Ipswich constituted yet another category of site. It is, therefore, no surprise to discover that by the early seventh century kings were constructing palaces as expressions in life of a status that was being expressed in death. At Yeavering (Northumberland) Brian Hope-Taylor excavated what might be termed the Sutton Hoo of a living leader. Hope-Taylor believes that the small cluster of later sixth-century buildings at Yeavering, at one point associated with a pagan temple, became an important palatial complex by 627. He identifies the site as *Ad Gefrin*, one of King Edwin of Northumbria's palaces, where according to Bede the missionary Paulinus preached and baptized the Northumbrian people.[39] The great hall and the associated ensemble of ancillary buildings, besides a possible church, indicate that the king was now attended by a retinue. Accommodation for the warrior band, recalled by the author of *Beowulf*, as well as for retainers, the king's wife and perhaps his concubines, illustrates the developing form that kingship was taking.

The remains of a putatative timber theatre at Yeavering offer further insight into kingship (Fig. 17). It was probably not built for Paulinus, but it may have been used by him. *If* indeed it is a theatre,

37. Wendy Davies & Hayo Vierck, 'The contexts of Tribal Hidage: social aggregates and settlement patterns', *Frühmittelalterliche Studien* 8 (1974), 223–93.

38. Wallace-Hadrill, op. cit. (n. 31), 41.

39. Brian Hope-Taylor, *Yeavering: an Anglo-British centre of early Northumbria* (London, 1977).

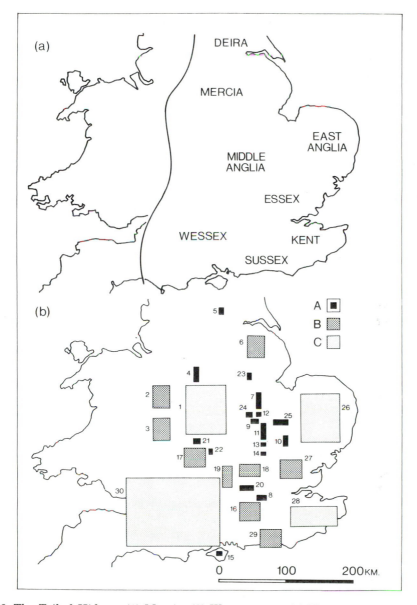

16. The Tribal Hidage: (1) Mercia; (2) Wocensaetna; (3) Westerna; (4) Pecsa-
etna; (5) Elmet; (6) Lindsey; (7) North and South Gyrwa; (8) East and West
Wixna; (9) Spalda; (10) Wigesta; (11) Herefinna; (12) Sweordora; (13) Gifla;
(14) Hicca; (15) Wihtgara; (16) Nox and Oht Gaga; (17) Hwinca; (18) Cilternsa-
etna; (19) Hendrica; (20) Unecung ga; (21) Arosaetna; (22) Faerpinga; (23)
Bilmiga; (24) Widerigga; (25) East and West Willa; (26) East Anglia; (27)
Essex; (28) Kent; (29) Sussex; (30) Wessex (drawn by Barry Vincent, after
Wendy Davies and Hayo Vierck). A = 300–1200 hides; B = 3500–7000 hides;
C = more than 7000 hides

it is a remarkable index of the use of a classical concept by Anglo-Saxon kingship, best paralleled by the period A churches. Its most likely use, however, was as an assembly point for the region. Hope-Taylor calculated that about 300 people might be seated within this structure.[40] Given the size of contemporary villages with estimated populations ranging from 25 to 50, the theatre might have held a population drawn from at least ten settlements, or alternatively the headmen from as many as 300. The latter would imply that Yeavering was a regional centre for a population of about 10,000. Yeavering, however, was occupied only briefly. By the mid-seventh century it was abandoned. Its transitory character, in common with several other royal sites recently discovered from this age, suggests that either the surrounding resources were considered insufficient, or its location as a central point in regional administration was unsatisfactory. Whichever was the case, when it was in use the largely peripatetic community at Yeavering had to be fed. Either this was undertaken by a permanent staff of servile cultivators, or by tribute to the dynasty from the population that attended the periodic assemblies. Certainly the composition of the palatial settlement at Yeavering was not unique.

Cowdery's Down, Hampshire, was the setting of a similar complex. Its excavator found a roughly linear spread of seventh-century buildings, seemingly 'planned', which superseded a small collection of fenced households. Building 12 in this palatial complex, in particular, is strikingly similar to the great hall at Yeavering, with the capacity to accommodate large numbers.[41] As the excavator Martin Millett shows, the skill of the carpenters enlisted to construct buildings like those at Yeavering, like the smiths responsible for the Sutton Hoo treasure, were part of a seventh-century artisanal *milieu* from whom the highest quality was demanded as the need to express status reached its zenith.

The discovery of these and other palaces is extremely important. Like the Sutton Hoo ship burial, they are illustrations of English kingship in its infancy from two ends of the country. Their histories embody the momentous occasion when hitherto unprepossessing places were rebuilt from scratch as architecturally imposing ensembles of buildings. From this point we might trace, to quote Nicholas Brooks, 'the development of royal authority in England [which] was directly connected with the successful enforcement of public works and general military obligations'.[42] Evidently, in the age of the

---

40. Hope-Taylor, op. cit. (n. 39), 119–22.

41. Martin Millett with Simon James, 'Excavations at Cowdery's Down, Basingstoke, Hampshire', *Archaeological Journal* 140 (1983), 151–279.

42. N.P. Brooks, 'The development of military obligations in eighth and ninth century England', in P. Clemoes & K. Hughes (eds.), *England before the Conquest* (Cambridge, 1971), 69–84, at 79.

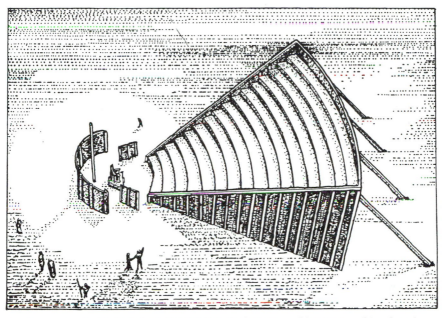

17. Reconstruction of the putative timber theatre at Yeavering (Northumberland) (drawn by Barry Vincent, after Brian Hope-Taylor).

missionaries the accumulation of credit in the gift-giving process appears to have created the existence as well as the need for retainers to protect, administer and work on a king's behalf.[43] Little wonder, then, that kings were concerned about their personal standing in society and their property rights.

The building of palaces evinced an attitude to property that was not confined to one section of society. Quite the reverse. It coincides with attitudes to property across the length and breadth of the English landscape which reveal the highly integrated nature of the English settlement systems. First, the concept of a farm enclosed by a fence or ditch is now introduced, mirroring the enclosure of the ensemble of royal buildings or the vallum around monasteries. Like the palace and the monastery, the property of a farmer was legally constituted. Hence, at West Stow in the seventh century, after nearly two centuries as a settlement, the property of each farm is formally designated by an enclosure (Fig. 18). At Catholme (Staffordshire), Chalton (Hampshire) and Raunds (Northamptonshire) the same sequence has been detected. In many cases, the life of these enclosed farms is short and gives way in the lowland, ecologically richer parts of England to

43. Gregory, op. cit. (n. 32).

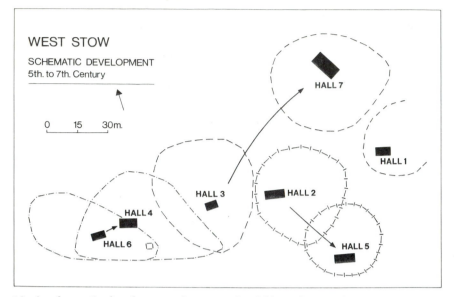

18. A schematic development between the fifth and seventh centuries of the Early Anglo-Saxon village at West Stow (Suffolk) (drawn by Barry Vincent, after Stanley West).

what has been dubbed the 'Middle Saxon shuffle'. The shuffle alludes to the desertion of many Early Anglo-Saxon villages during the seventh or early eighth century, among them Bishopstone (Sussex), Cassington (Oxfordshire), Chalton (Hampshire), Thirlings (Northumberland), West Stow (Suffolk) and Witton (Norfolk). In fact all these sites have one thing in common: they occupy ground that was not the best available. Bishopstone and Chalton were sited on exposed chalk downland promontories, while West Stow and Witton were on heathland.[44] None of this ground was strictly marginal, but equally none was located in an optimum situation. The Middle Saxon shuffle appears to reflect a new attitude to territory, causing the abandonment of lands which previous generations had found suitable.

In an interesting analysis of this evidence Arnold and Wardle point out (Fig. 19) that 'the major shift in location is concerned not merely with the relocation of settlements *within* a defined land unit, but with the reorganisation of such territorial units, some of whose new

44. M. Bell, 'Excavations at Bishopstone', *Sussex Archaeological Collections* 115 (1977); for Cassington see reports by E.T. Leeds in *Archaeologia* 72 (1923), 147–92; 72 (1927), 59–79; 92 (1927), 79–93; for Chalton see reports in *Medieval Archaeology* 16 (1972), 13–32; 17 (1973), 1–25; S. West, *West Stow. The Anglo-Saxon village* (East Anglian Archaeology, Ipswich, 1985); Andrew Lawson (ed.), *The Archaeology of Witton* (East Anglian Archaeology, Norwich, 1983), 50–69.

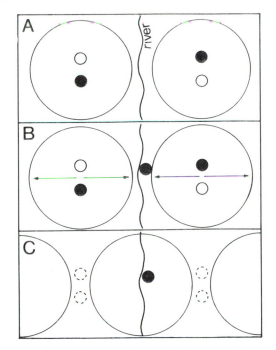

19. Three stages in the shifting pattern of villages in the seventh century, and the changing relationship between settlements (black dots), cemeteries (open dots) and land units (large circles) (drawn by Barry Vincent, after C.J. Arnold and P. Wardle).

boundaries later became fossilised as parish boundaries. It is suggested that the change is the result of new land-use requirements. . .it is to these new settlements that the majority of early place-name elements belong, irrespective of the pattern of usage of such names before that time. . .'[45] In their view, communities were uprooting themselves or being uprooted in a bid to control superior resources. Tributes demanded by the elite as well as the Church, it may be concluded, compelled communities to evaluate the long-term potential of their lands in a way which was unthought of before about 600. Aethelberht's interest in values, like Ine's later codes devoted to tribute, finds its reflection, we may surmise, in local adaptation strategies. Furthermore this new ethos was not restricted to the heartlands of old Roman Britain. The seventh century witnessed fresh colonisation of lands that had been deserted for many generations.

45. C.J. Arnold & P. Wardle, 'Early medieval settlement patterns in England', *Medieval Archaeology* 25 (1981), 145–9, at 148. Note the criticisms of this model made by Martin G. Welch, 'Rural settlement patterns in the Early and Middle Anglo-Saxon periods', *Landscape History* 7 (1985), 20–1.

Archaeologists of the Fenland Research Committee have now charted the spread of settlement into the Lincolnshire Fen Edge.[46] Here, in what was to become Middle Anglia, Roman sites had been very dense. They were mostly abandoned in the later third or fourth centuries. Traces of Early Anglo-Saxon activity have proved to be most elusive. The seventh- to ninth-century archaeology of the region, as we shall see in later chapters, marks a significant change in resource strategies (p. 20). The reoccupation of the Peak District by the *Pecsaetan* appears to be part of the same movement. Seventh-century burials in prehistoric and Roman-period barrows, if the recently excavated Wigber Low (in Derbyshire) is an accurate illustration, comprised family groups, though only for one or two generations. Wigber Low was the cemetery of an estimated 10–20 individuals (Fig. 20).[47] The fine grave goods, all belonging to the phase of climax burials, date to the middle or later seventh century. Wigber Low may have been the burial-place for settlers occupying the verdant valley below it. By contrast, the rich Benty Grange barrow, situated higher up on the White Peak, close to the Neolithic henge at Arbor Low, poses more problems. Could it have been the focus or boundary of a grazing territory? Or was it, like Wigber, a graveyard serving a nearby settlement? Only future surveys will decide whether Benty Grange pertained to a marginal community – the upland counterpart of those in the fen-edge.

Place-names and the first land-charters also reflect the importance now attached to land. Hayo Vierck has shown how the forests and woodlands of the Midlands were colonised in a small way at this time.[48] But the pre-eminent documentary illustration of the new attitude to land, and its central importance to aspiring kings, is the Tribal Hidage. This early precursor of Domesday Book lists the tributes raised from Mercia and the twenty-eight territories (Northumbria is omitted) surrounding it. In the survey a Mercian king divided the Anglo-Saxon tribes into three basic types of taxable community.

The largest group of territories amounted to 7,000 or more hides; a medium group was in the order of 7,000; and a third essentially comprised small territories of multiples of 300.[49] Each group had different political functions, roughly approximating to kingdoms, dependent administrative units and miscellaneous small groups respectively. Kingdoms and social groupings seem not to have been

46. P.P. Hayes, 'Roman to Saxon in the south Lincolnshire Fens', *Antiquity* 62 (1988), 321–6; and 'Relating Fen Edge sediments, stratigraphy and archaeology near Billingborough, south Lincolnshire', in N.R.J. Feiller et al. (eds.), *Palaeoenvironmental Investigations* (Oxford, 1985), 245–69.

47. John Collis, *Wigber Low. A Bronze Age and Anglian burial site in the White Peak* (Sheffield, 1983).

48. Davies & Vierck, op. cit. (n. 37).

49. ibid., 236–9.

20. Burial 4 in the seventh-century secondary barrow at Wigber Low (Derbyshire) (courtesy of John Collis).

straightforward alternatives as such. In some cases groups of people existed alongside, but not completely outside, the kingdom structure.

The Tribal Hidage is the first indication of the fragmented state of Britain after the Roman withdrawal. It is also a valuable illustration of the complex cultural foundations of the English, and of the myriad opportunities for inter-tribal competition. But the survey, as was claimed above, must also be viewed in the light of the settlement shuffle, the emergence of centralised authority and the changing attitudes to resources.

The conundrum of language

The thesis presented so far lays little emphasis on the part played by Angles, Saxons and Jutes in the beginnings of English society. Instead, it has been argued, following nearly a century of aboriginal social and economic conditions, a small nucleus of aliens was moulded into a cultural history that was substantially shaped by Continental interventions and peer-polity interaction. But how are the vast numbers of Anglo-Saxon place-names to be explained? Indeed how is it that the Anglo-Saxons spoke English rather than some form of Welsh?

It is tempting to fall prey to history once the sources survive: to chart events, the spread of language, and the use of place-names as our sources direct us to do. But we should beware. The sources for seventh-century England are essentially ethno-history written for an explicit purpose. With writing – with the domestication of the savage mind – came new approaches to formulating thoughts, and new horizons, both spatial and temporal. The sociologist Anthony Giddens directs our attention to this aspect of the transition towards statedoms, and to what he terms the *storage capacity* invoked by writing. He asserts that 'storage of authoritative resources is the basis of the *surveillance* activities of the state, always an undergirding medium of state power'. 'Surveillance' involves two things: the collation of information relevant to state control of the conduct of its subject population, and the direct supervision of that conduct. The formation of agrarian states is almost everywhere associated with the invention of writing and notation. Writing seems to have originated in most cases as a direct mode of information storage: as a means of recording and analysing information involved with the administration of societies of increasing scale.[50] The Tribal Hidage is a good illustration of Giddens' point: it is an Anglo-Saxon interpretation of a classical device (the survey) for managing land resources. The Church as a pan-European institution may have introduced this new storage capacity to the Anglo-Saxons, just as it seems to have introduced the concept of the land charter.

At the same time we should note that connections with a non-classical heritage were also being emphasised. Southern Scandinavian and Germanic symbols abound in the rich ornamentation of the finest jewellery and other artefacts of the period. One interpretation of these motifs would be as material symbols deployed by the artisans of the elite to propagate the concept of a common (albeit mythical) past. Such symbols, it might be argued, powerfully promoted sectional interests at a time of potentially stressful social change.

These circumstances may help to account for the curious alchemy which gave rise to the English. But the biggest obstacle to this conclusion is inevitably the language itself.

Language, it needs to be emphasised, is first and foremost a mechanism for communicating within and between peoples. In this respect it is not unconnected with other cultural traits such as dress and artistic expression, as structural anthropologists have long argued. In the case of English, though, we are poorly informed about its seventh-century form. But in theory, at least, it is not difficult to see why the English do not speak Welsh. The social and economic transformations in Britain between about 450 and 650 were much greater than those

50. Giddens, op. cit. (n. 2), 94–5; 169–70.

in Gaul, Italy or Spain, for example. There classical antiquity was never wholly extinguished as it was in Britain. Consequently linguistic change, illustrated especially in terms of place-names as well as written and spoken forms, occurred more slowly than in England. None the less Edward James has cogently demonstrated how ubiquitous sixth-century Frankish place-names found throughout northern France may connote political, ideological and economic movement rather than a migration/invasion by an ethnic group.[51] James's thesis is supported to some extent by a range of archaeological evidence, some of which was discussed on p. 30. As a result, we may speculate (and I admit it is no more than speculation at present) that, detached from late antique influences, many languages and dialects existed in Britain. Later in the sixth century, however, a common language, with its concurrent evocation of distant and mythic connections with the pioneers and founders who made the great adventure across the North Sea, may have begun to evolve as a medium of prestige and status which, in common with other material symbols, was manipulated to advance sectional interests. With the arrival of the Church and the intensification of peer competition, the definition of language, like all symbolic devices, would have been encouraged rather than opposed, and Anglo-Saxon may have evolved as the means of communication between the elites. At the same time, besides inadvertently fostering a new grammar, the Church may have fuelled the belief that the disparate English tribes, long since deserted by the Romans, shared a common heritage.

*

At the end of the sixth century those Anglo-Saxon tribes within the sphere of Frankish and perhaps North Sea connections were on the brink of a political catharsis. But without the advent of the Church at this time the Anglo-Saxons would probably have forged a very different society. It is tempting to speculate that, as in Denmark, political power would have evolved slowly, with cultural levelling mechanisms constraining the creation of dynastic leadership and this in turn proving an enduring hindrance to the development of production and regional distribution. In tenth-century Denmark, as in seventh-century England, the domestication of the savage mind was part of a complex package of classical ideas ranging from writing

51. Edward James, 'Cemeteries and the problem of Frankish settlement in Gaul', in P. Sawyer (ed.), *Names, Words, and Graves: early medieval settlement* (Leeds, 1979), 55–90, esp. 84–5; see also Patrick Perin, 'A propos de publications récentes concernant le peuplement en Gaule à l'époque mérovingienne: la question franque', *Archéologie Médiévale* 11 (1981), 125–45.

to church-building to notions of resource management.[52] As in tenth-century Denmark, the moment of transition from a pagan ideology to a Christian one was more than a change in ritual. It involved a new perspective of the present and, more importantly, of the future and the past. The inflation in the withdrawal of prestige goods in traditional funerary rites reflects the uncertainty, if not the trauma, of the age. In such circumstances the Church may be expected to have profited enormously from the stress. In England, though, the patchwork of territories in the seventh century forced the Church to be highly regionalised, thus diminishing its authority. It also had to compete with a highly integrated society. As we have noted, an archaic, often atomistic attitude to resource management was forsaken at all levels of society for methods that owed their genesis to classical antiquity. Herein lies a clue to the character of English society at this time, and in particular the dialectic between individualism and tribal order. Not surprisingly, therefore, when Bede was born, late in the seventh century, there was an emergent awareness – perhaps little more – of being English.

52. Klavs Randsborg, *The Viking Age in Denmark* (London, 1980); Anders Andrén, *Den Urbana scenen. Städeroch samhälle i det medeltida Danmark* (Lund, 1985).

4

The Age of Emporia

The age of Mercian supremacy has been studied less than any other
period of Anglo-Saxon history, and unless new materials come to light,
its details will always be uncertain.   (Sir Frank Stenton)[1]

In this and the next chapter I shall consider the 'age of Mercian
supremacy', to discover what happened to English society as it came
to terms with the emergence of ranking. Stenton, like most historians
after him, took the view that the achievement of the Mercian kings
was to make 'the first advance. . .on a great scale towards the political
unity of England. It showed that the particularism of the smaller
kingdoms was not an insuperable obstacle to the creation of a greater
state.' Under Penda, Wulfhere, Aethelbald and Offa, overlordship was
transformed in Stenton's opinion, into autocracy, and charismatic
chiefs induced local kings to exchange independence for the 'security
of a provincial ealdorman under Mercian patronage'.[2] But with new
materials can we reinterpret the bellicose character of the Mercians?
The archaeological evidence, I shall contend, reveals a different
picture of English history, in which King Ine of Wessex plays an
instrumental part, and in which, put simply, the Mercians felt
compelled to emulate their neighbours.

Before examining these new materials it is necessary to recall a few
features of the social and economic context. First, the Church had
encouraged great changes. By the late seventh century, for instance, it
had assumed exclusive control over funerals. Community cemeteries,
characteristic of the Early Anglo-Saxon period, were abandoned in
favour of multi-community cemeteries often located around minsters.
This meant that a regional or sub-regional clerical elite now largely
controlled mortuary practice and, as Jack Goody has shown, played a
powerful part in inheritance issues.[3]

Yet the authority of the Church was not unbridled. By altering
Early Anglo-Saxon values, it contributed to the gradual demise of the

1. Frank Stenton, *Anglo-Saxon England*, 3rd edition (Oxford, 1971), 236.
2. ibid., 202.
3. Jack Goody, *The Development of the Family and Marriage in Europe* (Cambridge,
1983).

deeply embedded systems of prestige goods exchange and hastened the concurrent introduction of resource strategies based upon property-ownership. As we have seen in Chapter Three, a feature of these changes was the crystallisation of existing political relations, and indeed the emergence of kingship. In place of traditional economic values, the Church fostered the right to accumulate wealth to personal or household advantage. This had lasting implications for the formation of the English aristocracy and was to prove detrimental to the Church.

It is as well to begin by considering these implications in abstract terms. In the eighth century England comprised numerous territories with regularly changing political complexions. In these circumstances, the apparatus was developed to set the leadership and the political structure apart both from subsistence and from commerce and wealth accumulated directly through the exchange of local products. Nevertheless, in the midst of rapid social change, some traditional constraints and blocks needed to be maintained upon free flows of wealth. Uncontrolled sources of wealth, particularly from outside England, could threaten the monopolies imposed by power-holders on the acquisition of tribal offices within the hierarchy. Indeed many anthropologists believe that the essence of this kind of society consists of rules to restrict the means of achieving political power and to perpetuate a ranking system.[4]

Elites, as anthropologists point out, generally experience considerable difficulty in maintaining blocks on the flow of imports, thus preventing the disruptive effects of imported wealth. Commerce is therefore controlled on boundaries, where it is easier to prevent lower-ranking groups from colluding with foreign merchants. Since this collusion destabilises an existing hierarchy, there is always the threat that lower-ranking groups may try to establish a new one. To subvert the political system effectively, lower-ranking groups would have to control both local and external sources of demand. The hierarchy must regulate not only trade with foreign merchants, but also the production of those goods that attracted the foreign trade in the first place. Control of production normally proves a critical factor if for some reason foreign trade declines, as native craft products may come to be circulated instead.

In complex systems, control of resources is invariably a violent task. This was especially true in Anglo-Saxon England, as the later *Anglo-Saxon Chronicle* illustrates. More often than not, polities were short-lived, lineage chiefs were murdered, and there was little opportunity to create a socio-political system in which kinsmen and tribesmen

4. A brief outline of this model can be found in M.J. Rowlands, 'Processual archaeology as historical social science', in C. Renfrew, M.J. Rowlands & B. Segraves-Whallon (eds.), *Theory and Explanation in Archaeology* (London, 1982), 155–74; see also Richard Hodges, *Primitive and Peasant Markets* (Oxford, 1988), 34–42.

walked in the chief's footprints (to paraphrase Elman Service; see p. 4).

The new materials: coinage and chronology

The archaeological study of Middle Saxon England is in its infancy. Only in the past decade has it become possible to form a picture of the age from its archaeology. In particular, evidence of long-distance trade has been amassed as a result of ambitious excavation programmes at Southampton and Ipswich. Recent excavations and research at Canterbury, London, Winchester and York also permit well-documented trade centres to be assessed from an archaeological angle. To this urban evidence must be added the results of excavations at monasteries such as Jarrow, Wearmouth and Whitby. New light on circumstances in the countryside is shed by current excavations of two elite sites at Brandon and Burrow Hill in Suffolk, together with invaluable data from the village project at Raunds (Northampton-shire). Last, but far from least, the numismatics of Middle Saxon England have received impressive attention in the past decade. Numerous discoveries (by metal-detector enthusiasts) of single coins, and a number of hoards, have transformed the monetary history of the eighth century. Middle Saxon coinage now throws a good deal of light on the chronology of the age, as well as on its economic history. In the following pages I wish to review its contribution to both. I shall begin with chronology.

The demise of the brief phase of Anglo-Saxon gold coinage, imitating Frankish tremisses, is now assigned to the 650s. There followed a pale gold epilogue to this phase – coins minted bearing the names 'Pada' and 'Vanimundus' which are usually attributed to the 650s or 670s. After these rare coins came a more important tradition. In about 670, following the example set by the Franks, silver sceattas were produced in significant numbers. The sceatta series puzzled numismatists in the nineteenth century and still confounds straightforward descrip-tion. Like the comparable Frankish coins, Anglo-Saxon sceattas were produced from pellets rather than from flattened flans. They are tiny coins, often richly ornamented. They occur in bewildering variety, defying the traditional norms of constancy which characterise later medieval and modern currencies.

Stuart Rigold cracked the peculiar code embodied in the great variety of these coins and formulated a typology which made it possible to date certain types. More recently D.M. Metcalf and others have endeavoured to make more detailed sense of the fast-growing assem-blage of sceattas. Nevertheless the purpose and the interpretation of the myriad types are issues of some contention. The interpretation offered here follows the scheme proposed by Philip Grierson and Mark

Blackburn, who have attempted to place the English coins in a European context.[5] As with the gold solidi, the idea of silver pennies was first introduced to England from the Frankish kingdoms of Neustria and Austrasia. The history of the sceatta series, therefore, has to be tied to circumstances in the Merovingian kingdoms. An important landmark in Merovingian history was the coalition of Neustria and Austrasia in the 670s by Pepin of Herstal, a formidable mayor of the Neustrian palace. The great trading emporium at Dorestad, to judge from the recent excavations, seems to have been founded at this time.[6] Coin finds as well as dendrochronology adequately date it to Pepin's age. The emporium lay on the old frontier between Austrasia and Frisia, at the point where the land fragmented into an archipelago. This sprawling urban settlement (and in all likelihood its twin to the south in the Pas de Calais at Quentovic: see p. 55) is one of the first medieval towns (what I have described elsewhere as a type B emporium) and as such an index of Pepin's ambitions. Another indication of his economic intentions can be found in the new silver denarial coinage issued at about this time. Silver fractions, based upon a new metrology, replaced gold bullion. Coinage, it must be presumed, was being minted in authorised conditions to facilitate exchange between non-kin groups. The pattern of sceattas and hoards from this era shows that currency was used to enable the elite to engage in commerce, perhaps to acquire prestige goods while disposing of local commodities.[7] Pepin died in 714. A brief phase of anarchy followed as the Frisians sought independence and attacked Austrasia, and this may have greatly reduced the scale of cross-Channel trade. Charles Martel restored control and over the subsequent two decades extended Carolingian authority into the areas north and east of the Rhine as well as into Aquitaine and Provence. During these annual military campaigns Anglo-Saxon missions ventured into the pagan territories of the Frisians and Saxons, tacitly supported by Charles. Archaeology adds a further dimension to our understanding of these times. On the one hand the Frisians seem to have been engaged in a phase of prominent economic activity. At Domburg on the western Frisian island of Walcharen a new emporium seems to have eclipsed Dorestad.[8] At this time, too, the Frisians minted great numbers of highly

5. Mark Blackburn, 'A chronology for the sceattas', in D. Hill & D.M. Metcalf (eds.), *Sceattas in England and on the Continent* (Oxford, 1984), 165–74. Philip Grierson & Mark Blackburn, *Medieval European Coinage*, vol. I: *The Early Middle Ages (fifth-tenth centuries)* (Cambridge, 1986), 164–89.

6. W.A. van Es & W.J.H. Verwers, *Excavations at Dorestad. 1. The harbour: Hoogstraat I* (Amersfoort, 1980).

7. Richard Hodges, *Dark Age Economics* (London, 1982), 111.

8. See the histograms of coin-finds from Domburg and Dorestad respectively in W. Op Den Velde, W.J. De Boone & A. Pol, 'A survey of sceatta finds from the Low Countries', in D. Hill & D.M. Metcalf (eds.), *Sceattas in England and on the Continent* (Oxford, 1984), 117–46, esp. Fig. 1 on p. 135.

distinctive sceattas. These are well-known from their wide distribution: there have been finds in the Rhineland, south-east England and Denmark.[9] It may be no coincidence that the first Danish sceattas attributed to this period are overtly modelled upon Frisian types.[10] Outside Frisia, there was a proliferation of mints producing sceattas, but although the hoards have been studied there is little information on the distribution of individual coins. The proliferation of denarial coinage between 720 and 755 points to a new pattern of commerce. Notably, it supports the view that the Frisians were operating chiefly from the westernmost edge of their territory, far from Austrasia, at island nuclei like Domburg. The hoards show that members of their community were readily amassing wealth in coinage. At the same time the numerous mints within the Frankish kingdoms themselves point to the political fragmentation of the community. By controlling the output of these mints, middle-ranking magnates could develop their own economic strategies, thereby posing a challenge to Charles. Much of his career was probably concerned with redressing the balance in favour of central authority. Pepin III's coin reforms of 755 bear witness to this Carolingian ambition.

On the other hand, there are signs that this was also a turbulent age. Large coin-hoards from Frisia throw light on the scale of the hostilities, as does the construction of the earthen frontier wall, known as the Danevirke, separating Jutland from North Germany, dated by dendrochronology to this time.[11]

In our chronological overview we must also consider a few features of the second half of the eighth century. First, Pepin III reformed the coinage in 755, introducing a lightweight denier made on a flan as opposed to the pellets of the preceding decades. Pepin's denier, along with Charlemagne's own version issued probably from about 771, is very rare.[12] Pepin, it appears, terminated the proliferation of silver denarial types issued in the reign of Charles Martel. The rarity of Pepin's c. 755 reform coins suggests that commerce was limited by the massive hauls of raided goods and tribute obtained by the Franks as they annually set about extending the frontiers of their territory. Power was restored to the Carolingian dynasty when it snatched back

9. ibid.

10. Kirsten Bendixen, 'Sceattas and other coin finds', in M. Bencard (ed.), *Ribe Excavations 1970–76*, vol. I (Esbjerg, 1981), 63–101; 'Skandinaviske fund af sceattas', *Hikuin* 11 (1985), 33–40; Grierson & Blackburn, op. cit. (n. 5), 154; Lene B. Frandsen & Stig Jensen, 'Pre-Viking and Early Viking Age Ribe. Excavations at Nikolajgade 8, 1985–86', *Journal of Danish Archaeology* 7 (1987), 164–73. I am grateful to Lene Frandsen and Stig Jensen for the opportunity to discuss these matters with them in Ribe in April 1988.

11. H.H. Andersen, H.J. Madsen & O. Voss, *Danevirke* 2 (Copenhagen, 1976).

12. J. Lafaurie, 'Numismatique: des Merovingiens aux Carolingiens', *Francia* 2 (1974), 26–48.

lands given to the aristocracy and re-awarded them temporarily for services. The cycle of warfare ended in the late 780s with the advent of a new and most significant period (see Chapter Five).

Starting from these European premises, Grierson and Blackburn believe that the kingdom of Kent and possibly the East Saxons introduced the primary sceatta series in the 670s. Primary sceattas, as their designs indicate, were closely modelled on Frankish and, to a lesser extent, Frisian coins. They are concentrated in south-east England, as were the gold coins from the early part of the seventh century. But by about 690 other Anglo-Saxon kingdoms were imitating them. The intermediate phase, as it is known, contains a number of enigmatic sceatta series, to which coins from the kingdoms of Wessex, Mercia, Hwicce, Northumbria and East Anglia belong. According to Grierson and Blackburn, this phase lasted until the second decade of the eighth century.

In about 720, however, the proliferation of series began to increase at a remarkable rate (Fig. 21). These are the so-called secondary sceattas, which are attributed to the quarter-century before Pepin III's reform of the denier in about 755. Secondary sceatta series have been found in most of the principal Middle Saxon territories, though their distribution patterns are unusual. In this period, too, an influx of Frisian sceattas has been identified, adding another dimension to an already complex history.

The secondary sceatta phase ends conventionally with Pepin's reform. This terminus is confirmed by recent finds of pennies minted in about 760 by an East Anglian king, Beonna, imitating Pepin's larger denarial issues. The Beonna coins illustrate how sensitive some English kings were to Frankish currency values (Fig. 32).[13] Nevertheless Northumbrian kings issued sceattas bearing their own names until the last decade of the eighth century. Whether or not theirs was an isolated tertiary phase of sceattas has been a subject of contention in recent years. In a paper written with Philip Andrews, director of several excavations at Hamwic, Saxon Southampton, D.M. Metcalf has proposed that a prolific type of sceatta from this emporium may in fact belong to a tertiary phase.[14]

A notable feature of the secondary sceatta series is the evolution of highly insular ornamentation in contrast to the devolved classical images found on the primary series. Analysis of the metal content of these coins indicates that the high amount of silver which distinguishes the primary and intermediate series declines sharply in the secondary sceatta phase, in which many types have been found to

13. For a useful summary on the Beonna coins see Grierson & Blackburn, op. cit. (n. 5), 277–8.
14. P. Andrews & D.M. Metcalf, 'A coinage for King Cynewulf?' in D. Hill & D.M. Metcalf (eds.), *Sceattas in England and on the Continent* (Oxford, 1984), 175–80.

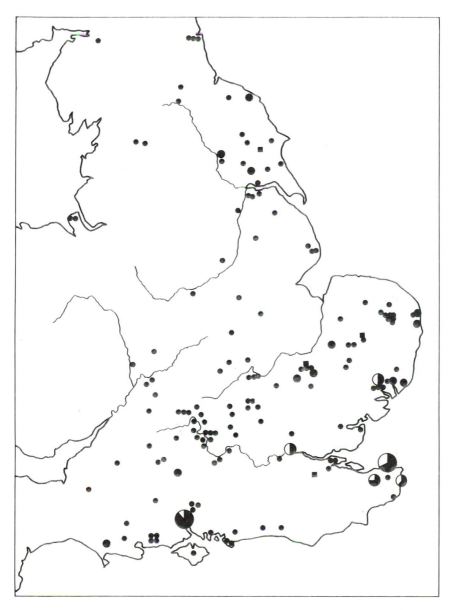

21. Finds of silver sceattas of the secondary phase (c. 720–755). Pie-diagrams at the major sites show the proportion of secondary coins among all the sceattas from the site; squares mark hoards or grave-finds (drawn by Barry Vincent, after D. M. Metcalf).

contain only 50 per cent or less silver. A similar decline had been a feature of the Merovingian gold tremisses in the first half of the seventh century. Does this show that silver supplies in the 750s were declining as, it is commonly believed, gold supplies had been in the early seventh century?

The coin types and the distribution of finds throw some light on the general configurations of the economies of this period. Elsewhere I have proposed that coins were special-purpose media of exchange, restrictively employed in non-kin circumstances.[15] The close imitation of Frankish and Frisian ornamentation, for instance, implies that they may have been intended for the closed sphere of foreign trade. However, the gradual adoption of coinage by most tribes, suggested by the ubiquitous discovery of secondary sceattas, lends weight to the argument that coins were increasingly used in all non-kin encounters, ranging from inter-tribal fairs to ceremonies. But despite their immense numbers, we must not be tempted to see them as anything more than an index of the gradual shift from the domestic mode of production towards the kind of monetisation envisaged by Marx and subsequent historians as a feature of a competitive market society. One of the aims of this chapter is to discover how far the English were along this economic scale by the eighth century.

At the beginning of the seventh century trade with the Merovingians enabled the earliest Anglo-Saxon kings to accumulate wealth. This helped them to consolidate their political ambitions. But the history of imported Frankish gold coins (tremisses) suggests that by the 630s international contacts were once more in decline. A renewal of these connections seems to have occurred in the 670s, at the instigation perhaps of Pepin of Herstal. Since the earliest Kentish silver pennies, the so-called primary sceattas, are imitations of Pepin's denarial coinage, there was probably some commercial link between the two territories. Bearing in mind the earlier connections between the Merovingians and Kent, the coinage may indicate a trading pact with Neustria. Similarly, the documentary references to London's mercantile activities in these decades may be interpreted as East Saxon connections via Frisia with the Austrasians.[16] However, as nearly all numismatists have pointed out, the death of King Hlothere of Kent in 685, and the savage attack on Kent made by Caedwalla, King of Wessex in 687, must mark a significant horizon in Kent's economic circumstances, perhaps bringing to an end its international pre-eminence among the English tribes. The cause of these hostilities eludes us, but control of the trade with the Neustrians may have been at stake. After succeeding Caedwalla in 688, King Ine of Wessex, a

15. Hodges, *Dark Age Economics*, 104–17; *Primitive and Peasant Markets*, 104–18.
16. Op Den Velde et al., op. cit. (n. 8).

towering figure in Anglo-Saxon history, was reputedly able to acquire thirty thousand pounds (? of silver) six years later as payment for the death of Caedwalla's brother Mul in the fighting of 687. This sum, if it really existed, was probably a good part of the Kentish treasury, and its loss must have been highly detrimental to the kingdom's political economy. Its real significance, however, lies in the swift rise of Ine to acquire the compensation, as well as the willingness of the Kentishmen to make the payment to the West Saxons. The later author(s) of the *Anglo-Saxon Chronicle* seems to have appreciated the importance of the payment for southern English affairs. He may have known that it was at this time that Hamwic was founded, involving great changes not only as far as cross-Channel trade was concerned, but also for the economy of the West Saxons generally (see below, pp. 85ff.).

The intermediate sceattas of c. 690 – c. 720 must be related to the increasing opportunities of several Anglo-Saxon kingdoms to engage in cross-Channel trade. The patterns of coin finds show that not only kings but other members of the Anglo-Saxon secular and ecclesiastical hierarchy were eager to be involved. With the exception of Wessex, the diffuse distribution of coins suggests that these special-purpose economic media were not rigorously monitored. Likewise the presence of Frisian coins belonging to this and the following secondary sceatta phase must be taken into account (Fig. 22). Frisian sceattas occur often in English contexts, especially in Kent, Essex and Mercia.[17]

This phase of English history, however, tends to be remembered for events which took place far from these south-coast shores. At the turn of the century Northumbria was the setting for an artistic vitality rarely paralleled in Anglo-Saxon times. Why a renaissance occurred in this kingdom at this time is difficult to explain. Outstanding church-men clearly played a critical role in fostering the artistic conditions, but it may perhaps be interpreted as a reaction to the kingdom's inability to share in the Frankish commercial orbit.

The secondary sceatta phase marks the beginning of widespread coin use. Metcalf has drawn up invaluable lists and maps of these coins.[18] They show a clustering of several types in eastern Kent; a concentration in London; a range of Mercian types in the territory of Middle Anglia and south-east Mercia and a marked incidence in the Thames Valley between Wallingford and Oxford; an extraordinary concentration of Metcalf's series H (BMC types 39 and 49) at Hamwic (Anglo-Saxon Southampton) (Fig. 23); several small concentrations of runic sceattas in East Anglia, notably at Ipswich, Barham and Burrow

17. ibid.; D.M. Metcalf, 'Monetary circulation in southern England in the first half of the eighth century', in D. Hill & D.M. Metcalf (eds.), *Sceattas in England and on the Continent* (Oxford, 1984), 27–69.
18. Metcalf, ibid.

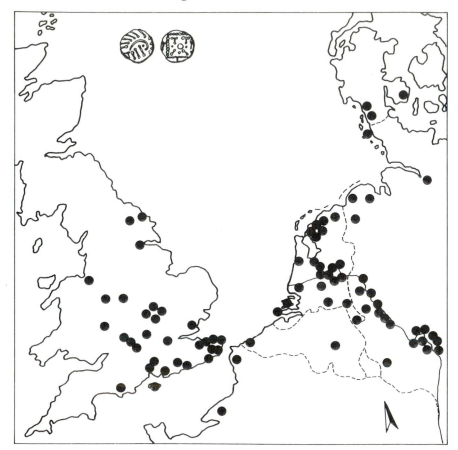

22. Finds of silver sceattas of the porcupine-standard series attributed to mints in Frisia (drawn by Barry Vincent, after W. Op Den Welde, W.J. De Boone and A. Pol).

Hill; a small distribution of Hwiccian types in the lower Severn Valley; and a largely exclusive use of Northumbrian types in many parts of this territory with notable concentrations at Sancton (a cemetery), and in the monasteries at Whitby and York. Metcalf has tried to interpret the pattern of finds, but like any objects they only become meaningful in their context. Therefore, bearing these sceatta distributions in mind, I shall consider first the emporia and then the other categories of sites from this period.

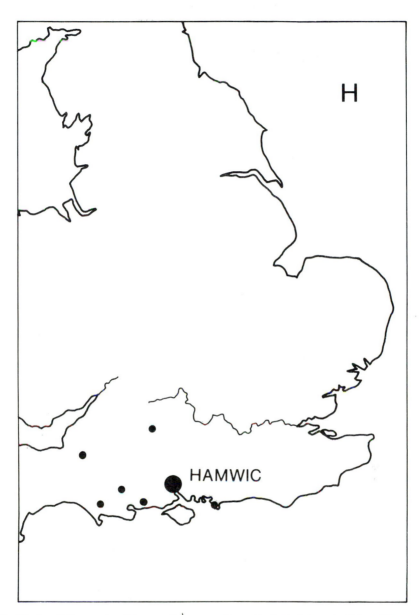

H

HAMWIC

23. Finds of the series H secondary sceattas attributed to mint(s) at Hamwic (drawn by Barry Vincent, after D.M. Metcalf).

Hamwic

Hamwic, Anglo-Saxon Southampton, is possibly the most important site of this period, and certainly the best known.[19] Since archaeological investigations began in 1946 an enormous amount of data has been collected, making it one of the best-studied towns in Europe. I shall attempt to show that the discoveries at Southampton are also of unrivalled importance in reconstructing the history of the English.

Hamwic lies on low ground beside the river Itchen, to the south of the Romano-British fort at Clausentum and due east of the much smaller Late Saxon and medieval town. It was probably chosen as an attractive place to beach the keel-less boats of the period, with good (Roman) roads leading into Wessex. Remains of two seventh-century cemeteries from the promontory point to a small earlier settlement here, though some of the graves may belong to the period in which Hamwic was being constructed. (One cemetery of this phase was also found at Clausentum; another was discovered in the heart of the Middle Saxon emporium at site XX.[20] Apart from the two cemeteries, traces of an earlier seventh-century settlement have so far proved elusive.

There have been nearly fifty large-scale excavations at Hamwic, encompassing some 4 per cent of the settlement. By far the most important are those recently concluded at the Six Dials site towards the north end of the Middle Saxon settlement. The Six Dials excavations reveal an altogether remarkable development dating from about the 680s or early 690s. In this decade about 45 hectares of the low ground were enclosed within a deep ditch (without a bank). Within the enclosure a gridded street system was laid out. The system consisted of three north-south streets and at least six interconnecting east-west streets. The main north-south street was nearly 14 metres wide, and was frequently remetalled, while the east-west streets were about 3 metres wide and were remetalled on fewer occasions.

These excavations show that much of the northern half of the 45 hectares was crammed with buildings. The buildings were constructed parallel to the streets, virtually end to end, and show a remarkable uniformity in size. Most are halls, 4-5 metres wide and up to 12 metres long, of a type similar to those found at the rural sites excavated in

19. The literature on Hamwic is now large; of particular importance are P.V. Addyman & D.H. Hill, 'Saxon Southampton: a review of the evidence', *Proceedings of the Hampshire Field Club* 25 (1968), 61–93 & 26 (1969), 61–96; Philip Holdsworth, *Excavations at Melbourne Street, Southampton, 1971–76* (London, 1980), containing a section by Alexander Rumble on the place-name itself; Richard Hodges, *The Hamwih Pottery* (London, 1981); Mark Brisbane, 'Hamwic, Saxon Southampton', in R. Hodges & B. Hobley (eds.), *The Rebirth of the Town in the West, AD 700–1050* (London, 1988), 101–8. For what follows I should like to express my gratitude to Phil Andrews, Jennifer Bourdillon, Mark Brisbane and Ian Riddler.

20. Holdsworth, op. cit. (n. 19), 35–9.

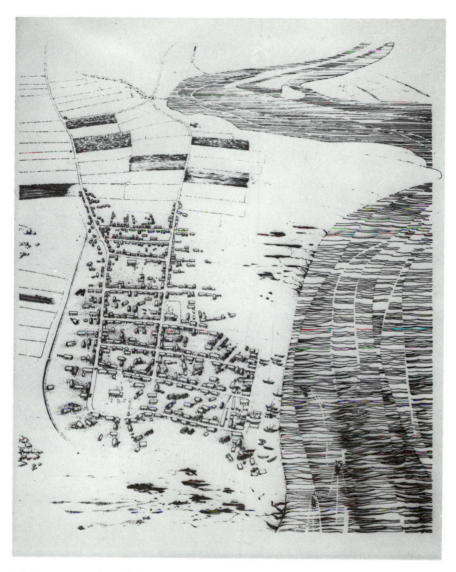

24. Reconstruction of Hamwic showing the street grid and settlement, with the perimeter ditch on the left-hand side and the river Itchen to the right (drawn by John Hodgson; courtesy of Southampton City Museums).

Wessex at Chalton, Cowdery's Down and Portchester Castle. But the post-holes of the Hamwic buildings are rather poorly aligned compared with the rural buildings, indicating either unseasoned timber or inexpert builders. Most buildings contain traces of industrial activities – principally metal-working or bone-working but also, to a lesser extent,

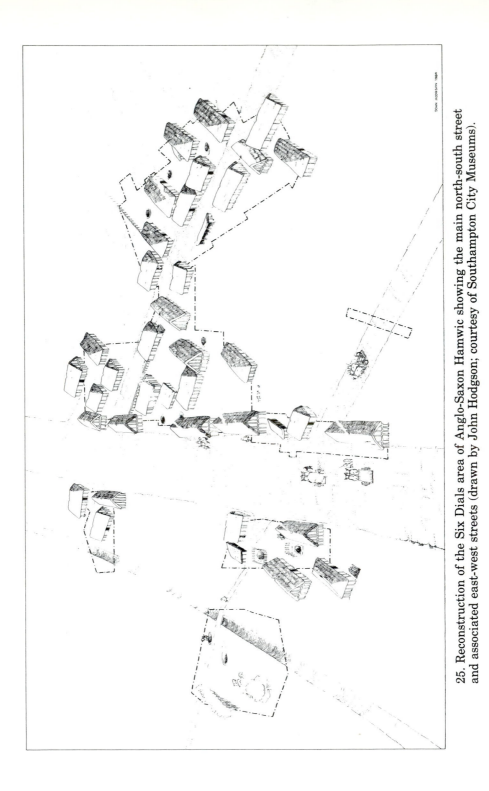

25. Reconstruction of the Six Dials area of Anglo-Saxon Hamwic showing the main north-south street and associated east-west streets (drawn by John Hodgson; courtesy of Southampton City Museums).

pottery manufacture. Most buildings appear also to have been rebuilt two or three times. Alongside some of the buildings are workshops. Sunken huts, a common feature in Early Anglo-Saxon villages, are absent. In the yards behind the buildings are numerous deep pits and skilfully constructed timber-lined wells. Interestingly, one of the most conspicuous features of early tenth-century towns seems to be generally absent. Instead of property boundaries marked out by fence-lines or shallow ditches, there are only fences alongside the roads to divide up areas of the settlement.

Traces of several small cemeteries have been found. At one site (SARC XIII), inter-cutting graves containing coffin burials have been discovered next to a timber structure (possibly a church). Here the ratio of adult males to females is 2:1 – a figure comparable to the ninth-century emporium at Haithabu, Denmark, possibly suggesting that Hamwic was primarily a male trading and production centre rather than a settlement of families.[21]

In this case, however, the graves and (?) church were abandoned, and were superseded by secular buildings in the late eighth century. This is a rare example of a change in the function of an area within Hamwic. It suggests that a new burial-ground was being developed elsewhere, perhaps for the whole community. The location of this cemetery remains speculative. St Mary's, a prominent church in the modern suburb and a minster as early as the tenth century, is the most feasible place. However, for the population of 4,000-5,000 estimated to have inhabited the town, the paucity of human remains in the long-running campaign of excavations is striking.[22] Hamwic lasted at least 150 years, from about 690 to 840-60, and taking into consideration an average life expectancy of 30 years, we might have expected over 20,000 burials.

The chronology of Hamwic is the subject of some debate. The planned layout of the site is fairly well fixed by coins, dendrochronology and carbon-14 dating to a decade or two before 700. Quite how long the settlement lasted, and in what form, is not so clear. A study of the coins suggests intense activity in the secondary sceatta phase (c. 720–50) when its own distinctive coin-issues (BMC 39 and BMC 49) minted in Hamwic were lost in extraordinary numbers. Far fewer coins occur after this period, particularly in the ninth-century phase. A good deal of evidence now confirms that the community was in

21. Philip Holdsworth, 'Saxon Southampton: a new review', *Medieval Archaeology* 20 (1976), 57–9; Brisbane, op. cit. (n. 19), 104.
22. Martin Biddle, 'The study of Winchester: archaeology and history in a British town, 1961–83', *Proceedings of the British Academy* 69 (1983), 123, n. 2; Brisbane, op. cit. (n. 19), 104.

decline before the Viking raids of the 840s and much reduced in size by Alfred's reign (see Chapter Five).[23]

The material culture is very rich. Great quantities of locally-made pottery in simple forms, as well as finer wheel-thrown Carolingian types, have been found in the pits. The local pottery appears to be the work of one potter, or at least one workshop, in the early years of the settlement, followed thereafter by a number of potters employing cruder production techniques. The imported Frankish pottery emanated mostly from sources in north-eastern France (Neustria), principally the environs of Quentovic, and is remarkably varied. Since these Frankish pottery types are rarely found elsewhere in southern England, and those found at Hamwic are mainly domestic wares, it may be that alien traders were equipped to stay there for long periods. Imported wares appear to be concentrated towards the southern part of the town, near the landing-places and (as it happens) St Mary's. Whether this was the traders' quarter is not known. But Frankish tablewares were circulated extensively throughout the settlement, and sherds occur in most pit-groups.[24]

Imported glassware, metalwork, ivory, bonework, quernstones and hones also occur throughout the settlement. Evidence shows that craft activities took place in almost every building. Only the final reports will confirm the scale of these activities by cataloguing, building by building, the debris left lying on the floors or in the back yards. Suffice it to say that, like other tenth-century towns, Hamwic was a centre of intensive craft production. The recent Six Dials excavations emphasise this aspect of the settlement, showing that previous interpretations of Hamwic solely as a settlement for trading with the Franks are questionable.

A great deal of research has been carried out on Hamwic's agrarian context. The animal bones reveal a high-protein diet, implying that there was a well-managed livestock economy. The diet consisted primarily of beef, mutton and pork being less common. The sheep bones come mostly from older beasts and are especially large for the period. One explanation could be that sheep were eaten after providing several good fleeces.[25] Strangely, little seafood was consumed.

Plentiful botanical evidence for cereal-production, including related weeds, led Michael Monk to conclude that the bulk processing of the field crop to produce flour was not taking place close to the rubbish pits. He speculated that the crops were processed outside the town

23. Hodges, op. cit. (n. 7), 157–9; but see Brisbane, op. cit., 103.

24. Hodges, *The Hamwih Pottery* (n. 19); I am indebted to Mark Brisbane for the additional information outlined here.

25. Jennifer Bourdillon, *Animals in an Urban Environment* (unpublished M.Phil. thesis, University of Southampton, 1983).

altogether.[26] According to Monk, barley and bread wheat were consumed in about equal quantities and were the main cereal foods. Some hulled wheats, wild oats and field peas indicated that the cereals were from spring-sown crops. Nevertheless numerous fragments of quernstones indicate that corn was ground throughout the town, presumably on a house-to-house basis. The range of dietary evidence, in fact, adds up to a picture of affluence, even if, according to Jennifer Bourdillon, the animal bones point to rather dull stews![27]

Interpreting Hamwic on the basis of a excavated sample of about 4 per cent is bound to be contentious. Yet the scale of the site and the diversity of the evidence leaves us in little doubt of its importance in Middle Saxon England. Hamwic represents a new stage in the evolution of the Anglo-Saxon town, being a planned centre in which craft production plays a great part – what I have previously termed a type B emporium, in contrast to the small trading-places or *wiks*, type A emporia.[28] Its size and overt planning must be attributed to the West Saxon king. We need to remind ourselves that the construction of an enterprise of this magnitude in the late ninth century is associated with King Alfred's governmental prowess.[29] A royal palace existed at Southampton from the eighth century and may help to explain how the settlement was constructed and maintained. The fact that Hampshire took its name from the port also points to its importance.

A foundation date in the late seventh century suggests that either King Caedwalla or King Ine was the architect. Caedwalla certainly created the circumstances for this enterprise by annexing the Isle of Wight to control the Solent in 685, a year after his accession, and by defeating the South Saxons and Kentishmen, hoping perhaps to monopolise cross-Channel relations with the Neustrians. But Caedwalla ruled for only three years before abdicating and journeying to Rome on a pilgrimage. It is hard to imagine that he could have crammed these campaigns *and* the building of Hamwic into such a short time. Furthermore, it is unlikely that he could have forced his tribe not only to take part in the wars but also to contribute to the building. It seems more likely that Ine was the architect of Hamwic. In his long reign he would have been able to ensure the future of this massive enterprise. In any case excavating the perimeter ditch,

26. Monk's work is cogently described by P.J. Fowler, 'Farming in the Anglo-Saxon landscape: an archaeologist's review', *Anglo-Saxon England* 9 (1981), 263–80 at 274–6; see also Frank Green, 'Iron Age, Roman and Saxon crops: the archaeological evidence from Wessex', in M. Jones & G. Dimbleby (eds.), *The Environment of Man* (Oxford, 1981), 129–53.

27. Bourdillon, op. cit. (n. 25).

28. Richard Hodges, *Primitive and Peasant Markets* (n. 4), 42–52.

29. See, for example, James Campbell, 'Observations on English government from the tenth to twelfth centuries', *Transactions of the Royal Historical Society* 25 (1975), 39–54.

constructing several kilometres of metalled roads, managing the development within the enclosure and administering the community would have required centralised leadership. In terms of area Hamwic was about 20 times larger than any other place in Wessex, and in demographic terms perhaps 40–80 times. In fact in most respects Hamwic was far more ambitious, for example, than Winchester as developed by Alfred two centuries later.

The model for Hamwic, however, remains a mystery. It is conceivable that such a site already existed in Kent or at London (though see below, p. 94) and provided the blueprint for the West Saxon enterprise. But the urban concept may have been imported from the Mediterranean rather like the royal theatre at Yeavering (noted in Chapter Three) or the water-mill(s) at Old Windsor (see below, p. 112). Was it Ine's answer to Pepin's new towns at Dorestad and Quentovic – set out however as if it was a version of a classical town? The street system certainly resembles the skeletal classical street systems that seventh-century visitors to Lucca, Pavia, Verona or Rome might have seen.[30] The broad high street (described in medieval Winchester by Martin Biddle as an *Einstrassenanlage*) strongly resembles the classical concept of a main thoroughfare on which markets were held.[31]

But Hamwic did not function like a classical town. In the first place it had no defences. The deep perimeter ditch served only as a boundary distinguishing those inside from those outside. Although the ditch was filled after a quarter-century or so, few buildings spread beyond the original confines. The ditch may define the limits of the settlement, rather as fences and ditches define other classes of settlement in this period, when royal sites, monasteries and most farms seem to have been enclosed (see p. 106). The enclosures were too flimsy to be defences and may be better interpreted as property boundaries defining the integrity of the community within.[32]

Property divisions inside Hamwic are notably rare. Unlike tenth-century *burhs* or Roman towns, there were no tenements as such. But the fence-lines alongside the roads may indicate that each insula was the property of a lord, just as early tracts of Late Saxon London and

30. See G.P. Brogiolo, 'La città tra tarda-antichità e Medioevo', in *Archeologia urbana in Lombardia* (Modena, 1985), 48–56.

31. Martin Biddle & David H. Hill, 'Late Saxon planned towns', *Antiquaries Journal* 51 (1971), 70–85.

32. The importance of property boundaries is considered in Chapter Three; see, however, Klavs Randsborg's interesting diachronic essay 'Rank, rights and resources: an archaeological perspective from Denmark', in C. Renfrew & S. Shennan (eds.), *Ranking, Resource & Exchange* (Cambridge, 1982), 132–40. For Anglo-Saxon England see T.M. Charles-Edwards, 'The distinction between land and moveable wealth in Anglo-Saxon England', in P. Sawyer (ed.), *Medieval Settlement* (London, 1976), 187.

26. Reconstruction of a workshop in Hamwic (drawn by John Hodgson; courtesy of Southampton City Museums).

Winchester appear to have been made over to the aristocracy.[33] The scarcity of keys, locks and latches further emphasises the absence of individual/household rights.

In the past, the imported finds and the prolific sceattas have led scholars to conclude that Hamwic was an emporium.[34] To what extent does this interpretation still hold? The imported objects reveal Frankish connections and the presence of traders periodically residing at Southampton. Most imported goods, it must be assumed, were regulated by the king, and seldom reach the archaeological record. But while the imports are prominent, it is the scale of urban production (glass-working, metal-working, pottery-making, bone-working, etc.) and the way the settlement was provisioned that distinguish it, for

33. On property divisions in Late Saxon London see Alan Vince, 'The economy of Anglo-Saxon London', in R. Hodges & B. Hobley (eds.), *The Rebirth of the Town in the West, AD 700–1050* (London, 1988), 83–92; on Winchester see Martin Biddle, 'The towns', in D.M. Wilson (ed.), *The Archaeology of Anglo-Saxon England* (London, 1976), 133.

34. Hodges, *Dark Age Economics*, 112–14.

example, from the small seventh-century trading place identified at Ipswich. As far as we can tell, these manufactured commodities were not produced on a large scale elsewhere within Wessex. It is reasonable to suppose, therefore, that they were commodities which had their own regional value.

The silver sceattas are another prominent feature of the site. Several dozen, for example, were discovered in the Six Dials excavations, some stratified in hearths, pits and between road surfaces. In all nearly 200 secondary sceattas have been found, principally of the BMC 39 and 49 sceatta types believed to have been minted at Hamwic itself. By contrast, sceattas are extremely uncommon outside Hamwic, suggesting that the economic activities for which these coins were minted were exclusive to the place.[35]

In sum, the topography of Hamwic is consistent with its being a royal settlement, run either as an extension of a royal household or as a collection of aristocratic holdings under royal aegis. Without doubt it constituted a massive and seemingly innovative enterprise in Anglo-Saxon England, which sheds fresh light on West Saxon society in the later seventh and eighth centuries. We must now focus a little more sharply on King Ine's capacity to undertake these works.

King Ine, to judge from his well-known laws, was familiar not only with Roman law-codes, but also with those modified by his Frankish neighbours.[36] Nicholas Brooks has demonstrated that Ine exacted military obligations from any ceorl or man of higher rank. Similarly, he was able to raise food-rents from his community which would have been sufficient to support the large population at Hamwic, as I have shown elsewhere.[37] It was not only the West Saxons who organised tribal resources on this scale. David Hill, for example, has argued persuasively that Offa's Dyke (another great enterprise of this age; see p. 144) was constructed by corvée labour, using well-equipped specialists mustered from each land unit within the kingdom. Similarly, Brooks notes that Aethelbald of Mercia exacted services of a more modest kind in the following century for the maintenance of a royal vill (estate). In the poem *Beowulf* we are told that when the Danish king Hrothgar built his great palace of Hereot he summoned

35. M. Dolley, 'The location of pre-Alfredian mints of Wessex', *Proceedings of the Hampshire Field Club* 27 (1971), 57–62; this coinage is also the subject of a new study by Michael Metcalf which will be published soon. For a counter view see Ian Stewart, 'The London mint and the coinage of Offa', in M. Blackburn (ed.), *Anglo-Saxon Monetary History* (Leicester, 1986), 29, n. 9.

36. J.M. Wallace-Hadrill, *Early Germanic Kingship in England and on the Continent* (Oxford, 1971), 39; 67.

37. N.P. Brooks, 'The development of military obligations in eighth and ninth century England', in P. Clemoes & K. Hughes (eds.), *England before the Conquest* (Cambridge, 1971), 69–84.

men from far and wide to help with the task.[38] These were services exacted by a king in return for land. It is not far-fetched to imagine that Hamwic was a public enterprise intended to regulate production and trade, maintained in large measure through food-rents.

In time we may also know who worked in Hamwic. We should note the absence of household property boundaries, the rarity of ancillary buildings alongside the halls in which surplus goods might be stored, and the general level of affluence. It is possible that each insula was managed by a member of the aristocracy or Church, as in Late Saxon England. Alternatively, it might be postulated that Hamwic was a community of specialists and traders, or craftsmen-traders with restricted rights within the town. A permanent community of the latter kind, however, would have produced immense amounts of commodities which should have transformed the material culture of Wessex. Such a workforce, too, might have posed a threat to royal authority by undermining the political economy, as I noted at the beginning of this chapter. In fact, the influence of Hamwic in Wessex *seems* to have been minimal in archaeological terms, and virtually negligible in any documentary sense. Could Hamwic have been partly a seasonal (late summer) fair, regularly administered by the king and his reeves, attended by thegns and higher aristocrats along with miscellaneous artisans, where each played host to Frankish traders (as in late medieval tradition)? This might account for some of the pits being open for decades, as they evidently were. It might account too for the comparatively small burial-grounds; for the anonymity of the church or churches in Hamwic; and perhaps for the gradual filling in of the ditch once the purpose of the place was regulated by an aristocracy pledged to the royal family and hence acknowledged by the West Saxon community.

But how would it have functioned? Porláksson offers a parallel from medieval Iceland, where at Gasar, Eyrar and Hvitarvellir, merchants came to trade between June and September. Local chieftains administered the trade, set prices and took steps to prevent competition.[39] This was also the place for the chieftains to interact with their leading rivals, so the trade had an integrating social function. The Icelandic system became increasingly difficult to administer as the economy expanded in the later Middle Ages and ultimately collapsed. Could the same have happened at Southampton?

Hamwic may have waxed and waned during its history, but evidence

---

38. David Hill, 'The construction of Offa's Dyke', *Antiquaries Journal* 65 (1985), 140–2; Patrick Wormald, 'The emergence of the Anglo-Saxon kingdoms', in L. Smith (ed.), *The Dark Ages* (London, 1984), 57; H.R. Loyn, *The Governance of Anglo-Saxon England 500–1087* (London, 1984), 34.

39. Helgi Porláksson, 'Comments on ports of trade in early medieval Europe', *Norwegian Archaeological Review* 11 (1978), 112–14.

for seasonal desertion, or even decade-long dereliction, has not been found. Instead, careful excavations on the Six Dials site suggest that the high street buildings were used (i.e. rebuilt) more than those on side streets, implying intensive use of the main thoroughfare.

The key to the history of Hamwic is to be found not only in the history of trade, but in its impact upon the West Saxon elite. Without doubt, however, Hamwic is an expression of the political economy to which ambitious kings like Caedwalla and Ine aspired as they sought to close the divide between themselves and their European counterparts. But if trade with Neustria declined after 714, when Pepin of Herstal died, how was West Saxon kingship to resolve the need for prestige goods? What were the implications for social relations in Wessex?

To some extent the sceatta coinage holds the answers to these questions. First, it may be no coincidence that in 710 King Ine extended his territory westwards to include Devon and Cornwall. He fought with the Mercians in 715, and the South Saxons in 722. It would seem rather bizarre that the first two decades of his kingship, according to the *Anglo-Saxon Chronicle*, were peaceful, while the final fifteen years or so involved him in a variety of battles. This reversal of the normal pattern may owe much to Ine's search for new land to compensate for the loss of imported resources. Yet Ine abdicated at about the time that secondary sceattas were first minted. The extensive loss of these coins is extraordinary, but in Wessex this occurred in Hamwic only, whereas in other kingdoms the sceattas were often distributed widely. Coins tend to be rare on archaeological sites because they are regarded as bullion in most peasant societies, employed for purchasing non-subsistence commodities. Only in the early tenth century, when a monetary economy was swiftly developed to encompass all levels of society, were coins lost in some numbers (see p. 162). In the tenth century perhaps their worth was not readily appreciated, and large numbers were minted to encourage the switch to an authorised, standardised unit of exchange. The economic historian Henry Misbach has interpreted high velocity in medieval coin-use as a product of rising prices.[40] This may not be inconsistent with the social mobility of the tenth century and the inherent uncertainty this generated, as we shall see in Chapter Six. But does it help explain the high loss of secondary sceattas in the rather different economic climate of Middle Saxon Southampton? Alternatively, bearing in mind the European circumstances, were sceattas minted to aid production of wares in Hamwic in the 720s (or before) as an explicit response to the decline in cross-

40. Henry L. Misbach, 'The balanced economic growth of Carolingian Europe: suggestions for a new interpretation', *Journal of Interdisciplinary History* 3 (1972), 261–73 offers some interesting ideas pertinent to these data.

Channel trade? Does the high number of coins lost indicate a phase of price-inflation induced by social change?

Whatever the answer, the high concentration of secondary sceattas in Hamwic, and their virtual absence outside it, seems to bear witness to the exclusive economic character of the place. Despite Ine's abdication, some efficient administrative hold was kept over the port. His legacy may have been the creation of enduring tributary relations within the tribe, permitting his successors to control both members of the aristocracy and specialised craftsmen.

Two generations after Ine's abdication the silver content of the sceattas declined sharply, and after this the mints ceased activity. The falling silver content of the sceattas may be interpreted as a mechanism, often used in Roman times, to retain silver without altering the value of the sceattas. Alternatively it may indicate that the royal treasury of silver had declined sharply, either as coinage was accumulated by lower ranks in society or simply because the supply of precious material had been exhausted. For reasons that will be outlined below, a combination of the two hypotheses is most likely.

What prevented the West Saxons from issuing a poor variant of their sceattas, as the Northumbrians did in these circumstances? The mid-eighth-century terminus for the secondary sceattas appears to coincide with Pepin III's coin reform of 757. With this monetary policy, the Carolingian king was almost certainly aiming to control Frisian as well as Frankish commerce. The rarity of his coins illustrates the impact of his reform: coins were not lost but continually recycled in one way or other. Perhaps the Franks courted new trade partners who appreciated the merits of a highly regulated monetary policy, such as King Beonna of East Anglia (see below, p. 101)?

Some light may be thrown on these circumstances by the *Anglo-Saxon Chronicle*. In 757 it first mentions Cynewulf when he deprives the newly elected King Sigeberht of Wessex of his lands, leaving him only Hampshire.[41] The logic of the phrasing suggests to the reader that Sigeberht was penalised by a bellicose competitor for power. But if Hamwic still existed, Sigeberht would have retained (albeit briefly) the most critical resource in his kingdom. The phrasing might be better explained if Hamwic had already fallen into decline and therefore Sigeberht's advantage was limited. This in turn might help to explain why kingdoms like East Anglia, Mercia and Kent issued reform pennies, modelled on Charlemagne's types, before Wessex followed suit in the 790s. It is tempting to think that these kingdoms outstripped Wessex in establishing trade partnerships with Charlemagne's mighty polity, though by this date the scale of cross-Channel commerce was not enormous (see p. 134).

41. Hodges, *Dark Age Economics* (n. 7), 112–14.

Ine's ruling on the obligations of the community, and the enduring nature of these customs, made it possible to sustain the regional centre at Hamwic through the turbulent decades of the eighth century. Hamwic's survival may offer an important clue to the success of the West Saxons in later centuries. Certainly, no further pleading is needed to establish the importance of Hamwic in the history of English kingship. What is more, the magnitude of the archaeological evidence confirms Wallace-Hadrill's impression that 'Bede knew nothing, or what amounts to nothing, about Ine'.[42] He did not even know that Ine was remembered and honoured in Rome as a saint.

Other sites

Bede was aware of mercantile activity in London and was doubtless familiar with similar activity in Kent. If Hamwic was not planned until about 690, is the model for this great experiment to be found in Kent, London, Ipswich or even York?

Kent

The evidence from eastern Kent is formidable for the seventh century. Augustine had landed on the Isle of Thanet in 597 and remained there, separated by the Wantsum Channel, until he was invited to Ethelberht's court. The cemeteries on the island that date from this golden age indicate an exceptional wealth connected with cross-Channel trade. It would be a mistake to project the uninterrupted continuity of this Early Anglo-Saxon trade into the later part of the seventh or even the eighth century. In Kent, as in other kingdoms, the changing configurations of the political economy have to be appreciated.

Two bodies of evidence have to be considered: first, the prolific numbers of sceattas from two monastic(?) sites at Reculver and Richborough stationed at each end of the Wantsum Channel; secondly, the documentary references to toll remissions on trade at Fordwich, Sandwich, Sarre and Minster, all places on the Wantsum Channel.

Kent was the first kingdom to mint not only gold coins (in the 630s), but also silver sceattas in the 670s or 680s. Finds of primary sceattas are concentrated around Thanet, though like the earlier gold tremisses individual coins occur in other territories. As was suggested above (p. 77), it is tempting to link these coins to a fresh phase of trade stimulated by Pepin of Herstal's expansionism in the late seventh century. But the large numbers of sceattas found at Reculver, a monastery, and Richborough, another Roman fort with a chapel, as well as

42. Brooks, op. cit. (n. 37), 52; Wallace-Hadrill, op. cit. (n. 36), 89–90.

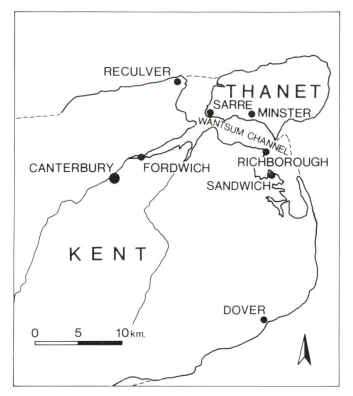

27. Location of the principal sites of the Middle Saxon period in eastern Kent (drawn by Barry Vincent).

at the nunnery at Minster-by-Thanet, reveal a markedly different pattern from that found in Wessex. If the sceattas were minted primarily for use in cross-Channel trade, their distribution implies that it was never concentrated wholly in the hands of the king of Kent. Toll remissions granted to various churches involved in commerce of some kind at Fordwich, Sandwich and Sarre (all in south-east Kent) reinforce this impression. If anything, the distribution of sceattas emphasises the part played by the Church in the economy of the kingdom.[43]

After about 690 the diverse variety of sceattas provides a striking contrast with Wessex. Kentish secondary sceattas occur in many

43. The sceattas are listed by S.E. Rigold & D.M. Metcalf, 'A revised check-list of English finds of sceattas', in D. Hill & D.M. Metcalf (eds.), *Sceattas in England and on the Continent* (Oxford, 1984), 245–68; on the early trading sites see Tim Tatton-Brown, 'The towns of Kent', in J. Haslam (ed.), *Anglo-Saxon Towns in Southern England* (Chichester, 1984), 1–36.

different types in association with Frisian porcupine and Wodan monster sceattas. The diversity may be due to the inability of the king to control the circulation of coinage in the kingdom. At the same time the Continental coins, especially the Frisian sceattas, suggest increasing contacts with merchants from the Low Countries. The sceattas confirm that the intervention of the West Saxons in Kentish affairs between 687 and 694 must have shifted the balance of power in southern England. As a result, it is tempting to speculate that no centre like Hamwic existed in Kent. Instead there were several small *wiks*, type A emporia, which were little more than trading-places fostered by competing factions within the kingdom.

London

London is altogether a more contentious issue. Despite the few familiar historical references to traders in Middle Saxon times, the archaeology of the period is not yet convincing. Very little has been found in the Roman city of London. Like most Romano-British towns it was abandoned during the fifth century, to be reoccupied on a small scale in the early seventh.[44] At that time a bishopric was established in London and, as at Canterbury, Winchester and York, the (East Saxon) king probably constructed a palace close to the new minster. It is evident that London was an important place in seventh-century England, but was it a mart in the sense of Ine's Hamwic?

Until recently the only archaeological evidence was for a string of 'farms' along the Thames running from the City to Windsor (and perhaps even further west).[45] However, Alan Vince and Martin Biddle have plotted the Middle Saxon finds from Greater London to make a case for claiming that Lundenwic, the emporium, was situated in Aldwyck on the Strand, immediately west of the largely derelict Roman city (Fig. 28). In their opinion sufficient evidence exists to postulate an an urban settlement covering about 86 hectares. Gold coins, primary and secondary sceattas, were almost certainly minted at London. By the end of the eighth century Offa probably had a mint here. In the turbulence of the mid to later ninth century, however, it appears that Lundenwic was abandoned in favour of the security of Lundenburg, the old fortified Roman city.[46]

44. On the bishopric see Patrick Wormald, *Bede and the Conversion of England: the charter evidence* (Jarrow Lecture, 1984).
45. On the string of royal and monastic farms (an idea originally proposed by John Hurst) see Hodges, *Dark Age Economics* (n. 7), 69–70.
46. Martin Biddle, 'London on the Strand', *Popular Archaeology* 6 (1) (1984), 23–7; Vince, op. cit. (n. 33); Timothy Tatton-Brown, 'The topography of Anglo-Saxon London', *Antiquity* 60 (1986), 21–8. I am grateful to Lynn Blackmore for the opportunity to study the Jubilee Hall imported pottery which lends limited weight to the Biddle-Tatton-Brown-Vince thesis; it seems to be late seventh-century material imported from Rhenish and northern French areas.

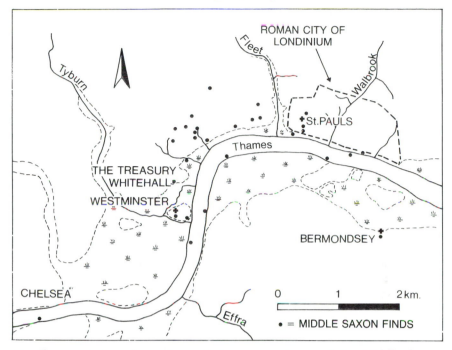

28. The general configurations of the proposed site of the Middle Saxon emporium of London, west of the Romano-British town (drawn by Barry Vincent, after Alan Vince).

But was London in the seventh and eighth centuries twice the size of Hamwic? Had the East Saxons established a trade partnership via Dorestad with the Austrasians, while Kent maintained Neustrian connections at this time?

Essex was evidently a pre-eminent kingdom in the late seventh century, as the Tribal Hidage shows. The bishop of London, in particular, was held in great esteem in the Anglo-Saxon orbit. But did the trading station take the form of a type B emporium on the Hamwic model? There are two reasons for doubting that an 86-hectare settlement evolved before the later years of Offa's reign. First, the absence of locally manufactured Middle Saxon pottery is rather curious if London was a town. Alan Vince has argued that chaff-tempered wares were the pre-eminent pottery in the seventh- and eighth-century settlement, as in most parts of the Thames Valley at this date. These were augmented by better-made Ipswich ware imported from East Anglia in the eighth and ninth centuries.[47] This

47. Alan Vince, 'New light on Saxon pottery from the London area', *The London Archaeologist* 16 (1984), 431–9.

is hardly very characteristic of an emporium created primarily to produce commodities.

A second problem is that Lundenwic fits awkwardly into the present picture of trade and commerce in southern England. This picture can be reconstructed from the historical references and, once again, the distribution of sceattas. In the 720s it is generally believed that London, like parts of the East Saxon territory, was annexed at some time or at least controlled, by the Mercian king Aethelbald (716-57), Offa's powerful predecessor. Under Aethelbald's jurisdiction in the 730s and 740s tolls on ships in the port of London were granted to the bishop of London, the abbess of Thanet, the bishop of Rochester and the bishop and church of Worcester. Together with the large numbers of Frisian sceattas from London, these gifts reveal how many parties were involved in commerce. This state of affairs must have been detrimental to royal power, in sharp contrast to circumstances at Hamwic.

But Anglo-Frisian trade in south-east England cannot be dissociated from the contemporary spread of secondary sceatta finds in the patchwork of Middle Anglian territories which separated Mercia from the Thames valley (Fig. 29). Surprisingly, sceattas belonging to Aethelbald's long reign occur mostly on his frontiers, not in the heartlands of Mercia itself (Fig. 30). His sceattas are very varied and are thickly distributed in a zone which must have contained several inter-tribal fairs, as D.M. Metcalf has noted.[48]

But if the Mercians were engaged in exchange with the West Saxons, East Saxons, East Anglians and Kentishmen, why was the trade conducted via Middle Anglia and not concentrated in one place, such as London? Furthermore the pattern of sceattas from the Middle Anglian territories, rather like those within Frisia in the period 700-750, gives the impression of a frontier population trying to take advantage of its location to accumulate wealth from Mercia's trade with other tribes. The pattern suggests that many lower-ranking figures in Middle Anglia were able to acquire silver and either hoarded it, or for some reason, discarded it freely within their homesteads. This evidence must weigh against the concept of Lundenwic as a great Mercian urban centre. Separated by the Middle Anglians from this emporium, the Mercians would have found it difficult to control London efficiently.

It is difficult to sustain the case for London's being not simply a string of (often important) Thames-side estates but a collection of (type A) periodic trading-places acting as a (type B) model for Hamwic. Instead it may in many respects have resembled the diffuse pattern

48. D.M. Metcalf, 'Monetary affairs in Mercia in the time of Aethelbald', in A. Dornier (ed.), *Mercian Studies* (Leicester, 1977), 87–106.

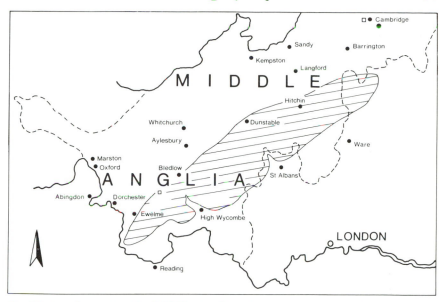

29. Finds of sceattas in Middle Anglia; the open squares indicate hoards (drawn by Barry Vincent, after D.M. Metcalf).

of aristocratic holdings along the Wantsum Channel in eastern Kent. It is worth noting that Pepin's effective reforms of the Carolingian economy could have been highly detrimental to London, whose trading connections appear from coin-finds to have been strongest with the Frisians. As these reforms took place shortly before Aethelbald's death in 757, it is not difficult to envisage the economic difficulties that greeted his eventual successor, Offa. In such circumstances Offa, with one eye on Wessex and the other on the marked ascendancy of the Carolingians, must have been conscious of the critical importance of Lundenwic as a means of instigating economic and social change. These are some of the issues considered in Chapter Five. All this leads to the conclusion that political relations within Mercia, in contrast to Wessex,[49] worked against the levying of services for developing and maintaining a large urbanised production centre.

Ipswich

A variation on this pattern occurs in East Anglia. Ipswich, it will be recalled, was a small (type A) periodic trading-place in the early seventh century. Its connections, however, seem to disappear in the subsequent recession of the 630s and to be re-established only in the

49. Brooks, op. cit. (n. 37).

30. Finds of sceattas in Mercia (drawn by Barry Vincent, after D.M. Metcalf).

secondary sceatta phase, to judge from the East Anglian R series coins which are distributed widely within the kingdom.[50] Some evidence exists, rather akin to that from Kent and London, showing that long-distance trade was not entirely focused at this site, but concentrated also at various other sites in the region.

Primary and secondary sceattas are comparatively uncommon in Ipswich itself, while at Barham a little to the north, and Burrow Hill,

50. Metcalf, op. cit. (n. 17), 58–9.

an island to the east, significant concentrations of these coins occur.[51] Excavations at Barham have produced little evidence of any occupation, suggesting that the coins were lost when some temporary activity – perhaps a fair – took place on the hill. By contrast, the investigations at Burrow Hill have uncovered an elite site with a large cemetery. An archaeological survey of the Sandlings region in which these sites are located, made in connection with the Sutton Hoo project, has brought to light many previously unknown sites and indicates the density of settlement in this part of the kingdom. In common with eastern Kent, therefore, it looks as if East Anglian regional exchange was conducted at several places in addition to Ipswich itself. But in contrast to the exclusive character of the coins in Hamwic, a mixture is found in these regions, possibly indicating the incidence of traders from other Anglo-Saxon kingdoms as well as from Frisia.

But the parallel with Kent cannot be taken too far. The long campaign of excavations in Ipswich has clearly identified a Middle Saxon emporium covering about 50 hectares.[52] The settlement spread on both sides of the river Orwell, having started from a small nucleus on the north shore. The pattern of streets gives the impression that the settlement has at least three parts. The first is the original seventh-century nucleus beside the river; the second, the zone immediately behind, in which there is no evidence of planned structure; and the third, under the heart of the modern shopping centre, seems to have some gridded structure to it. It has long been supposed that there was a royal palace on the northern flank of the third part close to the Thingstead (Fig. 31). In this area lay the pottery kilns producing Ipswich ware. Waste heaps of pottery amounting to several tons are known to spread over much of this part of the town. In contrast to Hamwic, no evidence of a boundary ditch has been found. Moreover, in the second zone, where most of the excavations have been concentrated until now, no traces of timber buildings have been found, although there are pits and timber-lined wells. Finally, as in Hamwic, property or tenemental boundaries are generally absent.

The continuous occupation of Ipswich impedes interpretation of the site, a problem which does not arise in the case of Hamwic. The morphology of the Ipswich emporium implies several phases. The following sequence is tentatively proposed. First, a riverside type A

51. I am indebted to Keith Wade for information on his 1983 Barham campaign; for Burrow Hill: Valerie Fenwick, 'Insula de Burgh: Excavations at Burrow Hill, Butley, Suffolk 1978–81', in D. Brown et al. (eds.), *Anglo-Saxon Studies in Archaeology and History* 3 (1984), 35–54.

52. I am indebted to Keith Wade and Cathy Coutts for information about Ipswich. See Keith Wade, 'Ipswich', in R. Hodges & B. Hobley (eds.), *The Rebirth of the Town in the West, AD 700–1050* (London, 1988), 93–100.

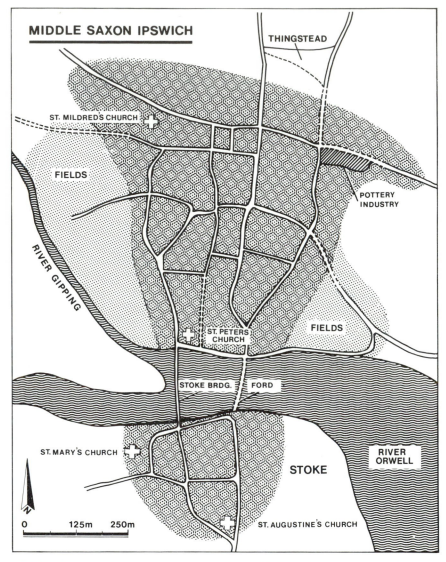

31. Middle Saxon Ipswich (courtesy of Keith Wade and the Suffolk Archaeological Unit).

emporium, which became, intermittently, the focus of trading activity from the seventh to the ninth century. Secondly, an area behind it, perhaps including impermanent facilities for periodic traders and craftsmen. Thirdly, adjacent perhaps to a royal palace at the north end of the settlement, a planned (type B) centre set out for controlled

32. Silver penny of King Beonna of East Anglia, c. 760 (photo courtesy of Ben Taylor).

regional production and exchange. The chronology of the second and third parts is a matter of debate at present. But, taking into account the imported pottery and the paucity of secondary sceattas, it is likely that these parts were not created before the middle of the eighth century. If so, the type B emporium, like London, falls within the scope of my next chapter. But it is worth drawing attention to the hitherto unknown King Beonna of East Anglia, suddenly made famous by the discovery of his coins by metal-detector enthusiasts (Fig. 32).

Beonna was the first king to order his moneyers to copy Pepin III's reform denier.[53] So, for a short while in about 760, East Anglia must have been within the reformed Carolingian monetary sphere, as Kent may have been towards the end of the same decade. The Carolingian connection may have allowed for the great changes at Ipswich. Such an agreement would explain the plentiful Frankish imported pots.[54] This, of course, presupposes that the East Anglian king could muster the same resources as his West Saxon counterpart had mustered some generations before. It also implies that the kingdom had broken free of its domination by the Mercians. This would lead us to suspect that, early in King Offa's reign (757-96), the Mercian polity which had intermittently included East Anglia was in disarray.

This interpretation of the history of Ipswich is still very speculative. New excavations within and around it should help to resolve the evolution of one of England's most important towns and hence shed light on the enigmatic history of the Mercians and their neighbours.

53. Grierson & Blackburn, op. cit. (n. 5), 164–89.
54. I am grateful to Cathy Coutts for information about the imported pottery.

Northumbria

Northumbria was the other great kingdom of the age. The history of its currency is rather eccentric. Despite the great cultural tradition of the kingdom and its ecclesiastical connections across Europe, it did not develop a distinctive coinage in the late seventh or early eighth century. The rare Northumbrian sceattas of this period betray an economic backwardness, in contrast to the great esteem in which Cuthbert, Wilfred and, of course, Bede were held. Was the renaissance that produced the Lindisfarne Gospels and a great range of sculpture a reaction to economic isolation, while the West and East Saxons along with the Kentish kingdom found prestige through mercantile connections? Was the Church the means by which Northumbria strived to command status?

The great age of Northumbria ended in the 730s and it may be no coincidence that, soon after his accession in 737, Eadberht introduced a distinctive and enduring sceatta series.[55] This is the age of Bede's lament for times past, and also the period in which, according to Professor Cramp, the great school of Northumbrian sculpture begins to become derivative.[56]

Eadberht's coinage occurs frequently on various sites, including the cemetery at Sancton (West Yorkshire) and the monastery at Whitby. Similarly the 'knick-knacks' (Patrick Wormald's word) from Whitby indicate developing production of manufactured commodities, but there are no signs of centralised production, such as pottery-making. It may be that the impoverished silver content of the later Northumbrian sceattas, like their continued use long after the type was defunct in other Anglo-Saxon territories, is an index of the complex and often bloody history of the kingdom.

Recent excavations in York offer new insights into the social and economic history of the kingdom at this formative period. Roman York was largely deserted in Middle Saxon times,[57] but a small nucleus with a royal palace almost certainly occupied the area of the Roman legionary headquarters – a spot lying beside as well as under the present minster. However, until recently the site of Eoforwic, in which, according to Alcuin, there was a community of Frisian traders in the 780s, had eluded archaeologists.

Excavations at 46-54 Fishergate to the east of the Roman and later Anglo-Scandinavian town have brought to light dense eighth- to

55. J. Booth, 'Sceattas in Northumbria', in D. Hill & D.M. Metcalf (eds.), *Sceattas in England and on the Continent* (Oxford, 1984), 71–112; E.J.E. Pirie, 'Finds of "sceattas" and "stycas" of Northumbria', in M. Blackburn (ed.), *Anglo-Saxon Monetary History* (Leicester, 1986), 67–90.

56. Rosemary Cramp, 'The Anglian tradition in the ninth century', in J. Lang (ed.), *Anglo-Saxon and Viking Sculpture and its Context* (Oxford, 1978), 6–7.

57. Richard Hall, *The Viking Dig* (London, 1984), 29–42.

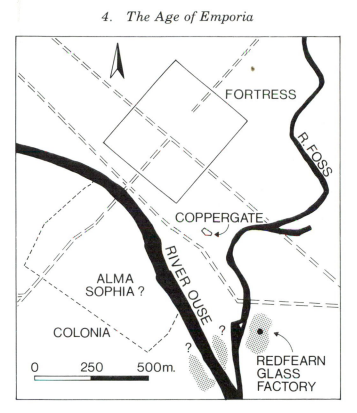

33. The proposed location of Eoforwic, Middle Saxon York, at the junction of the rivers Foss and Ouse, following the discoveries made beneath the Redfearn Glass factory at 46–54 Fishergate (drawn by Barry Vincent, after R. Kemp and the York Archaeological Trust).

ninth-century features that surely indicate the site of Eoforwic (Fig. 33).[58] The small trial trenches lead us to suppose that the settlement spread around the confluence of the rivers Ouse and Foss. A hoard of four sceattas including a series L London type and traces of craft activities have been found.

If this site was used in Eadberht's age, when sceattas were introduced to Northumbria, it may be viewed as an imitation of Hamwic, created some 50 years after the West Saxon town. By this time Bede was dead. By this time, too, the Northumbrians may have been able to find only a small share in the international trading system, largely because the freelancing Frisians were occupied principally with the competing elites of Kent, Mercia and East Anglia. Given these circum-

58. Richard Kemp, ' "Pit your wics" or How to excavate Anglian York', *Interim* 11 (1986), 8–16; Richard Hall, in R. Hodges & B. Hobley (eds.), *The Rebirth of the Town in the West, AD 700–1050* (London, 1988), 125–32.

stances, Eadberht may have attempted to develop a regional economy, as the West Saxons had done.

So far the details of these important excavations at York are limited. It is interesting to note that an urban settlement was established outside the Roman and Early Christian (seventh-century) nuclei, as may have happened also at London. Furthermore, the *wik* appears to be separated from another nucleus of eighth- to ninth-century date which was probably situated in the Bishopshill district of the old Roman colonia. Here, Richard Morris has speculated, Alcuin may have built a monastery called Alma Sophia modelled upon Santa Sophia at Benevento (Fig. 33). Coincidentally, concentrations of eighth- and ninth-century objects in this district led Joan Moulden and Dominic Tweddle to broadly similar conclusions.[59] If they are right, York by the end of the eighth century was a thriving settlement, comparable with Hamwic, London and Ipswich.

In sum, trade may have given Anglo-Saxon kings access to Carolingian commodities to sustain their tradition of gift-giving, but it also became a threat to centralised kingship. The evidence from Hamwic, however, reveals that the early (innovative) steps were taken by West Saxon kings not only to control trade, but also to initiate the production of their own commodities. At the same time, it is argued, this urban community became the focus of highly regulated regional marketing. It would be arrogant not to assume that the West Saxons kings perceived the political advantages of their enterprise. Above all, as far as the central theme of this book is concerned, Hamwic remains a tribute to West Saxon social relations which made it possible to muster support to build and maintain this great place. But was Wessex alone in taking this innovative step? On balance, the archaeology of Kent, London, Ipswich and York suggests that urbanism came to these places a fraction later. The chronology is important, as there can be no doubt that the powerful political implications of the concept would not have been lost on neighbouring kings. Yet there is some reason to suppose that the age of Mercian supremacy marks a period in which this land-locked territory sought in vain to catch up with its neighbours. The reasons for this become a little clearer when we consider how the transformation from a gift economy to a commodity economy was greeted outside the emporia in the monasteries and homesteads of this time.

59. Richard Morris, 'Alcuin, York, and the *alma sophia*', in L.A.S. Butler & R.K. Morris (eds.), *The Anglo-Saxon Church* (London, 1986), 80–9; Jean Moulden & Dominic Tweddle, *Anglo-Scandinavian Settlement South-West of the Ouse* (*York Archaeological Trust Report 8/1*, York, 1986), esp. 5–14.

Bede's world: ideal and reality

Bede's later years were dominated by his preoccupation with what he regarded as the interdependent problems of the spiritual and temporal decline of the English. According to Patrick Wormald, his works were not concerned with charting reality but with idealism.[60] His aim was to initiate a general reform of Church and society, 'the instruments of which were to be an instructed king and aristocracy, a rejuvenated episcopate and, above all, a reformed monasticism'.[61] He wanted a return to the ethics of his youth. Few would now doubt that his 'best-seller' had its required impact and to some extent achieved its ends.[62] Boniface, archbishop to Charles Martel in the German territories, shared Bede's views and convinced Charles, as well as the early Carolingian aristocracy, of the virtue of reform. Boniface's successor among the Germans, Chrodegang of Metz, was later to put them into effect and to lay the foundations of the spirit underpinning the Carolingian renaissance. That spirit, as we shall see in Chapter Five, was not lost on King Offa of Mercia, his successor Coenwulf or the ninth-century West Saxon kings Egbert, Aethelwulf and Alfred. Carolingian reformers enshrined Bede's ideals in their doctrines, and this proved an essential ingredient in the eventual transformation of warrior-kings into dynastic rulers.

Bede's overview of the late seventh and earlier eighth centuries appears to be endorsed by the available archaeology. For example, the late seventh century was an age of controlled primary sceattas; the earlier eighth century by contrast is notable for the sceatta types. The challenge to a generation of kings in the early eighth century came not only from the changing character of trade, but from attitudes to trade in England. Power could be hijacked if wealth could be manipulated. Power depended not only on the supply of valuables, but on control of resources which generated services. At the same time the Church proved an obstacle to the rise of strong centralised kingship. Its lands were immune from services and obligations, yet it appears to have invested poorly. The Northumbrian renaissance was a brief *floruit* enacted by energetic, fresh converts, sensitive to the creative opportunities of the age. A generation later Bede expressed concern about counterfeit monasteries administered by false abbots sidestepping services owed to their kings. These rogues had gained land from their kings in perpetuity rather than for their lifetimes. As a result their sons did not have to serve in a royal household before becoming eligible for gifts of land. Burial, moreover, appears to have been virtu-

---

60. Patrick Wormald, 'Bede, the *Bretwaldas* and the origins of the *Gens Anglorum*', in P. Wormald (ed.), *Ideal and Reality in Frankish and Anglo-Saxon Society* (Oxford, 1983), 99–129.
61. Alan Thacker, 'Bede's Ideal of Reform', in ibid., 145.
62. Wormald, op. cit. (n. 60).

ally the monopoly of minsters; it was in their power to control the 'rites of passage', exacting gifts of lands and goods from the living before they could hope for salvation in the afterworld.

Archaeology reveals a few of the reasons for Bede's shattered ideals. No royal sites can be ascribed to his lifetime, but a variety of monastic and quasi-monastic sites are now known. Whitby was the first to be excavated; although the results are confusing some conclusions may be drawn from the re-examination of the original records by Cramp and Rahtz.[63] First, the monastic settlement was small but probably comprised many separate units rather than an integrated complex. Cramp's excavations at Jarrow revealed a similar aggregated plan (Fig. 34).[64] The prevalence of stone buildings in both places is striking, in contrast to their absence on other categories of sites in this period. Secondly, the material culture of Whitby was extraordinarily rich. Styluses for writing, decorated metal tags, brooches, sceattas and a good collection of pottery were retrieved from comparatively poorly-executed excavations. As at Hamwic, the material possessions of the community were far from negligible. Similar finds have been discovered in the excavations of Burrow Hill and Brandon. Burrow Hill is an island site close to the Suffolk coast, south-east of Sutton Hoo. Recent excavations show that the hilltop was enclosed by ditches. In the enclosed area there is not only a large cemetery (mostly of coffin graves), but also evidence of industrial activities.[65] This was an elite site, suitable for burial and, to judge from numerous sceattas and Beonna pennies, concerned with exchange (see p. 98). Was it a minster or a rogue minster of the type which challenged Bede's ideals?

The same question mark hangs over Brandon in north-west Suffolk, on the eastern edge of the Cambridgeshire Fens. Again it is an island site (in the Little Ouse), with a great variety of timber buildings set within several compounds (Fig. 35). It had a small timber church, at least two cemeteries and a remarkable material culture.[66] The cemeteries are separated; the larger one contains shroud burials, while the smaller has coffin burials. Styluses, rich metalwork, good quantities of pottery and bonework imply an elite settlement, possibly with monastic functions. Linen production seems to have taken place on the

63. Rosemary Cramp, 'Analysis of the finds register and location plan of Whitby Abbey', and Philip Rahtz, 'The building plan of the Anglo-Saxon monastery at Whitby', in D.M. Wilson (ed.), *The Archaeology of Anglo-Saxon England* (London, 1976), 453–8 & 459–62.

64. Rosemary Cramp, 'Monkwearmouth and Jarrow: the archaeological evidence', in G. Bonner (ed.), *Famulus Christi. Essays in commemoration of the thirteenth centenary of the birth of the Venerable Bede* (London, 1976), 5–18.

65. Fenwick, op. cit. (n. 51).

66. R.D. Carr, A. Tester & P. Murphy, 'The Middle-Saxon settlement at Staunch Meadow, Brandon', *Antiquity* 62 (1988), 371–7.

34. Reconstruction of the Bedan monastery at Jarrow (drawn by Barry Vincent, after Rosemary Cramp).

island. However, despite its position, no evidence of its involvement in trade has been found; no sceattas have so far come to light.

In contrast, a large number of secondary sceattas have been discovered at Reculver, a minster founded inside the old Roman fort in 669 by a priest named Bassa. The report of its foundation by the author(s) of the *Anglo-Saxon Chronicle* two centuries later certainly implies that the site and the priest were special. Some importance was evidently attached to this Kentish place by the ninth-century West Saxon historian.[67] Finally, the monastic site at Nazeingbury (Essex) betrays a similar affluence.[68] The material culture is not so spectacular, but the palaeopathology of the skeletal remains reveals the

67. On its ninth-century history see Nicholas Brooks, *The Early History of the Church of Canterbury. Christ Church from 597 to 1066* (Leicester, 1984), 199–200.
68. P.J. Huggins, 'Excavations of Belgic and Romano-British farms with Middle Saxon cemetery and churches at Nazeingbury, Essex', *Transactions of the Essex Archaeological Society* 10 (1978), 29–117.

presence of many healthy women. A preliminary study of the small sample of skeletons available indicates tentatively that women lived longer here, as in other places in England, than in Roman or later medieval times and were comparatively tall.[69] Diet, to some extent, must be the cause.

There is every reason to suppose that monasteries and convents were as sensitive as royal families to the management of their resources – perhaps it is not so surprising to discover that a great illuminated book like *The Lindisfarne Gospels* used the hides of over 100 calves.[70] No doubt we should be suspicious of those monks who sought hermits' lives in the Fens and other places 'in the wilderness'. Places like Crowland, Ely and Medehamstede were indeed located where the freshwater fen was greatest, but Peter Hayes of the Lincolnshire Archaeological Unit has now demonstrated that in Roman and later medieval times these zones were recognised as constituting major ecological resources.[71] It is clear that many enterprising 'colonists' in Middle Saxon times settled in these areas, where stock could graze, freshwater fish could be trapped and salt, a valuable resource, could be made.

Finally, we must remember that all these monastic sites were small in area and must have supported small populations. After the age of missionary churches, the ecclesiastical monuments of the late seventh and eighth centuries were diminutive. Jarrow minster, like the Old Minster at Winchester. was designed on the scale of contemporary Frankish churches.[72] There was hardly anything resplendent about them. Evidently the urge to imitate classical form no longer existed. One can argue therefore that the Church was less concerned with its 'home' than with its manipulation of moveable wealth. Books, reliquaries, crosses and even the 'knick-knacks' constitute its prominent material culture in this period. For this reason it is no surprise that St Cuthbert was buried with a collection of grave goods in ancient rather than early Christian tradition (see p. 46). Seemingly he was removing gifts from worldly circulation, much as pagan members of the elite had done. The advantage of controlling treasure and concomitant inheritance strategies was not lost on this saintly man any more than on the king associated with Sutton Hoo.

69. ibid., 62–3.

70. Janet Backhouse, *The Lindisfarne Gospels* (Oxford, 1981), 27; I am indebted to Ian Riddler for some enlightening conversations on this issue.

71. Peter Hayes, 'Relating Fen Edge sediments, stratigraphy and archaeology near Billingborough, south Lincolnshire', in N.R.J. Feiller et al. (eds.), *Palaeoenvironmental Investigations* (Oxford, 1985), 245–69; see also J. Le Goff, 'Le désert-forêt dans l'Occident médiéval', in J. Le Goff, *L'imaginaire médiéval* (Paris, 1985), 59–75.

72. Eric Fletcher, 'The influence of Merovingian Gaul on Northumbria in the seventh century', *Medieval Archaeology* 24 (1980), 69–86.

35. Brandon Staunch Meadow: a view of excavated remains at post-built timber structures (courtesy of Bob Carr and the Suffolk Archaeological Unit).

Archaeologists of the Church have often been deceived by the ideals of Bede's youth, as well as by the great crosses and fine bibles. There has been a failure fully to appreciate the dissipation of these ideals as minsters began to concern themselves with wealth in the present and failed to make preparations for the afterlife. This spiritual conflict was not lost on eighth-century society. Aethelbald of Mercia was denounced for his unchaste behaviour towards nuns and his seizure of church property. In fact Aethelbald himself drew attention to the decadence in Anglo-Saxon monasteries.[73] None the less he was prepared, we may be sure, to condone polygyny, while at the same time challenging the immunities which undermined the social foundations of royal power. Boniface's letters to Aethelbald leave us in little doubt that Anglo-Saxon society had entered a highly unstable phase.

Two archaeological illustrations reveal the depths of this instability. The splendid eighth-century helmet recently located at Coppergate, York, along with a small assemblage of weaponry, links the spiritual confusion to secular conflict. These regalia were evidently in the possession of a member of the hierarchy. But why were they deposited so ignobly alongside the river Foss in a simple wood-lined pit? May they have represented looted or stolen goods, hastily disposed of to avoid detection?[74] The fact that the pit was lined makes this an improbable explanation. More probably it was a ritual deposition – an expression of a virtually redundant system of withdrawing wealth from circulation which had been common a hundred years earlier (see p. 41). The objects, it is proposed, were intentionally pledged as gifts to the gods, just as prestige goods had been ritually removed in the Early Anglo-Saxon funerary rite. The regalia, almost certainly associated with the tribe and its land, were being deployed in opposition to the concept of gifts to the Church for future salvation.[75] As it is dated to the age of Bede, the deposit reflects the spiritual and secular tension affecting the volatile ranks of the Northumbrian hierarchy.

At an altogether lower level in Middle Saxon society, alterations to the plan of Raunds – a village in Northamptonshire on the Mercian frontier with Middle Anglia – reflect other cultural mechanisms at work in the eighth century. The remarkable excavations have revealed a sequence of farms, running on one site from the sixth to the sixteenth century (Fig. 36).[76] The first timber halls probably date from the early part of the sixth century. There follows an interesting sequence including a large bow-shaped hall (A), around which a fenced enclosure containing two or three dispersed halls has been added. Towards the end of the century, the large enclosure around the early eighth-century farmhouse was replaced by a smaller one containing a tightly arranged line of structures. The sequence is of signal interest. Building A – a grand hall erected a generation or so after the construction of grand halls at Cowdery's Down and Yeavering (in the seventh century) – seems to indicate the social aspirations of thegns (or even possibly ceorls), some way down the social ladder. It also marks the

73. Thacker, op. cit. (n. 61).
74. Hall, op. cit. (n. 57), 36.
75. Jonathan Parry, 'The gift, the Indian gift and the "Indian gift" ', *Man* 21 (1986), 453–73 at 464 describes tribal attitudes to heirloom valuables in Oceanic contexts.
76. Graham Cadman, 'Raunds 1977–1983: an excavation summary', *Medieval Archaeology* 27 (1983), 107–22.

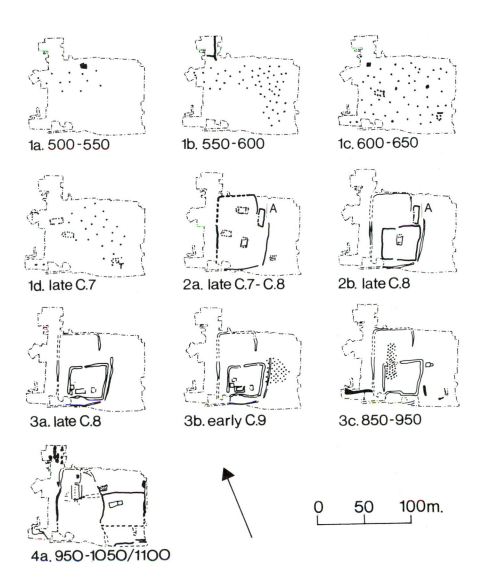

1a. 500-550

1b. 550-600

1c. 600-650

1d. late C.7

2a. late C.7-C.8

2b. late C.8

3a. late C.8

3b. early C.9

3c. 850-950

4a. 950-1050/1100

0   50   100m.

36. The sequence of excavated plans found at Raunds (Northamptonshire) showing how post-built structures in period 1c were enclosed by a ditch in period 2a, and thereafter replaced by new buildings in period 2b, and later still by a church (see Fig. 54) in periods 3c and 4a. The bow-shaped building A is a feature of periods 2a and 2b. The dots in periods 1a–1d indicate scatters of potsherds (drawn by Barry Vincent, after the Northamptonshire Archaeological Unit).

break with a dwelling form that had commonly existed since Roman times, suggesting a modification to the household unit. At this level in society, as Charles-Edwards has noted, the house was distinguished within the ranked structure of society as a familial possession, as opposed to land, which invariably belonged to the tribe.[77] Dwellings of similar scale to building A at Raunds have also been discovered in the excavations of the Middle Saxon village at Catholme (Staffordshire).[78] Raunds is therefore not unusual.

At this date facilities for storage were apparently absent at both sites. Separate buildings, alongside the farmhouses, only appear in the late eighth and ninth centuries. Elsewhere, the apparent absence of storage facilities appears to contradict Ine's familiar West Saxon laws, which describe well-managed agrarian regimes. Yet several archaeological studies of food refuse from Middle Saxon sites (p. 108) confirm the general tenor of these laws. The apparent contradiction therefore needs to be reconciled. The most likely explanation is that the refuse was left over from the social consumption of produce, little of the agrarian output being set aside for storage. In this connection it is pertinent to recall Wormald's opinion that 'royal halls such as those in *Beowulf* were not only scenes of upper-class jollification but also centres which exploited a king's agricultural resources'.[79] The food-rents never posed the problem that arises from the EEC's agricultural policy; nor did individual farmers face such crises. Instead the images from *Beowulf* suggest that the hall was the scene of conspicuous consumption. It was the locus of tribal competition, probably accelerated by social instability in the early eighth century.[80]

Production, in other words, was not maximised in the capitalist sense; it was generated to meet the needs of the political economy. Surplus was consumed for integrative purposes, as were commodities. Hamwic is a reminder that the significance of production as well as trade was comprehended by at least one royal household and upheld by its aristocracy, but it is not the only one. In 1956 Brian Hope-Taylor discovered a remarkable watermill at Old Windsor with well-preserved timbers still in place, dated by dendrochronology to the late seventh century.[81] His investigations showed that the mill lay at the

77. T.M. Charles-Edwards, 'The distinction between land and moveable in Anglo-Saxon England', in P. Sawyer (ed.), *Medieval Settlement* (London, 1976), 184.

78. S. Losco-Bradley & H.M. Wheeler, 'Anglo-Saxon settlement in the Trent Valley', in M.L. Faull (ed.), *Studies in Late Anglo-Saxon Settlement* (Oxford, 1984), 101–14.

79. Wormald, op. cit. (n. 38), 58.

80. W.G. Runciman, 'Acclerating social mobility: the case of Anglo-Saxon England', *Past and Present* 104 (1984), 3–30.

81. I am indebted to Brian Hope-Taylor for discussing the Old Windsor excavations with me. Full publication is forthcoming; meanwhile see *Medieval Archaeology* 2 (1958), 183–5 and 3 (1959), 288–90 and for a discussion of the dating: J.M. Fletcher & M.C. Tapper, 'Medieval artefacts and structures dated by dendrochronology', *Medieval Archaeology* 28 (1984), 112–32 at 119–20.

end of a deep canal-like leet, a kilometre long, which had been cut across a tongue of land jutting into the river Thames. The excavated mill, perhaps one of several along the leet, was driven by a substantial vertical wheel, quite out of character with the primitive technology of the age. Hope-Taylor's skilful excavations reveal that it lasted for a short time only, before the mill race silted up. The site then lay abandoned until the later ninth or tenth century when a fresh, more modest mill race was cut. The documentary sources are few, but there can be little doubt that this great enterprise lay within West Saxon territory and was probably once again the work of Ine. Like the timber theatre at Yeavering and the planned street grid at Hamwic, this remarkable technological innovation must owe its genesis to Mediterranean influence. The scale of the work, after the discovery of Hamwic, comes as no surprise. The excavations reveal a plan to intensify agricultural production, as we have already noted from the Hamwic evidence, over and above the needs of consumption. The brief history of the mill tells its own story. Ine's achievements were short-lived, and the will to contrive new social and economic experiments may have been stifled in the aftermath of his death. Yet, as we have seen, his legacy was enshrined in West Saxon laws and in the streets of Hamwic. Old Windsor may reflect the tentative nature of change in the short term, but it was part of an achievement that was bound to have implications for the development of Anglo-Saxon society as a whole.

*

Slight though the archaeological sources are, a picture has emerged of social tension at most levels of society in the generations after the conversion. The seventh-century doctrine of the Church had been hijacked by the early eighth century, and social process grew increasingly more complicated once the flow of valuables essential to social integration diminished. If the trading sites are a true reflection of the political economy in the territories examined in this chapter – and it must be stressed that this is by no means certain – then the kings of Wessex exercised greater social authority than their neighbours. It is difficult for the archaeologist to assess why this should have been so. The answer must be sought in the tribal constitutions of the English, and their curious development since the fifth century. Even so, the West Saxon kings, like their Mercian counterparts, repeatedly failed to secure inheritance for their siblings. Throughout the eighth century both the regulated, modestly integrated West Saxon economy and the policies of conspicuous consumption practised elsewhere failed to work to the advantage of the elite. The eventual arbiter in matters of succession was the sword', as one historian concludes.[82] Yet Offa's moment was to come. Drawing upon Carolingian experience, the political configurations of the English were bound to change, and with these changes the concept of a nation began to emerge.[83]

82. David Dumville, 'The Aetheling', *Anglo-Saxon England* 8 (1979), 1–33 at 33.
83. B.A.E. Yorke, 'The vocabulary of Anglo-Saxon overlordship', in D. Brown et al. (eds.), *Anglo-Saxon Studies in Archaeology and History* 2 (1981), 171–200.

5

The Carolingian Connection

Twice in her history England has exercised a broad, deep, and lasting influence upon continental ways of thought and life. During the last two centuries of modern history, since the days of Montesquieu, her constitution has directly or indirectly served as a standard and given direction to the popular struggle for participation in and a control of government, for a constitutional balance of powers, for an adjustment between the efficiency of the state and the liberty of the individual. A millennium earlier English missionaries and scholars...left their native country to work in foreign lands and made a large contribution to the spiritual foundations and unity of Western civilisation. (W. Levison)[1]

In his seminal account of eighth-century England, Wilhelm Levison attributed pride of place not to the warrior-kings, but to the missionaries. He contended that Alcuin, Boniface and Willibord together introduced the Bedan ideal to their Frankish brethren, sowing the seeds of ecclesiastical and political change. The Carolingian kings were evidently impressed by these Englishmen, and Alcuin was to become an influential minister in Charlemagne's government. From this point it was a short step to the negotiation of marriage alliances between the children of Charlemagne and Offa in the 790s. Hence, Levison concluded, 'the devotion and enterprise of English emigrants had a large share in creating this common soil and atmosphere', enabling the Anglo-Saxons to flow into 'the greater river that is usually called the Carolingian renaissance'.[2]

The climax of Offa's long reign is marked by these negotiations with the greatest ruler Europe witnessed between the demise of the Roman Emperors and Napoleon. An English king could now command respect in Europe. Moreover, by the later eighth century, the Mercians appear to have rejected the political apparatus that had stifled the ideals of Bede's youth as well as the governmental machinery introduced by King Ine. But within a generation the Mercian ascendancy had been eclipsed by the West Saxons, who under Egbert and his son Aethelwulf established the dynasty around which the nation was to be built. We

1. Wilhelm Levison, *England and the Continent in the Eighth Century* (Oxford, 1946), 1.
2. ibid., 170–1; 151 respectively.

may speculate that Levison, with his roots in German historiography, would have ascribed the brief Mercian supremacy to the Carolingian connection. Unfortunately the written sources for this period are at best sketchy. No substantive sources equivalent to those documenting Charlemagne's age describe England in this period. As a result it is tempting to ignore the creation of a common soil and atmosphere as mere conjecture, and thus to lose sight of the moment of Offa's greatness as well as the all-important roots of the West Saxon dynasty. But such a perspective is necessary for any enquiry into the beginnings of English society, for it is clear that, at the height of the Carolingian age, the Anglo-Saxons rediscovered the political and economic momentum that had resulted in the building of Hamwic. In this chapter I wish to explore the three themes which have emerged, using 'new materials' (to quote Stenton). First, we must identify whether the Anglo-Saxons did flow into the greater river that is called the Carolingian renaissance. Secondly, we must explain how Offa's great rise to historical fame was possible in a period in which social restrictions prevented the accumulation of wealth and power. Thirdly, bearing in mind the first two themes, we must look for the source of the enduring political success of the West Saxons.

The Carolingian renaissance and the Anglo-Saxons

Writing of the Carolingian renaissance, the eminent art historian Erwin Panofsky commented: 'When Charlemagne set out to reform political and ecclesiastical administration, communications and the calendar, art and literature, and – as a basis for all this – script and language...his guiding idea was the *renovatio imperii romani*.'[3] As Lawrence Nees has recently pointed out, Panofsky belonged to a period of historiography that was greatly influenced by imperial concepts.[4] In particular the experience of Bismarckian and Nazi Germany had left a considerable impression upon Panofsky, as it had on Levison. A post-war generation has tended to play down the powerful role taken by empires, giving greater emphasis instead to provincial histories.[5] The swing of the pendulum of historiography invariably obfuscates the past. As far as the Carolingian Empire is concerned, its history stands in need of reappraisal as 'new materials' begin to indicate aspects of this age which lay beyond the horizons of historians studying it 50 years ago. Likewise its relations with its neighbours

3. Erwin Panofsky, *Renaissances and Renascences in Western Art* (Stockholm, 1960), 44.

4. Lawrence Nees, 'The plan of St. Gall and the theory of the program of Carolingian art', *Gesta* 25 (1986), 1–8.

5. Frank Stenton's classic history of *Anglo-Saxon England* (Oxford, 1947), like many of its imitators, paid little attention to the impact of the Carolingian renaissance upon the Anglo-Saxons.

need to be reassessed in terms not only of Carolingian influence, but also of how these connections influenced the history of the Empire. I shall begin this section, therefore, by presenting a brief overview of the Carolingian renaissance, drawing upon these 'new materials'. I shall then examine how the Anglo-Saxons interpreted this movement.

In the second half of the eighth century Pepin III, followed by Charlemagne, conquered almost all of western Europe. Each summer, as the *Frankish Annals* record, the Carolingian kings led their war-bands in search of new conquests and fresh plunder.[6] Yet this great polity was administered by war-bands and primitive ministries as opposed to Augustan legions or Napoleonic armies. Charlemagne may have attempted to establish a small permanent army, but it is quite unrealistic to believe that, with such forces, he could manage regions stretching from south Jutland to the Sabine Hills, from Bavaria to Aquitaine. As the Empire became bigger, so the problems of managing it increased. In these circumstances, the English monks may have helped to formulate a policy. What was needed was an ideological revolution, facilitating such social and economic transformations as would enable the king to control potentially hostile members of the aristocracy and to raise taxes to enlarge his governmental and military forces. No blueprint for such a policy existed, of course, but in many cases the means for change could be found simply by drawing upon existing under-developed traditions.

An ideological revolution was the keystone of this policy. A fundamental aspect of the Carolingian reform was the central role of the king in a united Christian society. Charlemagne manipulated the Church so as to alter the structure and basis of society. In short, Christianity became the basis of a 'reborn' society.[7] The legislation necessary for effecting this social revolution was formulated at reforming synods where king and bishops sat together. Symbolically, the climax of this transformation occurred when Charlemagne was formally anointed with oil by Pope Leo III in Rome. Thereafter he possessed the theocratic status of the great Roman emperors. As the Lord's anointed ruler, refusal to follow him could be treated as sacrilege, punishable by excommunication.

The promotion of public ritual to enforce the place of the Church in society was a central theme of the *renovatio*. Symbolic significance was consciously incorporated in the design of abbeys, churches, monasteries and palaces.[8] But the Carolingian renaissance was more than

6. Timothy Reuter, 'Plunder and tribute in the Carolingian Empire', *Transactions of the Royal Historical Society* 35 (1985), 75–94.

7. W. Ullmann, *The Carolingian Renaissance and the Idea of Kingship* (London, 1969).

8. Richard Krautheimer, 'The Carolingian revival of Early Christian architecture', *Art Bulletin* 24 (1942), 1–38; idem, 'Die Karolingische Wiederbelebung der frühchristlichen Architektur', *Ausgewählte Aufsätze zur europäischen Kunstgeschichte*, Cologne 1988, 272–6.

a phase of ritual fervour. Maintaining this polity was only possible through adherence to the centre. Charlemagne therefore set out to redevelop classical government as well as the early Christian imagery of a Holy Roman Empire. The imperial palace at Aachen was not only constructed from Roman materials but made to appear as if it were a classical rather than a Germanic residence. Its design, and the technology employed to achieve it, belonged to an earlier empire. The past took a new shape in the Carolingian world. Charlemagne was represented on coins as if he was Constantine; while the chronicler Paul the Deacon, influenced indubitably by Frankish dynastic chroniclers, traced back the history of his peoples and elevated the Lombards to a new ethnic importance as peoples with a biblical past. Memory became an important tool in the administering of the regime.[9] The Carolingians were consequently fascinated by tradition as a means of achieving their enormous aspirations. The aristocracy was ideologically bound by a shared Christian ethos to uphold Charlemagne's secular authority as well as the future of his dynasty.

It is hardly surprising that these ideological instruments have captured the imagination of historians. The political history of the times, the annals, biographies and poetry, the architecture and the art, have been enduring grist to the mill of debate about this brief but highly significant period. Yet to understand the age properly we need to know whether the *renovatio* enabled Charlemagne to introduce the social and economic changes on which the future of the Empire depended. In an important study of these changes, Georges Duby argued that Charlemagne's strategy was misapplied.[10] He contended that the dynasty invested enormous landed and labour resources in the Church but the Church used them poorly and as a result vast wealth was accumulated by the monasteries to the detriment of the dynasty. This ultimately contributed to the civil war which broke out barely twenty years after Charlemagne's death. The civil war in turn led to the break-up of the Empire and a long phase of turmoil as the political factions came to terms with the eclipse of Charlemagne's aspirations.

The basic tenor of Duby's overview still has much to commend it, but archaeology now permits us to measure three aspects of this age which are important in assessing not only the scale of change in the Empire, but also its influence on neighbours such as the Anglo-Saxons.

First, excavations and recent architectural studies confirm that

9. Most recently discussed by Chris Wickham, 'Lawyer's time: history and memory in tenth- and eleventh-century Italy', in H. Mayr-Harting & R.I. Moore (eds.), *Studies in Medieval History presented to R.H.C. Davis* (London, 1985), 53–71.

10. For a stimulating overview of the Carolingian period see Georges Duby, *The Early Growth of the European Economy* (London, 1974), and note Rodney Hilton's review of it, 'Warriors and peasants', *New Left Review* 83 (1974), 83–96.

monastic life was transformed in this period. Small retreats of the Merovingian age were substantially altered to become centres which spread the cultural renaissance to visiting members of the aristocracy. Small armies of lay workers were drawn to the monasteries in order to free the monks for spiritual duties. This influx of workers turned the monasteries into demographic centres of urban proportions with a marked division of labour. The new monastic plans seem to date from the 780s, long before the St Gall Plan – a schematic blueprint of a south German monastery – was drawn up in about 817.[11] Like the shift from type A to type B emporia described in previous chapters, this was bound to have implications not only for ecclesiastical matters, but also for the control of resources.

Secondly, in about 790 the volume of long-distance trade increased, coinciding with a decline in summer campaigns to obtain territory and plunder. Elsewhere I have linked this boom in commerce to the rise of Abbasid trade connections through western Russia and the Baltic Sea.[12] By way of this circuit of trading networks, oriental silver and a range of fine goods travelled westwards. Haithabu in south Jutland seems to have been the Baltic terminus for Frisian entrepreneurs trading Carolingian produce. From here the Frisians returned to Dorestad, which flourished at this time, providing the Carolingian elite not only with silver which could be used to develop a monetary economy but also with a rich array of prestige goods that could be employed as gifts to sustain important relations within the aristocracy. In addition to this sinuous northern connection between the Abbasids and the Carolingians, it now seems likely that there was at least a subsidiary connection linking the two nations via the Aghlabids of the Maghreb and Beneventum.[13] This system of global trade, connecting the Chinese, Indian Ocean peoples, Arabs, Vikings and Carolingians, was inevitably short-lived. For reasons I have discussed elsewhere, a serious decline in the volume of trade seems to have set in by about 820.[14] This threatened the stability of the elite in all the communities that had adapted their economies to the commerce. It weakened Carolingian society in particular, and it hindered the development of the Carolingians' trade partners in Denmark and North Africa. It may also have had serious implications for the Anglo-Saxons.

Thirdly, in 793/4 Charlemagne reformed the coinage; this was inter-

11. Walter Horn & Ernest Born, *The Plan of St. Gall* (Berkeley, 1979) make this point most vividly.
12. Richard Hodges & David Whitehouse, *Mohammed, Charlemagne & the Origins of Europe* (London, 1983), 102–22.
13. Richard Hodges, 'Charlemagne's elephant and the beginnings of commoditisation in medieval Europe', *Acta Archaeologica* 59 (1988), forthcoming.
14. Hodges & Whitehouse, op. cit. (n. 12), 158–68.

preted by Duby as an attempt to create a monetary economy.[15] The minting of coins was now more rigorously controlled, while the amount of silver in them was increased by as much as a third. Similar reform deniers were minted soon afterwards by Pope Leo III, by Grimoald, king of Beneventum, by the Danes at Haithabu and by the Anglo-Saxons. Other techniques were also improved and widely adopted. A standardised type of cement-mixer was used to make the lime concrete needed to construct the grand new churches.[16] The concepts of building technology must also have been widely diffused if we are to account for the emergence of a standardised Carolingian basilican plan. Glass, tile, iron, bronze, soapstone and pottery production were also improved.[17] In essence Roman technology was revived and greater emphasis was laid on producing large quantities of goods (leading to increased wastage), using more expedient materials. New industries were not founded in every region; instead there appear to have been some areas that were well provisioned, while in others the underdevelopment of the preceding centuries went unchanged. This pattern can also be seen in agrarian intensification. Historical geographers, for instance, have attributed the introduction of the open field system to ideas from the newly conquered eastern Frankish lands in this period.[18] Likewise agrarian historians in Italy believe that many great monasteries set about developing their lands Archaeological evidence of intensification and the adoption of new agrarian practices has been identified in areas as different as the Rhine delta, the Po valley and the coastal littoral of Beneventum.[19] But the rate of change evidently varied, and changes were invariably short-lived compared with the agricultural intensification in the later tenth century. However the Carolingian *renovatio* not only encompassed a revival of Roman science, it also released an energy, as Jacques Le Goff describes it, as craftsmen were given individual rights and the division of labour

15. Philip Grierson, 'Money and coinage under Charlemagne', in *Karl der Grosse* 1 (Dusseldorf, 1965), 501–36; Philip Grierson & Mark Blackburn, *Medieval European Coinage*, vol. 1: *The Early Middle Ages (fifth-tenth centuries)* (Cambridge, 1986), 206–10.

16. D.B. Gutscher, 'Mechanische Mortelmischer', *Zeitschrift für schweizerische Archäologie und Kunstgeschichte* 38 (1981), 178–88.

17. Richard Hodges & Helen Patterson, 'San Vincenzo al Volturno and the origins of medieval pottery in Italy', in R. Francovich (ed.), *Ceramica Medievale nel Mediterraneo Occidentale* 3 (Florence, 1986), 13–26. John Moreland, 'A monastic workshop and glass production at San Vincenzo al Volturno, Italy', in R. Hodges & J. Mitchell (eds.), *San Vincenzo al Volturno* (Oxford, 1985), 37–60. Richard Hodges, 'The beginnings of the medieval iron industry in western Europe', in *Medieval Iron-making and the Role of the Oldest Process Industry in Medieval Society* (Stockholm, 1985), 299–307.

18. H-J. Nitz, 'Settlement structures and settlement systems of the Frankish central state in Carolingian and Ottonian times', in Della Hooke (ed.), *Anglo-Saxon Settlements* (Oxford, 1988), 249–74.

19. Richard Hodges, 'Charlemagne's elephant' (n. 13).

began to assume a new form.[20] Since craftsmen as far away as Beneventum responded to this scientific transformation, it is unlikely that such changes passed unnoticed in Anglo-Saxon England.

A final point is that archaeology now confirms Pirenne's famous remark that the Carolingian age was the scaffolding for the Middle Ages. Despite the breakdown of centralised government and the sharp decline in international commerce, the traditions and technologies of the age endured to become vital aspects of many regional cultures after the later tenth century.

It is often assumed that Anglo-Saxon society, with its strong Germanic tradition, had little in common with the revival of classical antiquity that was fundamental to the Carolingian renaissance. Yet individual Anglo-Saxons such as Alcuin and his pupil Fridugis played central roles in the management of the Carolingian Empire. At the same time archaeological evidence confirms that Frankish merchants continued to visit Hamwic, London and Ipswich, though perhaps in smaller numbers than before. In these circumstances, therefore, the question is not so much whether the Carolingian movement in all its diverse forms was assimilated by the Anglo-Saxons, as what form these cross-Channel relations took.

In 781 Charlemagne sent his sons Louis and Pepin to Rome to be anointed by Pope Hadrian. In a striking imitation of Carolingian form, Ecgfrith, son of Offa, was consecrated king in 787. It did Ecgfrith no good, of course. His reign lasted only a few months in 796. In Alcuin's words, 'he has not died for his own sons; but the. . .vengeance for the blood shed by the father has reached the son. For you know very well how much blood his father shed to secure the kingdom on his son.' The consecration of his son was one of the issues debated by Offa at the great council held at Chelsea in 786. On this occasion two papal legates attended to furnish the assembly with a European status. It seems that Offa, like Charlemagne, was attempting to harness ecclesiastical authority to sanctify his dynasty. Decrees compiled at the council condemn conspiracies against royalty and all threats to kill the king.[21]

But these occasions brought the Mercian king face to face with the other side of the Carolingian movement: the aspirations of the European Church. It has been suggested that Archbishop Jaenberht of Canterbury refused to anoint Ecgfrith. This was almost certainly one motive for Offa's plan to create a metropolitan see at Lichfield in the heart of Mercia. His action was in direct opposition to Canterbury, and Ecgfrith was consecrated only after Hygeberht had been chosen

20. Jacques Le Goff, *Time, Work, and Culture in the Middle Ages* (Chicago, 1980), 86.

21. Patrick Wormald, 'The age of Offa and Alcuin', in James Campbell (ed.), *The Anglo-Saxons* (Oxford, 1982), 101–31.

as Offa's Mercian archbishop. The conflict reveals how important the consecration was to Offa, and at the same time how much of a threat it posed to the Kentish primate. The dispute outlasted Offa, for Archbishop Wulfred of Canterbury and King Coenwulf, Offa's successor, were in intermittent conflict for more than two decades. Wulfred is known to have been a keen reformer, sympathetic to the rule of Chrodegang of Metz, but he and Coenwulf both wanted control of the monasteries on the Wantsum Channel at Reculver and Minster-in-Thanet (see p. 92).[22]

Despite these conflicts, Nicholas Brooks believes that kings were 'seeking to secure the support of the Church for their dynasty' by granting land and immunities.[23] They were following a Carolingian model. Offa, for example, granted Jaenberht the right to mint pennies in the 790s, despite the dispute over the consecration. Coenwulf returned lands to the archbishop of Canterbury which had been snatched by Offa in these conflicts. Until 817 Coenwulf of Mercia mostly supported Wulfred, and in the 820s Coenwulf's successor Coelwulf resumed the flow of benefices. It only ceased when the West Saxons annexed Kent during 825–7. But by 838 the West Saxons were once again showing marked royal generosity to the Church, unlike the beleaguered Carolingians.

Canterbury was not the only great church to profit from royal largesse. King Egbert forged close ties with the West Saxon Church in the later years of his reign, possibly influenced by his period of exile spent at Charlemagne's court.[24] His son and successor, Aethelwulf, maintained this policy, giving considerable lands and endowments to Swithun, bishop of Winchester in the mid-ninth century. Yet by the 860s the donations had diminished in number, and it is surprising to discover that King Alfred was referred to as an enemy of the Church in the first years of his reign.[25]

To what extent do the written sources reveal the real impact of Carolingian ideology on the Anglo-Saxons, as opposed to selecting some celebrated moments in a volatile relationship between England's warrior kings and the Church? A range of archaeological data has begun to shed some light on this question.

The archaeology of the Anglo-Saxon Church rests upon a good many assumptions, as Richard Gem has recently shown.[26] The basis of these assumptions is that 'the architecture of the Anglo-Saxons forms an

22. Nicholas Brooks, *The Early History of the Church of Canterbury. Christ Church from 597 to 1066* (Leicester, 1984), 156; 175.

23. ibid., 129–36; 180–97.

24. ibid., 197–203.

25. ibid., 150.

26. Richard Gem, 'ABC: how should we periodize Anglo-Saxon architecture?', in L.A.S. Butler & R.K. Morris (eds.), *The Anglo-Saxon Church* (London, 1986), 146–55.

integral part of the culture of the period and that, if a framework is established on an examination of other aspects of that culture, a pattern may be postulated which may (or may not) explain the architectural history as well'.[27] Gem acknowledges that this method has been employed, albeit not always explicitly, in the study of Anglo-Saxon architecture since the days of G. Baldwin Brown. For example, the chronology of the architecture has been derived from key descriptions of churches by Anglo-Saxon authors themselves. Bede set the scene, describing the Church and church-building in the century before and during which he was writing. Next, the writings of Boniface and Alcuin, together with incidental letters and biographical accounts of the period, offer rare insights into later eighth- and ninth-century ecclesiastical history. A century later, in the 890s, King Alfred of Wessex is represented by his biographer, Asser, as the champion of the Anglo-Saxon Church. Later eleventh- and twelfth-century written sources describe the monastic reform movement of the later tenth century when the Anglo-Saxon Church re-established itself as a powerful force in society, modelling itself on Carolingian ideas.

This simple synopsis of the history of the Anglo-Saxon Church, as Gem shows, becomes less satisfactory as more churches are subjected to architectural and archaeological scrutiny. The traditional thesis takes little account, for example. of Boniface's European fame or of Alcuin's political achievements in Charlemagne's court. Furthermore, it would be very strange if the Anglo-Saxons were unaffected by the great rebuilding of churches in Carolingian times and by the liturgical and social forces that were the real motor of the monastic *renovatio*. Indeed the great age of the Anglo-Saxon Church in the tenth century occurred when the Frankish Church was at a low ebb, and when in addition cross-Channel mercantile relations between England and the Continent had diminished from an early ninth-century peak to a comparatively low level (p. 134). Richard Gem proposes a number of stages to take account of these circumstances within a continuous development. His tentative groupings are

(1) c. 600–750/800	Period of conversion and consolidation
(2) c. 750/800–900/940	Period of attempted reform, parallel to the Continental Carolingian reform
(3) c. 900/940–1010/1045	Period of successful monastic reform
(4) c. 1045–	Period of papal reform.

The second stage in Gem's sequence is of special interest, as it is often underemphasised in recent analyses of Anglo-Saxon Church history. If the Carolingian liturgy and reform rules were adopted during this period, we might expect Canterbury and the other prin-

27. ibid., 147.

cipal minsters of the kingdoms to have been enlarged, redesigned and redecorated. Gem himself has found hints of this. More recently Nicholas Brooks has advanced the case that alterations of this kind took place at Canterbury early in the ninth century under the guiding hand of Archbishop Wulfred, a man often at odds with the Mercian overlords of Kent and Canterbury. Brooks uses a mixture of archaeological and historical sources to support his argument.[28] (Sadly none of the evidence is very substantive.)

In contrast to Canterbury, Martin Biddle's excavations of the Old Minster alongside the present cathedral at Winchester are on a scale suitable to the needs of this investigation.[29] Here we have a remarkable opportunity to examine a major monument in West Saxon history. The sequence of rebuilding is bound to shed light on relations between the kings of Wessex and the Church.

Biddle's masterly excavations revealed the great church as a jumble of robbed walls (Fig. 37). These walls, he decided in his fullest review of the evidence in 1975, belonged to three major building-phases obscured by many minor alterations. What I shall refer to as phase A was a small church built by King Cenwalh of Wessex in about 648. Phase B consisted of an enlarged church with a western addition built upon a crushed chalk foundation. This was dated to about 971. Phase C represented a far grander building with a great rectangular westwork as well as an extension of the apse to the east. Biddle proposed that this church was constructed after about 974. The building was demolished in 1093–4 to make way for the new Norman cathedral.

Early in the 1962–9 excavations Biddle postulated that the phase B enlargement of the seventh-century church, with its conspicuous chalk-founded west front, might belong to the Carolingian age. But after paying special attention to the sequence of graves associated with the building, he concluded that phase B belonged to the tenth rather than the ninth century. This was consistent with the interpretation of the sequence made by the historian Roger Quirk using the

28. Brooks, op. cit., 51–2; 55–6; 129–74; see also A.D. Saunders, 'Excavations in the church of St. Augustine's Abbey, Canterbury, 1955–58', *Medieval Archaeology* 22 (1978), 25–63.

29. The literature on the Old Minster is considerable: there are interim reports in the *Antiquaries Journal* 44 (1969), 312–23; 50 (1970), 311–21; 52 (1972), 115–25; see particularly Martin Biddle, *'Felix urbs Winthoniae*: Winchester in the age of monastic reform', in D. Parsons (ed.), *Tenth-Century Studies* (Chichester, 1975), 123–40; note his recent reappraisal in idem, 'Archaeology, architecture, and the cult of saints in Anglo-Saxon England', in Butler & Morris (eds.), op. cit. (n. 26), 1–31, esp. 20–5 (hereafter Biddle 1986), and Birthe Kjolbye-Biddle, 'The seventh-century minster at Winchester interpreted', in Butler & Morris, op. cit., 196–209; on the cemetery see B. Kjolbye-Biddle, 'A cathedral cemetery: problems in excavation and interpretation', *World Archaeology* 7 (1975), 87–108; on the painting found in the foundations of the New Minster see J. Backhouse et al. (eds.), *The Golden Age of Anglo-Saxon Art* (British Museum, London, 1984), 44 and David Wilson, *Anglo-Saxon Art* (London, 1984), 155–6.

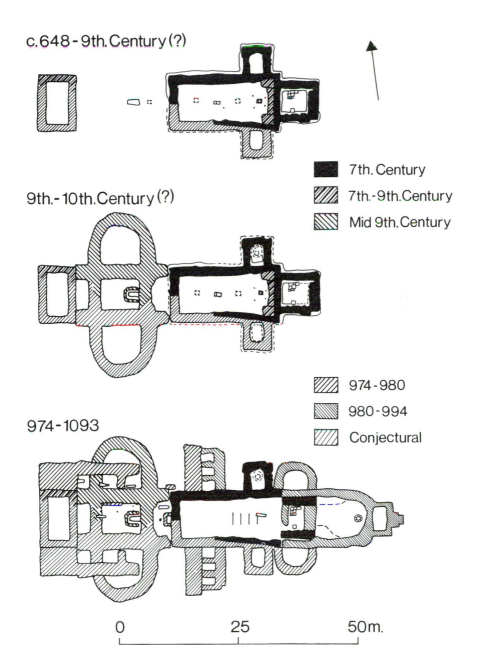

c.648 - 9th. Century (?)

9th. - 10th. Century (?)

974 - 1093

■ 7th. Century

▨ 7th. - 9th. Century

▨ Mid 9th. Century

▨ 974 - 980

▨ 980 - 994

▨ Conjectural

0   25   50m.

37. A modified version of Martin Biddle's 1975 interpretation of the phases of the largely robbed remains of the Old Minster, Winchester. These are described in the text as phase A (top), B (middle) and C (bottom) (drawn by Barry Vincent, after Martin Biddle).

later documentary sources. More recently, with the benefit of fifteen years in which to examine the question, Biddle has broadly confirmed the latter interpretation. The Old Minster, in his opinion, was a comparatively small church in the ninth century and had been so essentially since Cenwalh's time.

The historical and archaeological sources pertaining to the Old Minster are extremely complex. In neither case do they offer an incontrovertible account of the building history. As a result, we can ask several questions about this special excavation. First, to what extent can the historical chronology of the Old Minster be trusted? Even Biddle acknowledges that an element of doubt exists in such critical aspects as the position of St Swithun's tomb within the minster.[30] Even if the present hypothesis is accepted, several puzzling questions must still be answered. Are we to assume that Bishop Swithun's (c. 852–62) minster was the small church founded in the seventh century? If so, what are we to make of the splendid fragment of ninth-century painted plaster found in the early tenth-century foundations of the New Minster nearby? Surely the painting is indication of major building(s) here in the early to mid-ninth century, when Kings Egbert and Aethelwulf had established West Saxon supremacy in England.

If Biddle's phasing is upheld (and it has been until now), we must conclude that, on the eve of Alfred's accession, the West Saxon dynasty was accompanied by an ecclesiastical authority with a strikingly modest cathedral. As an expression of the bishop's status, the Old Minster would attest the failure of the West Saxon Church to assimilate Carolingian ideas. Furthermore it shows that one of the major churches in Wessex was not even architecturally compatible with lesser minsters being built at that time elsewhere in England (see below). These are clearly important issues, and I shall return to them later in the chapter.

In Mercia the pattern was different. Biddle's excavations of the minster at Repton (Derbyshire) illustrate an entirely different history (Fig. 38). Repton was founded in the late seventh century and was the burial place of King Aethelbald of Mercia after his assassination in 757. In 839 it was again a royal burial-ground when Wiglaf was interred here, and ten years later Wystan of Mercia was also brought to rest at the minster.

Biddle's excavations show that the minster was assimilating Frankish ideas before the tenth century.[31] This is borne out in particular by a detailed study of its well-known ninth-century crypt

30. Biddle 1986, 24.

31. Martin Biddle, public lecture, Sheffield University 14/3/84; Biddle 1986, 16–22 & fig. 8; see also H.M. Taylor, 'Repton reconsidered' in P. Clemoes & K. Hughes (eds.), *England before the Conquest* (Cambridge, 1971), 391–408 and 'St Wystan's church, Repton, Derbyshire: a reconstruction essay', *Archaeological Journal* 144 (1987), 205–45.

38. View of the chancel and crypt at Repton (Derbyshire).

which cut through an earlier (late seventh- to early eighth-century) cemetery beyond the east end of the first church. Originally, in fact, the crypt was a detached structure, similar to the Roman mausolea favoured by the Carolingian aristocracy in the later years of the eighth century.[32] Subsequently the freestanding building was linked to the church. The distinctive vaulting and columns of the crypt appear to belong to this phase. Later still side passages were added for processional purposes, permitting pilgrims to pay homage to relics in the crypt.

The freestanding building (the first phase of the crypt) was not the only structure of its kind within the minster's cemetery at this time. In the gardens to the west of the church as many as six earthen barrows appear to be covering rectangular sunken structures. The one fully-excavated barrow contains a stone-built mausoleum divided into two chambers, which may have been decorated with stucco and lit by glazed windows. In Biddle's words: 'At Repton there may have been not one but two or even more tombs crest-sited along the low cliff of the south bank of the Trent. Like the earthen tombs of old, these were sunk into the ground, but one at least rose above the surface in monumental plinths which recall the mounds, perhaps even stone pyramids, appropriate to the burial of princes.'[33]

These barrows seem to represent the wish to be interred in chambers which might be visited. Displayed as such, the dead were expected to play a part in the future of their descendants. The ritual is quite compatible with the Carolingian ethic and its pronounced fascination with relics and their display. Furthermore since Repton was associated with the Mercian kings these discoveries tend to confirm the influence of Carolingian ideas on the highest ranks of this kingdom.

Other parallels for this mortuary rite with public display of relics occur elsewhere within Mercia. The crypt at Wing (Buckinghamshire) has many features in common with Repton,[34] though it remains to be seen whether mausolea also existed in the cemetery around the church. At Winchcombe (Gloucestershire) and Worcester cathedral, Steven Bassett has made a plausible case for royal Mercian mausolea of the same type.[35] Elsewhere in Mercia the construction of the large basilican churches at Cirencester and Deerhurst is considered to resemble the stonework at Wing. The well-preserved basilican church at Brixworth (Northamptonshire) may also belong to this group. Finally, at St Oswald's Priory, Gloucester, recent excavations by

32. Eric Fernie, *The Architecture of the Anglo-Saxons* (London, 1983), 116–21.

33. Biddle 1986, 22 (n. 31).

34. Harold M. Taylor, 'The Anglo-Saxon church at Wing in Buckinghamshire', *Archaeological Journal* 136 (1979), 43–52.

35. S.R. Bassett, 'A probable Mercian royal mausoleum at Winchcombe, Gloucestershire', *Antiquaries Journal* 65 (1985), 82–100.

Carolyn Heighway have revealed a phase with apses at either end of the nave. This classic Carolingian feature has been found beneath the remains of the church constructed in the early tenth century by Queen Ethelflaeda, Alfred's daughter, to house St Oswald's relics.[36]

The case for a regeneration of ecclesiastical fortunes in Mercia is strengthened further by the revival of monumental art at this time. Several collections of sculpture, for instance, betray the influence of Frankish artists. The friezes from Fletton (Northamptonshire), associated with the minster at Medehamstede (modern Peterborough), like those from Breedon-on-the-hill (Leicestershire) were originally designed to decorate grand buildings. The friezes blend indigenous and Carolingian motifs in a distinctive hybrid (Fig. 39).[37] Most importantly, though, like the solitary fragment of painted fresco from Winchester, these friezes betray an ambition quite consistent with the spirit embodied in the monumental basilicas of the Carolingian age.

It is now being appreciated that a similar artistic eclecticism also runs through various other ecclesiastical works from this time. Mildred Budny believes that the great illuminated book Royal 1.E.VI was inspired by Carolingian workmanship.[38] The Book of Cerne, probably made at Canterbury, stems from much the same heritage. In common with the makers of stone crosses, metalsmiths were developing a distinctive sinewy interlace ornament, derived from the Hiberno-Saxon tradition, which was threaded through vinescrolls of classic Carolingian form. Offa's pennies show a similar motif, as do the Witham Pins and Fuller brooch (Fig. 45), two of the finest works of art of this period.[39] In sum, art historians tend to concur that the confused styles of the early eighth century, best illustrated on secondary sceattas, were superseded at the end of the century by a common motif that was readily distinguished and, it seems, gaining international renown.

The Carolingian connection is also beginning to be identified in the archaeology of the Middle Saxon aristocracy. At Northampton remains of a sequence of Mercian palaces have recently been excavated (Fig. 40).[40] Here traces of a substantial stone palace belonging to the early ninth century overlie a timber hall of Yeavering form. The timber

36. C.M. Heighway and Richard Bryant, 'A reconstruction of the tenth-century church of St. Oswald, Gloucester', in Butler & Morris, op. cit. (n. 26), 188–95.

37. Rosemary Cramp, 'The Anglian tradition in the ninth century', in J. Lang (ed.), *Anglo-Saxon and Viking Sculpture in its Context* (Oxford, 1978), 1–32; R.H.I. Jewell, 'The Anglo-Saxon friezes at Breedon-on-the-Hill, Leicestershire', *Archaeologia* 108 (1986), 95–116.

38. Mildred Budny, 'The Anglo-Saxon embroideries at Maaseik: their historical and art-historical context', *Academiae Analecta* 45 (1984), 57–133.

39. Wilson, op. cit. (n. 29), 108–11.

40. John H. Williams, Michael Shaw & Varian Denham, *Middle Saxon Palaces at Northampton* (Northampton, 1985).

39. Ninth-century panel showing a pair of figures from Breedon-on-the-Hill
(Leicestershire) (courtesy of John Mitchell).

40. The excavated remains of the ninth-century stone hall at Northampton (courtesy of Mike Shaw and the Northampton Archaeological Unit).

hall, according to its excavators, dates from the second half of the eighth century. It had annexes at each end and measured 29.7 metres by 8.6 metres overall. The timber palace was situated next to the minster of St Peter's, close to the summit of the hill on which Northampton now sits. It was replaced by a large stone hall which dates to about 820–75. The foundations of this once grand building measure 37.6 metres by 11.4 metres. Remains of mortar-mixers (of typical Carolingian type) were discovered in the excavations close by, and the building itself incorporates material robbed from other stone structures (Fig. 41). The width of the walls tends to indicate a two-storey structure of the well-known triclinium type. Close parallels have been found by the excavators in France, Germany, Italy and Spain, showing that it is a typical palace of the Carolingian age. Stone halls of this type on the Continent often incorporated small chapels as well as accommodation on the first floor, while facilities for stabling and storage were commonly located on the ground floor. The ritual character of the first floor chapel, showing the close ties between Church and state, has been pointed out by several Continental scholars. Whether this association holds true for the Northampton example is of course a matter for speculation. None the less, the technology and the form of the structure are explicitly alien to Middle Saxon England. We cannot doubt that the Mercian architect was striving to emulate a Carolingian model.

An important incidental discovery in these excavations was of the remains of several cement-mixers, associated with the construction of a royal hall. These cement-mixers are of a type well-known from the Carolingian age and invariably associated with the large new buildings of the renaissance.[41] Building technology of this kind is perhaps the clearest illustration of the exchange of information and science during this time.

There is some evidence to suggest that the Northampton palace was not an eccentricity. In his biography of King Alfred, Asser describes the royal halls which were constructed in stone and timber at Alfred's command, or moved from ancient sites and beautifully reconstructed in more suitable places.[42] Barbara Yorke selected this quotation to explain the transfer of administrative functions from Hamwic to Winchester in the ninth century.[43] The stone-built tower set in an enclosure found in the Brook Street excavations at Winchester is of related interest. Biddle, who excavated the building, interprets it as part of a residential compound of thegn-status. Similar residences from the eleventh century are thought to belong to this status, a notable example being the one excavated some years ago at Portchester Castle. However, stone secular buildings were extremely uncommon before the tenth century. A likelier explanation is that the stone tower belonged to a higher ranking member of the elite, possibly even a family that retained the property from the seventh to the tenth century, as Biddle implies. It is tempting to interpret the stone construction as a conscious representation of the classical world and its place in Carolingian ideology, as on the Continent.

The grandeur of monumental stone buildings was not lost on the Anglo-Saxons, as is illustrated by the short poem from this epoch entitled *The Ruin*, in which the poet refers to stone buildings as the work of giants.[44]

The West Saxon palace at Cheddar does not fit this picture. Although it is dated to the later ninth or early tenth century, its form is rather more reminiscent of the age of Yeavering.[45] Inside it may have been designed like the stone hall at Northampton, but this is a matter for speculation. Similarly the complex excavated at Wicken Bonhunt (Essex) (see p. 137), which may have been a royal vill in the eighth and ninth centuries, resembles in form the seventh-century

41. Gutscher, op. cit. (n. 16).
42. Dorothy Whitelock (ed.), *English Historical Documents* (London, 1955), 272.
43. Barbara A.E. Yorke, 'The Bishops of Winchester, the Kings of Wessex and the development of Winchester in the ninth and tenth centuries', *Proceedings of the Hampshire Field Club* 40 (1984), 61–70.
44. Cf. Martin Biddle, 'The study of Winchester: archaeology and history in a British town, 1961–83', *Proceedings of the British Academy* 69 (1983), 118; S.A.J. Bradley (ed.), *Anglo-Saxon Poetry* (London, 1982), 401.
45. Philip Rahtz, *The Saxon and Medieval Palaces at Cheddar* (Oxford, 1979).

41. Reconstruction of a hand-driven mortar-mixer found beside the stone hall at Northampton (drawn by Barry Vincent, after John Williams).

elite settlement discovered at Cowdrey's Down (Hampshire) (see Chapter Three).[46]

To sum up, archaeology has revealed the influence of Carolingian ecclesiastical ideas and indeed Carolingian royal ideology in Mercia, but the evidence is less satisfactory for the other kingdoms. As far as we can tell, with the possible exception of Canterbury, no large urban-like monasteries were fostered in England. The promotion of ritual, it seems, was considered important by kings like Offa and Coenwulf, but craft-production and distribution remained prominent in the control of secular authorities.

Nevertheless it is in the production sector that the influence of Carolingian royal policy is best illustrated. In common with the Danes, Pope Leo III and the Beneventans, several Anglo-Saxon kings imitated Charlemagne's reform of the silver denier in 793/9. Offa of Mercia and Berhtwulf of Wessex minted heavier versions of the rare pennies first struck by the East Anglian King Beonna and subsequently by two

46. Keith Wade, 'A settlement site at Bonhunt Farm, Wicken Bonhunt, Essex', in D. Buckley (ed.), *Archaeology in Essex to AD 1500* (London, 1980), 96–102.

obscure Kentish kings, Heaberht and Ecgberht. Even the Northumbrians followed the reform, switching from sceattas to the new penny.[47] But none of these coins are commonly found. They were seemingly minted at controlled (royal?) mints by far fewer moneyers than had operated in the age of sceattas. Offa's fine pennies are the best known, but like the bulk of English liturgical objects of this time they occur most often on the Continent. This is in sharp contrast to the dense distribution of sceattas within England.

The Carolingian monetary reform was intended to stimulate long-distance and regional trade. However, at Hamwic the paucity of imported Carolingian tablewares from this period implies that fewer merchants stayed in the port than had a century earlier.[48] In other respects Hamwic remained as large as it had ever been and was certainly flourishing in the Carolingian age.

The creation of the emporium at London could well belong to the years after the battle of Bensington in 779, when Offa captured the Thames valley, or at the latest to 785, when he conquered Kent. The series of councils held at Chelsea in 785, 786, 788, 789 and after strongly imply that Offa considered this an important part of his kingdom. Similarly it has recently been proposed that a mint was established here in the later part of Offa's reign. Imported objects, though, seem to be uncommon. Instead, Alan Vince, in a survey of the settlement, has drawn attention to the prevalence of pottery made in neighbouring regions of England, mostly Oxfordshire shelly wares and Ipswich wares.[49] If London was becoming a centre for craft production, like Hamwic, spread over 80 or more hectares, it is strange that potters were not present in the community.

Ipswich, by contrast, flourished as a trading centre in this period. Considerable numbers of imported Carolingian pots are associated with this phase, reminiscent in some respects of the earliest phase at Hamwic. As in earlier periods, these imported domestic wares can be traced back to production centres in the Middle Rhineland as well as the Low Countries. As with Hamwic a century before, it is tempting to overemphasise these commercial connections.[50] The great part of the emporium was undoubtedly concerned with craft production for regional purposes. The pre-eminent industry in Ipswich in this respect was pottery-making. Excavations in Cox Lane revealed that the Ipswich potters were using single-flue kilns, like their Carolingian counterparts. Kilns of this kind could be controlled more readily than

47. Grierson, op. cit. (n. 15).

48. Richard Hodges, *The Hamwih Pottery* (London, 1981).

49. Alan G. Vince, 'The Saxon and medieval pottery of London: a review', *Medieval Archaeology* 29 (1985), 25–93.

50. Information from Keith Wade and Cathy Coutts; Hodges, *Dark Age Economics*, 70–3.

the traditional primitive clamp variety. The distribution of these wares was extensive, crossing several territorial frontiers. More than 70 per cent of the pottery found at the royal vill (?) of Wicken Bonhunt (Essex) in the territory of the East Saxons stemmed from Ipswich, while notable quantities occur in London and as far afield as Canterbury.[51]

The archaeology of Ipswich may help to throw light on the otherwise enigmatic history of the East Anglians at the end of the eighth century. According to Christopher Blunt, Offa established a mint in the kingdom in about 790. Then in about 794 he had the East Anglian king Aethelberht beheaded. Shortly afterwards, however, East Anglian runic pennies were once again being minted.[52] Having identified the particular significance of Ipswich at this time and its contacts with the heartlands of the Carolingian Empire, it may be surmised that it was regarded as an important asset by the Mercians as long as it could be controlled. None the less it is curious that the Mercians should have exercised control over London as well as Ipswich. Competition must have developed between the two places, and this was bound to create political problems.

The discovery of a comparable settlement at York also merits a word. The excavations at 46–54 Fishergate to the east of the Roman and Anglo-Scandinavian town confirm the existence of some kind of urban community at Eoforwic, much as Alcuin implied.[53] In addition a good deal of Middle Anglian material has been identified in Bishophill, the area immediately south of the walled city (see p. 104). But in both cases Frankish and Frisian objects are rare. The strength of York's Frankish connections must remain open to doubt.

The archaeology of Hamwic, London, Ipswich and York compels some reconsideration of international trade at this time. Their archaeology tends to emphasise their importance as centres of craft production rather than of international commerce. Of course trade in prestige goods is unlikely to have remained static for two centuries. Reflecting on this in Chapter Four, I questioned whether there had been some inflation in the exchange of prestige goods during the course of the eighth century. At present neither the archaeology nor the historical sources shed any light on the matter. In fact the archaeology of these ports suggests that too much emphasis has been accorded to the commercial significance of the letters exchanged

51. Keith Wade, 'Ipswich', in R. Hodges & B. Hobley (eds.), *The Rebirth of Town in the West, AD 700–1050* (London, 1988), 93–100.
52. C.E. Blunt, 'The coinage of Offa', in R.H.M. Dolley (ed.), *Anglo-Saxon Coins* (London, 1961), 39–62.
53. Richard Hall, 'York' in R. Hodges & B. Hobley (eds.), *The Rebirth of Town in the West, AD 700–1050* (London, 1988), 125–32.

between King Offa and Charlemagne mentioning black stones – possibly Neidermendig lava quern-stones – and English woollen cloaks.[54]

However, two categories of traded objects can be identified by the archaeologist. First, the large volume of silver circulating in Anglo-Saxon England implies that this precious metal may have been imported from the Franks. Silver strap-ends and tags,[55] as well as fine silver pennies minted in reform weights (see above), are a conspicuous feature of the period (Fig. 42). The seventh century was notable for its gold, as tribal competition required its lavish use in funerary rites. The eighth century is distinguished by the use of silver-alloys in such things as the secondary sceattas. But after the coin-reform at the end of the century silver seems to have existed in boundless quantities, except in Northumbria. The striking loss of the fine strap-ends, for example, like the loss of sceattas a generation previously, indicates the quantity of silver that must have been in circulation. Some of this silver may have been acquired by the chain of networks stretching to the Baltic and via western Russia to the Abbasid Caliphate in the east. Two Offan pennies minted in imitation of Arabic dirhems offer modest support for this.[56]

The other notable feature of cross-Channel trade in this period is the large variety of Anglo-Saxon liturgical objects circulating on the Continent. Mildred Budny has compiled an impressive list of these to illustrate the Carolingian connection.[57] It includes the Maaseik *casula*, the Gandesheim casket and the Tassilo chalice. But why were these items in demand at Carolingian courts and monasteries? Their craftsmanship was outstanding and highly influential in Carolingian circles. Likewise most of them were made with precious materials rather than the alloys which were more frequently used within the Carolingian kingdoms. Perhaps, as images of the world from which Alcuin, Bede and Boniface were drawn, they conferred status. Competition between the numerous Carolingian monasteries was intense, and these works of art may have served as status symbols within the clientage systems.

In contrast to the limited evidence for commerce, there are plentiful data to illustrate the expansion of agrarian and craft production at this time. Hamwic, London, Ipswich and York, to judge from the great bulk of domestically produced material, were the principal centres of controlled craft production in this period. Some light has been shed

54. Hodges, *Dark Age Economics*, 117–29; for the correspondence see Whitelock, op. cit., 781–2.
55. David M. Wilson & C. Blunt, 'The Trewhiddle hoard', *Archaeologia* 98 (1961), 75–122 discuss these strap-ends and tags on pp. 120–2.
56. Ian Stewart, 'Anglo-Saxon gold coins', in R.A.G. Carson & C.M. Kraay (eds.), *Scripta nummaria romana: essays presented to Humphrey Sutherland* (London, 1978), 142–72.
57. Budny, op. cit. (n. 38), 89–97; 104–33.

42. Ninth-century silver strap-end from excavations at Portchester Castle (Hampshire) (courtesy of B.W. Cunliffe).

on Hamwic's shift in function by Jennifer Bourdillon's analysis of its animal bone remains. Increasing numbers of cattle and a concomitant fall in the consumption of pigs distinguish this phase of the settlement's history.[58] Bourdillon's seminal study of the livestock economy, while only in a preliminary form, hints that Hamwic had access to a balanced stock economy. This shift in emphasis would have necessitated a longer-term agrarian strategy involving an increase in the number of fields for grazing cattle at the expense of woodland.

Corroborating evidence has been found in several recent excavations of rural sites. The settlement at Wicken Bonhunt (Essex), considered tentatively to have been a royal vill, comprised a line of timber buildings, associated with which were excavated pits and ditches crammed with refuse. The refuse contained, among other things, 600 pigs (mostly heads), 200 cattle (all bones) and 100 sheep (all bones). Such offal suggests that it was a meat production site, but for whom were the carcases or joints intended?[59] More significantly, the excavator claims that many of the buildings were workshops, barns and byres. A single nine-post structure, for example, is identified as a granary

58. Jennifer Bourdillon, *Animals in an Urban Environment* (unpublished M.Phil. thesis, University of Southampton, 1983).
59. Wade, op. cit. (n. 46).

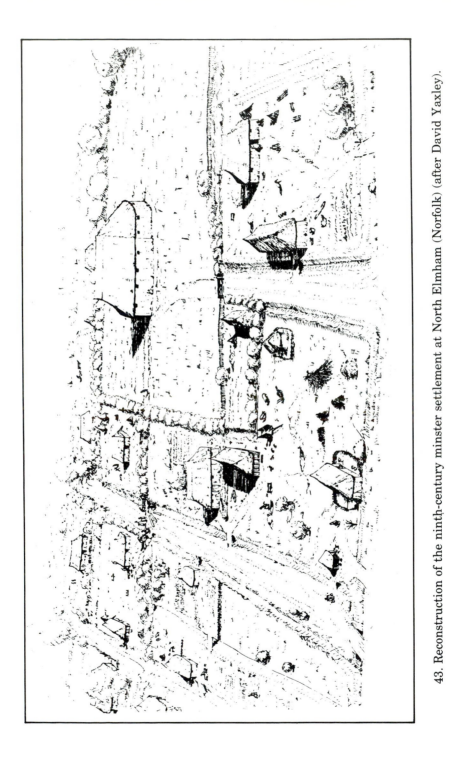

43. Reconstruction of the ninth-century minster settlement at North Elmham (Norfolk) (after David Yaxley).

or hay-loft. This pattern of buildings is not unique. At North Elmham (Norfolk), a minster whose importance is not yet known, a similar line of buildings has been discovered (Fig. 43).[60] Both places, it might be concluded, reflect new attitudes to agrarian production in which storage is now considered essential.

The pattern is not confined to elite sites. At Raunds (Northampton-shire) the enclosure around the farm diminished in size at this time, as did the sizes of the buildings within it.[61] Alongside the hall are new structures, not unlike those noted at Wicken Bonhunt, which must be associated with storage of surplus grain and hay. Similarly the later phases of the excavated village at Catholme (Staffordshire) reveal a multiplicity of buildings within the settlement, followed by the eclipse of the grand bow-sided halls. At Goltho, a clayland village east of Lincoln, the same picture emerges.[62]

These buildings must represent a new ethos in Anglo-Saxon society, marking a growing shift from conspicuous consumption to increased production for storage and exchange. The long bow-sided halls, which had replaced the Romano-British house type, appear in turn to have been replaced, possibly indicating yet another alteration to the house-hold. The significance of these findings, recalling the uniform changes to the settlement system as a whole in the seventh century, is that the shift encompassed not only the elite, but the peasantry as well. But the new buildings cannot all have been simply for storage. Some structures in these diverse settlements are associated with domestic refuse, implying the presence of servile labour accommodated separately from the principal family. This slight evidence affirms the views of the sociologist W.G. Runciman, who speculated that the replacement of kinship by service as a criterion of status in Anglo-Saxon society may trace its origins to this period.[63]

Changing attitudes to production are also revealed by the rich material culture of the time. As in agriculture, there are signs of long-term investment and technical advance. Offa's pennies are as a good an illustration of this as any. Unlike the sceattas which were made from pellets of silver, the new pennies were minted from flans. The dies used for the heavy reform pennies late in Offa's life were enlarged, and there were increased numbers of individual issues. Standardis-

60. Peter Wade-Martins, *North Elmham* (East Anglian Archaeology, Norwich, 1980), 37–124. On mills see P. Rahtz & D. Bullough, 'The parts of an Anglo-Saxon mill', *Anglo-Saxon England* 6 (1977), 15–38.

61. I am indebted to the Raunds team for this information; on Raunds generally see Graham Cadman, 'Raunds 1977–1983: an excavation summary', *Medieval Archaeology* 27 (1983), 107–22.

62. Guy Beresford, *Goltho. The development of an early medieval manor, c. 850–1150* (London, 1987), 22–8.

63. W.G. Runciman, 'Acclerating social mobility: the case of Anglo-Saxon England', *Past and Present* 104 (1984), 23.

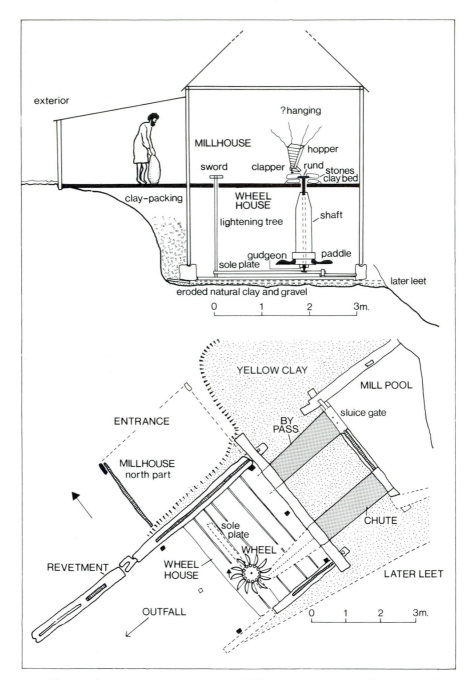

exterior

MILLHOUSE

?hanging

hopper

sword   clapper   rund

stones
clay bed

clay-packing

WHEEL
HOUSE

lightening tree   shaft

gudgeon   paddle

sole plate

later leet

eroded natural clay and gravel

0   1   2   3m.

YELLOW CLAY

MILL POOL

ENTRANCE

BY
PASS

sluice gate

MILLHOUSE
north part

CHUTE

sole
plate

WHEEL

REVETMENT   WHEEL
HOUSE

LATER LEET

OUTFALL

0   1   2   3m.

44. Plan and reconstruction of the Middle Saxon water-mill excavated at Tamworth (Staffordshire) (drawn by Barry Vincent, after Philip Rahtz).

ation of individual issues was a guarantee both of purity and of protection against fraud. The coins also boldly depict the Mercian king; they were a means of disseminating propaganda and asserting authority widely throughout the population. Above all, the organisation of coinage was rigorously controlled. New technology and better social conditions meant that unit costs decreased while the volume and distribution of individual issues could reach most sections of the community.

The unit costs of producing certain pottery types also dropped in this period. As noted above, the use of single-flue kilns by the Ipswich-ware potters may reflect Carolingian influence.[64] Whether or not that is the case, the intention must have been to produce more standardised wares by exercising greater control over oven temperature. Similar changes in the industry took place at Hamwic as well. In the early eighth century fine sand-tempered ware (class 3) was produced exclusively for the settlement. Later in the eighth century, however, this ware was replaced by various chalk-tempered and flint-tempered coarse wares (classes 2 and 4). These were far cruder, being made from poorer widely available materials, yet such vessels were distributed throughout Hampshire. The chalk- and flint-tempered wares may have been more durable, but unit costs had none the less been lowered, enabling a rise in production and wider distribution. Middle Saxon pottery production at Canterbury also follows this pattern, with poorer quality materials being fired to a higher temperature in the late eighth or early ninth centuries. Lowering unit costs and increasing output may also account for the origination of the so-called shelly wares of Lincolnshire at this time. A crushed limestone filler was easily obtained and bound together poor clays with acceptable refractory properties. The Lincolnshire potters began to use a mould to make their wares, thereby broadening their range of products.[65]

The trend towards greater productivity was not confined to pottery manufacture. The production of iron almost certainly followed suit. In about 800 Carolingian smiths developed a harder carbonised iron, especially suitable for weapons. Hitherto it had been a month-long enterprise to make pattern-welded (damascene) seaxes and swords; now they could be made in a matter of hours. Like potters, smiths realised that control over kiln or furnace temperatures was critical. The important discovery of a smithying site, possibly on a royal estate, at Ramsbury (Wiltshire) illustrates these changing circumstances.[66]

64. Blunt, op. cit. (n. 52).

65. Richard Hodges & John F. Cherry, 'Cost-control and coinage: an archaeological approach to economic change in Anglo-Saxon England', *Research in Economic Anthropology* 5 (1983), 131–84; Glenn Foard & Terry Pearson, 'The Raunds area project; first interim report', *Northamptonshire Archaeology* 20 (1985), 3–21 at 12–13.

66. Jeremy Haslam, 'A Middle Saxon iron smelting site at Ramsbury, Wiltshire', *Medieval Archaeology* 24 (1980), 1–68.

Here three traditional bowl hearths were superseded in about 800 by a smaller hearth with efficient slag-tapping facilities. The new technique, as the excavator noted, points to the rediscovery of a technological process lost from Britain since Roman times. Thus a growing body of evidence indicates that a new phase of technological development began in the later eighth century. Yet, while the stimulus for this must have come from the Continent, it is unlikely that Carolingian craftsmen came to England. Instead, as in the case of coin and pottery production, the insular typology and technology show that the English were sensitive to new needs but sometimes a little unfamiliar with modern Carolingian skills.

The archaeological evidence shows that the Anglo-Saxon kingdoms were receptive to Carolingian ideas. Both the secular elite and the Church, especially in Mercia, seem to have been influenced by the ideological themes of the *renovatio* and to have constructed buildings appropriate to the promotion of relics, for example. Similarly, it appears that coinage was reformed in all the principal kingdoms, and at the same time agricultural and craft production was intensified, affecting all levels of society. In other words the Anglo-Saxons were experiencing the pre-conditions of an agrarian 'take-off'.

The pre-conditions for 'take-off'

The Anglo-Saxons as islanders were able to interpret Carolingian ideas largely free of any compulsion, unlike the Beneventans, Bretons and Danes. There is a good deal of evidence that, as Levison put it, they shared the common soil of the age. Consequently the rule of King Offa of Mercia, and indeed the age of Mercian ascendancy, begin to come into focus. To appreciate the opportunities presented to Offa by the greater river of the renaissance, we need to remind ourselves briefly of the circumstances prevailing in England when Charlemagne became king.

First, in the late seventh century the West Saxons appear to have developed a more stable tributary system than their neighbours. The Mercians, for example, were compelled to seek land and plunder, rather as the Carolingians did at this time, to sustain a loyal warband and prevent insurrection by members of the aristocracy.[67] The vulnerability of the Mercian kingship is best illustrated by the emergence of the otherwise unknown King Beonna of East Anglia in the aftermath of the long reign of Aethelbald of Mercia. Beonna, it was argued in Chapter Four, may even have enlarged Ipswich in imitation of Hamwic. East Anglia may well have had far more advanced production and distribution systems than its better-known and far

67. Reuter, op. cit. (n. 6).

grander neighbour Mercia. However, Offa's longevity and success in war may have gradually altered the balance of power in Mercia's favour by about 780/5, when Offa was in a position to exploit Carolingian ideology. In these years, it will be recalled, he captured the Thames valley after the battle of Bensington (779) and annexed Kent (785).[68]

Offa's later fame may rest on his actions as an old man, supported by his crucial successes in war after 779, and influenced by his relations with the Carolingians. With ecclesiastical support he sought the trappings of a theocratic king. By commercial alliances with the Carolingians he obtained silver as well as other noble goods, including an Avar sword captured by Charlemagne. Like Charlemagne, he was politically strong enough to use the silver to reform the mechanisms of regional and long-distance trade. The emporium at London may date from this period, while Ipswich, though East Anglian, fell within Mercia's hegemony. During Offa's reign agrarian and craft production were intensified, while the conspicuous consumption of surplus was eschewed in favour of its distribution through networks of tribute systems and small-scale markets. Jeremy Haslam has argued that many towns in Mercia owe their origins to this period. He begins by placing unacceptable emphasis upon the hypothesis that these burhs were designed for the systematic defence of Greater Mercia against Viking sea-borne attacks. However, drawing upon recent excavated evidence from towns as diverse as Bedford, Cambridge, Hereford, Northampton and Worcester, he then develops a contentious and attractive case for a second tier of Mercian trading sites 'for interior regions'.[69] It is certainly tempting to see these places as forerunners of the second-tier burhs of the tenth century (see Chapter Six). However, one important caveat must be borne in mind: none of these places has produced evidence of craft production such as has been readily identified at London and Ipswich. If his model is correct, the archaeology reveals that these were controlled periodic markets at which craft production did not take place on any scale.

Overall, the archaeological evidence suggests that the last decade of Offa's reign was in sharp contrast to the previous decades. In these last years, when the royal household was prospering through Frankish alliances, it was no longer necessary for the Mercians to maintain their earlier military zeal. Like the Beneventans and Danes, the Mercians had to come to terms with the implications of Carolingian ideology. The new Mercian churches and their now fragmentary decorations are evidence that clerics officiating in even minor minsters succeeded in translating the Frankish concepts into reality. Initially

68. Wormald, in Campbell, *The Anglo-Saxons*, 116ff.
69. Jeremy Haslam, 'Market and fortress in England in the reign of Offa', *World Archaeology* 19 (1987), 76–93 at 89.

this may have helped the Mercians, but in common with the abbots and bishops of the Empire, the leaders of the Mercian Church sought gifts of land and increasing privileges. The long-running dispute between Offa (and later Coenwulf) and successive archbishops of Canterbury may be some modest illustration of the ascendancy of the Church. Offa's threat to create the premier see of England at Lichfield may reflect the beginnings of a frustration that was to become all too familiar to Charlemagne's descendants. By contrast Carolingian ecclesiastical ideology appears to have been adopted in a more temperate manner in Wessex. West Saxon kings, it may be deduced, had less to gain from the promotion of 'reborn society' at this time.

Yet it would be a mistake to imply that Offa's achievement was ephemeral. Describing the dyke dividing Greater Mercia from Wales, Patrick Wormald has commented: 'The historian's imagination is defeated by the capacity of an apparently illiterate government to organise this sort of enterprise, but the prehistorian is quite used to such things . . . To a real extent it marks not the first great public work of English government, but the last great prehistoric achievement of the inhabitants of Britain, in a tradition stretching back thousands of years.'[70] There has been much speculation about whether the 98 miles of earthwork were modelled upon the Danevirke or Hadrian's Wall. But two aspects of the construction seize our attention. The first, as Wormald remarks, is the scale of the enterprise. David Hill has recently calculated that it might have been constructed in two summers if Offa was able to exact 4.125 feet of fortification from each holder of a hide in Greater Mercia.[71] If he is correct, this reflects Offa's mighty vision and his powerful hold over the kingdom. Secondly, underlying this vision was a concept of fixed frontiers reminiscent of Roman times. (Indeed Paul Buckland speculates that the Roman Rig in South Yorkshire may have served as a northern border for Greater Mercia; perhaps the North Sea and the Thames formed the other sides.[72]) This was surely the vision of the first Anglo-Saxon king to describe himself as King of England, and to promote himself as if he were of imperial standing.[73]

The political propaganda of the Carolingians must have impressed Offa too. Essentially, this taught that it was important for the community to appreciate its past, its traditions and its sense of ethnicity. For this purpose the Carolingians had memories and traditions committed to parchment, and pictorial form became

70. Wormald, in Campbell, *The Anglo-Saxons*, 121.
71. David Hill, 'The construction of Offa's Dyke', *Antiquaries Journal* 64 (1985), 140–2.
72. Paul Buckland, personal communication.
73. B.A.E. Yorke, 'The vocabulary of Anglo-Saxon overlordship', in D. Brown, J. Campbell & S. Chadwick Hawkes (eds.), *Anglo-Saxon Studies in Archaeology and History* (Oxford, 1981), 171–200.

45. The Fuller Brooch: epitome of the distinctive ninth-century Anglo-Saxon ornament (courtesy of the British Museum).

immensely important. In England, following in Charlemagne's steps, Offa may have sponsored the beginnings of secular culture. The great English poem *Beowulf*, despite the vigorous debate about its date, still seems most likely to have been the work of a Mercian court poet at about this time. It reflects on a distant heroic past in terms of the Christian values of the community at the time of writing. As an epic, it spans the themes of change, the recognition of deep-rooted memories and above all the central importance of kingship. *Beowulf*, however, is surrounded by so much controversy that it would be unwise to lay too much emphasis upon it in this context.[74] Instead we should pay attention to the great outpouring of decorated works from this period

74. I see no reason to accept Chase's belief that Beowulf belongs to the turn of the millennium: Colin Chase (ed.), *The Dating of Beowulf* (Toronto, 1981).

which clearly project the makings of a common identity. According to Mildred Budny, it is an identity which evolves from a variety of sources: 'At this stage in Anglo-Saxon art the different categories of ornament – above all interlace, fretwork, animal and spiral ornament – merged with one another, with one type leading directly into another or assimilating it; asymmetrical arrangements predominated; and spiral ornaments, previously a highly distinctive feature in Anglo-Saxon (and Hiberno-Saxon) art, disappeared from use altogether.'[75] This style is amply illustrated on the Ormside bowl, the Witham pins, the walrus-ivory casket from Gandesheim, the Hedda stone at Peterborough, the Barberini Gospels and the Maaseik *casula*. It was an art form, moreover, much admired in the Frankish kingdoms, and in some cases adapted by Carolingian craftsmen to suit their taste. The elite on both sides of the Channel may have understood the symbols as well as the artistic merits of the new Anglo-Saxon visual arts, but were these designed merely to manipulate sectional interests or to reach all levels of society?

As I noted above, silver was frequently used in Middle Saxon England for the production of decorated strap-ends and tags.[76] These beautifully ornamented pieces occur at Ipswich, at Wicken Bonhunt and at more than a hundred other locations. The strap-ends and tags reflect not only the diffusion of wealth at all levels within the social spectrum, but also the dissemination of a distinctive cultural artefact well beyond the confines of the elite. The common loss of these objects, resembling the loss of sceattas a century earlier, implies a high velocity of circulation, and to some extent reflects their short-lived value. It is tempting, therefore, to identify them as an Anglo-Saxon cultural fossil giving some small expression of this brief period. Controversial though that might be, it is nevertheless worth noting that comparable artefacts do not occur within the Carolingian Empire. In the Empire copper-alloy buckles and strap-ends, and occasionally gilded variants, propagated Frankish styles to limited elite circles.[77] Furthermore, in contrast to the unity of style of the Anglo-Saxon pieces, those from the Empire display many regional variations.

Despite these achievements, Offa remained a war-lord until his death, unable to ensure his son's accession or the future of his dynasty. The evolution of English society may have been advanced in his age, but it owed a good deal to temporary influences absorbed from the Continent. Not until the West Saxons gained their supremacy over the English polity after Coenwulf's death in 821 did a genuine dynasty emerge in any Anglo-Saxon kingdom.

75. Budny, op. cit., 85.
76. Wilson, op. cit. (n. 55).
77. Neeke Fraenkel-Schoorl, 'Carolingian jewellery with plant ornament', *Berichten ROB* 28 (1978), 345–97.

The supremacy of the West Saxons runs against the grain of European history. After the 820s civil war caused the division of the Empire and contributed to political instability in Beneventum and Denmark. The central decades of the ninth century, moreover, are best remembered for the series of Viking and Saracen raids on the largely undefended strongholds of Latin Christendom. Nor were the West Saxons without problems. Excavations in Hamwic show that the decline of Wessex began in the 820s, doubtless hastened by political events across the Channel. In these circumstances the West Saxon kings may have opted to find prestige goods through the conquest of Devon and Cornwall, much as Ine had done in the early eighth century to compensate for the loss of Frankish trade. Yet Ine had clearly protected Hamwic's role as a centre of regional production. The fact that Hamwic diminished in size during the central decades of the ninth century, despite the apparent absence of any turmoil in Wessex, suggests that alternative means were found to sustain existing economic institutions.

Quite what the alternative strategy was remains a mystery. Archaeology offers only tantalisingly slight insight into this critical period. For example, the evidence for the dispersal of Hamwic's many craftsmen in the 830s and 840s to other West Saxon towns does not seem to exist. Did the craftsmen of Hamwic seek safety within the old Roman walls of Winchester, for example? Martin Biddle believes that there may have been some small nucleus by the 850s and 860s, but the famous planned town belongs at the earliest to the 880s. Biddle contends, however, that the high street at Winchester was in use throughout much of the ninth century.[78] Was this street a conscious imitation of, and replacement for, the main street in Hamwic?

A charter of 838 refers to urban property boundaries in Canterbury, which was then within Wessex. Unfortunately excavations in the town shed no fresh light on these incipient tenements. In this year too a cnicht's guild is referred to in Canterbury. This was probably a group of noble merchants who felt it necessary to form a corporation to defend their rights in the face of the growing authority of the West Saxon kings.[79] In Chapter Three it was postulated that the insulae within Hamwic belonged to members of the elite, prefiguring the arrangements well-documented in Late Saxon London and Winchester. If the same arrangement was present in Canterbury, some of Hamwic's craftsmen may have found sanctuary inside the Roman walls in the new urban holdings of the aristocracy. At present the paucity of the archaeological evidence can only mean that their enterprise was small. Yet the West Saxon kings suffered neither from the

78. Biddle, op. cit. (n. 44), 120–3.
79. Hodges, *Dark Age Economics*, 158.

apparent decentralision of production nor from its diminished scale. In both respects it testifies to the deep-rooted political structure of the kingdom.[80]

Once again the Old Minster at Winchester may offer some clue to this enigmatic period. King Egbert, who had spent many years at Charlemagne's court, evidently patronised the West Saxon Church. Aethelwulf followed suit.[81] Yet according to Martin Biddle, the Old Minster – the premier church of Wessex – had scarcely altered since the seventh century. This is an extraordinary indictment of the state of the West Saxon Church, running counter to the history of royal patronage at this time. Moreover, while Anglo-Saxon churches with explicitly Carolingian features do not exist (or perhaps have not been preserved), the decorated wall-plaques at Britford church near Salisbury are reminiscent of ninth-century North Italian workmanship.[82] It makes one wonder whether the second great building phase (Phase B) of the Old Minster (Fig. 37) belongs to this period in the ninth century rather than to the tenth century, as the excavator proposes. It is certainly strange to imagine aspiring characters like Egbert, Aethelwulf, Alfred and even Bishop Swithun arranging major ceremonies in Cenwalh's tiny seventh-century minster.[83] Such speculation serves to emphasise how little we know about Wessex on the eve of its greatest moment.

To find out about production in mid-ninth-century Wessex, we must consider what was happening in the neighbouring kingdoms. Sadly the Mercian reaction to the Carolingian collapse cannot be reconstructed. At London, however, references to Lundenwic cease in the 860s and are supplanted by those to Lundenburg.[84] In neighbouring East Anglia there are traces of increased activity in Ipswich and possibly at Norwich too, on the eve of the Viking attacks. At York pre-Viking features betray increasing concentrations of people assembling within the old Roman colonia. Traces of mid-ninth-century activity at Coppergate, including glass-making,[85] may show that people were beginning to prefer the walled Roman town to the open settlement of Eoforwic at the confluence of the rivers Foss and Ouse. In common with Canterbury, Winchester and London, it appears that it was here deemed essential to protect craft production in the face of Viking aggression. Prolific numbers of copper stycas dating from this time

80. Wormald, in Campbell, *The Anglo-Saxons*, 132–59.

81. Brooks, op. cit. (n. 22).

82. I am grateful to Richard Gem and John Mitchell for pointing out the significance of Britford to me.

83. Yorke, op. cit. (n. 43).

84. Alan Vince, 'The economy of Anglo-Saxon London', in R. Hodges & B. Hobley (eds.), *The Rebirth of the Town in the West, AD 700–1050* (London, 1988), 83–92.

85. Richard Hall, *The Viking Dig* (London, 1984), 43–8; 'York', in Hodges & Hobley (eds.), *The Rebirth of the Town in the West*, 129.

have been found in the city, indicating that with the devaluation of the silver Northumbrian penny a kingdom-wide monetary system was being adopted. This fragmentary picture leaves us in no doubt that England as a whole weathered the collapse of the Carolingian Empire. Yet the curious ninth-century history of Hamwic, running counter to the political history, forewarns the historian that West Saxon society was about to undergo substantial institutional changes.

*

The common atmosphere that the Anglo-Saxons shared with the Carolingians undeniably fostered changes. Anglo-Saxon kings well appreciated the significance of the new ideology, as the palace at Northampton illustrates. The recent work at Repton shows that some great minsters were equally responsive to the movement. In this way new meaning was given to Anglo-Saxon culture without substantially altering it. The search for an identity gave rise to the emergence of writing over oral tradition. To judge from the archaeological evidence, an agrarian 'take-off' was in progress, while efforts were simultaneously being made to ensure the continued integration of the community as a whole. The evidence is slight and the argument slender, but to challenge the impact of the Carolingian renaissance on the English would necessitate an explanation that considered the available evidence to be unusual, eccentric or misleading.

Even buffered by its island status, ninth-century England was bound to be affected by the fragmentation of the Carolingian polity. The response is difficult to measure, due to the anomalous quality of the archaeological information. Even so, we may safely predict the stable persistence of the West Saxon community and the inception of a new political economy despite, or perhaps because of, the slow desertion of Hamwic. But the symbolic messages of the Carolingian age, trapped between antiquity and its warring factionalism, between the ideal of the Roman age and the kin-based ethos of Dark Age communities, were not the means to trigger any substantial Anglo-Saxon movement. The Carolingian connection was a prelude, an important chapter before an outstanding individual made history by grasping the circumstances of his choosing.

6

The First English Industrial Revolution

Etymologically speaking, a revolution is the movement made by a
rotating wheel or a revolving planet: a rapid movement, once it begins it
is sure to stop rather quickly. Yet the Industrial Revolution is a perfect
example of a slow movement that was barely noticeable at the beginning.
Adam Smith lived in the midst of the first portents of this revolution, yet
did not realise it.   (Fernand Braudel)[1]

Adam Smith, of course, did appreciate the growing complexity of the
English economy, and his studies prepare the historian for its transformation. No such analyst prepares one for the quantum leap in
English economic affairs after King Alfred's victory over the Danes
in 878. Planned towns, an explosion of craft industry and the intensification of agriculture appear to be expressions of a movement that
embraced all levels of society. Furthermore, while Wessex was once
more in the forefront of this revolution, the potential to develop was
also present in the Danelaw – the former kingdoms of East Anglia,
Mercia and Northumbria. In the history of England the foundations
of the unified state, established symbolically when Edgar was anointed
king in 971, must be sought in the first Industrial Revolution.

Before considering the foundations in detail, I shall make a brief
interpretative excursus to search for parallels in the history of the
eighteenth-century Industrial Revolution. The Industrial Revolution
is still the subject of unresolved questions. Was Britain in some ways
special at this time, as many historians believe? Did the Protestant
work-ethic provide the basic materials for the economic and social
miracle in Britain, in contrast to Catholic France and Holland,
as Max Weber once argued? Why was there what T.H. Ashton has
termed 'the impulse to contrive': that is, men prepared to wrestle pur-
posefully to break the bottlenecks in fuel supply for iron-making,
in spinning, in the efficiency of steam-engines and so on? Such
questions fire the historical debate. Yet some features of the late
eighteenth- to ninteenth-century economic take-off are now well
documented.

---

1. Fernand Braudel, *Afterthoughts on Material Civilization and Capitalism* (Balti-
more, 1977), 105.

England changed from a country of small urban populations in the sixteenth century to one with the largest in Europe by the nineteenth century. In the same period there was a 30 per cent increase in agricultural production to cope with the growing number of town dwellers. In the spirit of Adam Smith's *Wealth of Nations*, E.A. Wrigley has argued that eighteenth-century agricultural expansion paved the way for urban and industrial development.[2] Agricultural production, in his opinion, was an essential pre-condition of take-off, since it had to be sufficiently elastic to support the sudden growth of non-agrarian communities. This systemic interaction between town and country allowed the exponential growth of the economy. Consequently, over the course of several generations, the fabric of society was transformed.

Archaeology offers a measure of this economic and social catharsis. The image is of vastly enlarged towns, urban planning on a great scale, new secondary and tertiary level industries, new scientific innovations, radical replanning of landed property, and investment in farms to increase production and storage. The revolution forced great changes on the English, ranging from the creation of new divisions within society to the emergence of new familial units. The archaeology and history of the period emphasise the slow build-up before the explosion of change, as well as the fact that the revolution affected society as a whole, not just sections of it. At the same time archaeology records the underlying tension of the age. The proliferation of non-conformist chapels and changes in the burial rite reveal not only extreme mobility, but a feeling of 'placelessness' as the community searched for meaning after the final eclipse of the medieval ethos.

The Industrial Revolution, then, provides an index against which to measure the history of the later ninth and tenth centuries. No historian denies that this was a period of considerable change, but is it an exaggeration to call these changes a revolution? In this chapter I intend to examine three aspects of the question. First, to link the Carolingian age to its aftermath, we must examine the moment of change. In particular, to what extent were the last great barbarian raids and migrations a catalyst, facilitating the reshaping of English society? Secondly, was it really a industrial revolution as such or simply an intensification of production? Thirdly, to what extent were old English traditions and values irrevocably abandoned in the tenth century in favour of a state society with a very different constitution? It is at this point that we need to consider Marc Bloch's belief that the English largely shunned feudalism and retained instead many of

2. E.A. Wrigley, 'Urban growth and agricultural change: England and the Continent in the Early Modern Period', *Journal of Interdisciplinary History* 15 (1985), 683–728.

the customs that evolved after the Anglo-Saxon migrations.[3] To find out whether this was the case, we need to examine the English peasantry and their prospects. It was they, after all, who first occupied the towns, the new manors and villages that many generations later formed the substance of the manorial rolls, wills and other documentation which caught Macfarlane's attention.

The rise of a virtuous prince

In a recent portrait of King Alfred, Janet Nelson concludes: 'Amid changing times, he could adapt policy to fortune; he was, in Machiavelli's sense, a virtuous prince.'[4] In facing the Vikings Alfred, unlike the other Anglo-Saxon kings, was able to obtain support from the men whom his biographer, Asser, called his 'noble followers and vassals', or as one tenth-century chronicler put it, 'men who used the royal feed'.[5] This may have been the foundation of Alfred's achievement, rooted in the evolution of a tribal constitution already two centuries old. In Machiavellian fashion this virtuous prince knew how to bend the rules. In 871, 876 and 877 he approached the Danes in an attempt to purchase peace.[6] This may have had lasting implications, as we shall see. He certainly had scant respect for the status and privileges of the Church – ironically, considering the Victorian respect for his piety. In particular, he seized many monastic lands after the treaty with the Danes, especially along the border between Wessex and the Danelaw. These lands were then given to his vassals as buffer estates to defend Wessex. This was a 'revolution in landholding', according to Robin Fleming, and one which sets the scene for the wider reorganisation of the English landscape.[7] Meanwhile Alfred set about emulating Charlemagne's achievements with a sense of purpose which has long since persuaded historians that the earlier Mercian and West Saxon kings had been but half-hearted imitators. Alfred assumed a theocratic status after the Carolingian model, backed up by various measures. The coinage was reformed,[8] the military was reorganised and a means of propaganda was fashioned in the manner devised by Charlemagne. Alfred's 'domestication of the savage mind' by his patronage of English written texts has won him great admirers. Until recently, these texts

3. Marc Bloch, *Feudal Society* (Cambridge, 1961), 183.

4. Janet L. Nelson, ' "A king across the sea": Alfred in Continental perspective', *Transactions of the Royal Historical Society* 36 (1986), 45–68 at 68.

5. ibid., 67.

6. Simon Keynes, 'A tale of two kings: Alfred the Great and Aethelred the Unready', *Transactions of the Royal Historical Society* 36 (1986), 195–217 at 199–200.

7. R. Fleming, 'Monastic lands and England's defence in the Viking Age', *English Historical Review* 395 (1985), 247–65.

8. Philip Grierson & Mark Blackburn, *Medieval European Coinage*, vol. 1: *The Early Middle Ages (fifth-tenth centuries)*, (Cambridge, 1986), 303–16.

have distracted historians from noticing the lack of Continental interest in his achievements – and indeed the isolation of Wessex at this period.[9] At the same time the texts have left the impression of a virtuous prince, in the fashion of the 'Last Lion',[10] leading the English back from the brink of disaster to become the natural inheritors of a great Christian realm.

The role of the Vikings

The Vikings provided the catalyst for these swiftly executed changes. But how real was the threat they posed? The answer depends on how many were involved in the invasion and settlement of eastern England and their political ability. Archaeological traces of the Vikings in England are negligible. Once again only the survival of Scandinavian place-names and words allows us to assert that, whatever the size of the invasion, its political implications should not be undervalued. There have been different estimates of the numerical strength of the Great Army of Danes who took York, East Anglia and most of Mercia and relentlessly badgered King Alfred in Wessex.

The discovery of a fort constructed around the Mercian minster at Repton (Derbyshire) may bring some measured consensus to the long-standing discussion. The Danes apparently wintered at Repton in 874–5 after defeating the Mercians in a battle nearby. It appears that they built a 3½-acre D-shaped encampment on the tongue of land jutting into the river Trent west of the minster. Martin Biddle estimates that it would have taken five weeks to construct this fort with two hundred men. Moreover the dead contained in the Anglian mausolea (see p. 128) seem to have been cleared out to house the dead from the battle.[11] The earthworks were not designed for an army the size of a Roman legion (as the distinctly partisan *Anglo-Saxon Chronicle* would have us believe), but rather for a cohort. A three- rather than four-figure number of men (and women) was involved. Warfare in these terms concentrated upon removing and replacing central persons rather than defeating the enemy.[12]

In these circumstances are we to believe that the success of the small Danish army paved the way for a migration of thousands of settlers? The place-names might suggest such a migration, yet this does not square with the notable absence of Danish material culture. The excavations at Repton seem to show that Scandinavian burial

9. Nelson, op. cit. (n. 4).

10. William Manchester, *The Last Lion; Winston Spencer Churchill. Visions of Glory 1874–1932* (London, 1983), esp. 3–18.

11. *The Times*, 27 August 1982 & 21 December 1985.

12. Alfred Smyth, *Scandinavian Kings in the British Isles, 850–880* (Oxford, 1977).

rites were transported to England. But why are pagan burial mounds not found more often?[13] The traditional thesis would have us believe that the Danes adopted Christianity far faster after the treaty made with Alfred than they did in Denmark a century later. This explanation must clearly be rejected. The number of settlers was surely limited, and the many Scandinavian place-names must be attributed to the new administrative apparatus introduced by the conquering elite. Place-name specialists may find this a specious and expedient solution, but the place-names need to be interpreted in the light of the achievements of the conquerors during this time.

The Danes were ceded the poorer half of England. Centralised authority in these territories was almost certainly less developed than in Wessex, Kent or central and southern Mercia, as we have seen in previous chapters. Yet, as will become apparent, the Anglo-Scandinavian kings undertook a programme of public works which was as impressive as that occurring simultaneously in Wessex. Viking York (Jorvik), Lincoln, Stamford and Ipswich – to name a few places – exploded into commercial life at the same time or shortly after their West Saxon counterparts. If, as many scholars believe, and as will be argued below, the planned towns of Wessex are a testament to the political prowess of King Alfred and his son Edward the Elder, the creation of new towns in the Danelaw must be seen as a far greater achievement in the face of reactionary cultural restraints.

The prolific numbers of Anglo-Scandinavian place-names in the Danelaw territories may be related to new attitudes to land-holding. Land had become an important resource in political *and* economic terms, and it needed to be controlled if it was to repay investment (see pp. 50–2). David Roffe, for instance, has attributed the origins of the hundred system in Lincolnshire to this period. Similarly Mary Harvey believes that the open-field system in much of Yorkshire was devised at this time. Excavations at Wharram Percy show that the dispersed Anglian homesteads in the valley were being aggregated together to form a nucleated village, while field survey in the Lincolnshire Fens attests the abrupt desertion of Middle Saxon farms for the Fen Edge villages which have survived to this day (Fig. 6). The many place-names may reflect the first occasion on which these

13. James Graham-Campbell, 'The Scandinavian Viking-Age burials of England – some problems of interpretation', in P. Rahtz, T. Dickinson & L. Watts (eds.), *Anglo-Saxon Cemeteries 1979* (Oxford, 1980), 379–82; Richard Morris, 'The Church in the countryside: two lines of enquiry', in D. Hooke (ed.), *Medieval Villages* (Oxford, 1985), 49–50; Klavs Randsborg, 'Burial, succession and early state formation in Denmark', in R. Chapman, I. Kinnes & K. Randsborg (eds.), *The Archaeology of Death* (Cambridge, 1982), 105–21.

new villages were taxed (and thus named) by the Anglo-Scandinavian government.[14]

The Scandinavian achievement may not have been fully appreciated; indeed the threat posed to the West Saxons may also have been misrepresented. It is not difficult to imagine how the speed of change surprised Alfred. He and his father before him had known Northumbria in the age of its copper stycas, when it had a largely isolated regional economy governed by a succession of weak kings. East Anglia in the mid-ninth century was barely more advanced. The preconditions of change existed in both kingdoms, influenced by traditions forged in Mercia and Wessex, but in neither was there the acumen to execute a take-off. The Scandinavian migrants, so it seems, provided that vital ingredient, and their success consequently posed a threat to Wessex. Alfred and his descendants were compelled to challenge this threat or else accept the rivalry. The rise of the virtuous prince and the subsequent unification of England appear to be responses to a common threat. The preconditions of social and economic change had existed in England, as in many regions of the Carolingian Empire, for several decades. In England, though, Alfred in the moment of victory was in the position to contrive new socio-political circumstances, and seemingly the Anglo-Scandinavian communities were able to follow suit.

An industrial revolution?

Urban development and the expansion of production

The most appropriate starting-point for examining the industrial revolution in Anglo-Saxon England is the archaeology of its towns. Towns, of course, contained only a fraction of Late Saxon society; the majority still lived outside. But the character and articulation of the urban markets, as well as their high archaeological profile, draws us to them first.

The archaeological documentation for the new towns is prodigious. In Alfred's capital, Winchester, a street grid was laid out in the 880s or early 890s; the defences of the ruined Roman *civitas* were refurbished; tenemental properties were marked out with ditches; and craftsmen began to lease or own these properties. At the same time new services were created in which the Church played a part. Alfred's New Minster was finished soon after his death and proved a vivid contrast to back-

14. David Roffe, 'The Lincolnshire Hundred', *Landscape History*, 3 (1981), 27–36; Mary Harvey, 'Planned field systems in eastern Yorkshire: some thoughts on their origins', *Agricultural History Review*, 31 (1983), 91–103; J.G. Hurst, 'The Wharram research project: results to 1983', *Medieval Archaeology* 28 (1984), 77–111; Peter Hayes, 'Relating Fen Edge sediments, stratigraphy and archaeology near Billingborough, south Lincolnshire', in N.R.J. Feiller et al. (eds.), *Palaeoenvironmental Investigations* (Oxford, 1985), 245–69.

street chapels like St Pancras (at Brook Street) built at the same time.[15] Winchester was a town not unlike Hamwic, now lying largely deserted 12 miles away. As at Hamwic there was a street grid with a major 'high street'; as at Hamwic an enclosure, in this case the refurbished Roman walls, defined the limits of the place; and as at Hamwic there was great emphasis on production and distribution. In common with most Late Saxon towns, Winchester was divided into numerous property parcels, each associated with a lord and commonly with a church. Commerce and production – the principal rationale for the place – were no longer the *lucri causa* which had hidden Hamwic from the historian's view. In Late Saxon Winchester, as in all Late Saxon towns, both lay and clerical authority were connected in the public eye with the expansion of economic activities.

The other great distinction between Hamwic and Winchester was that Hamwic was a monopolistic centre, complemented perhaps by a second tier of periodic markets elsewhere in Wessex. Winchester, by contrast, formed part of a ranked hierarchy of markets – a capital linked to middle-ranking markets like Chichester and Southampton where craft-production was limited until the mid to late tenth century, and to lower-order markets where until King Edgar's time there were probably no craftsmen, only facilities for periodically administering sub-regional trade in surplus commodities.

The hierarchy did not come into being at once. The concept may have existed as early as Alfred's reign, but it was still taking shape in the later tenth century. In Alfred's and Edward's time there occurred a transition from the monopolistic regional centres of the Middle Saxon period towards the ranked competitive markets that distinguish medieval England. The passage of this transition is not yet well documented. Even so, a recent case-study of London's Anglo-Saxon pottery revealed that in the tenth century the city was served by potters who were marketing their wares throughout the Thames valley and who were superseded in the eleventh century by an industry based in or near the city which provided pottery for only a sub-regional area (Fig. 47).[16]

Canterbury, Exeter, Gloucester, Oxford and London grew almost as rapidly as Winchester during the tenth century. So too did the Danelaw towns, such as Ipswich. Dwellings and workshops have proved elusive in Middle Saxon Ipswich, but numerous examples have been discovered belonging to the tenth and eleventh centuries. There was similar progress at Norwich, where the dispersed (polyfocal)

15. Martin Biddle (ed.), *Winchester in the Early Middle Ages* (Oxford, 1976), 329–35; for a general discussion of Late Saxon urban church history see James Campbell's paper in *Studies in Church History* 16 (1979), 119–35.

16. A.G. Vince, 'The Saxon and medieval pottery of London: a review', *Medieval Archaeology* 29 (1985), 25–93, esp. 30–4.

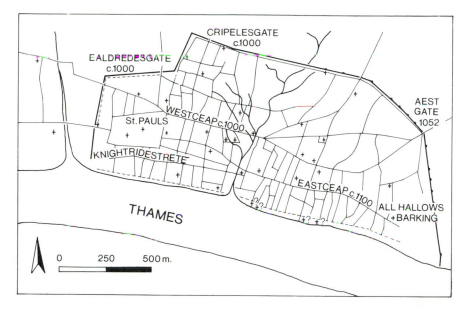

CRIPELESGATE
c.1000

EALDREDESGATE
c.1000

WESTCEAP c.1000

St. PAULS

KNIGHTRIDESTRETE

AEST
GATE
1052

EASTCEAP c.1100

ALL HALLOWS
(+BARKING

THAMES

0   250   500 m.

46. Late Saxon London (drawn by Barry Vincent, after Alan Vince).

pattern of small Middle Saxon sites became aggregated into a nucleus soon after 900. By the eleventh century Norwich was a large sprawling port. Thetford and Lincoln followed the same pattern. At York the growth was even more impressive.

Before the Vikings arrived at York, the eighth- to ninth-century emporium seems to have been abandoned in favour of settlement inside the old Roman walls. The excavations at Coppergate, some distance from the heart of the new town, vividly illustrate the course of events. As Richard Hall, the excavator of this large site, points out, it is as if a town-planner was at work in the early tenth century.[17] Small tenements were set out in rows, each with workshops. Behind the tenements heaps of refuse, including large amounts of pottery, attest to industry. Craft-production in this and neighbouring towns was in motion from the moment the builders left. Many other excavations, moreover, chart the extension of Jorvik into the suburb south of the river where, according to Richard Morris, Alcuin's monastery once stood.[18] Urban churches like St Mary Castlegate next to Coppergate, and St Mary Bishophill Junior, in the southern suburb where Alcuin's monastery may have been, remain as markers of this tide of expansion, which clearly created one of the most industrially-active places in tenth-century Latin Christendom.

17. Richard Hall, *The Viking Dig* (London, 1984), ch. 5.
18. Richard Morris, 'Alcuin, York, and the *alma sophia*', in L.A.S. Butler & R.K. Morris (eds.), *The Anglo-Saxon Church* (London, 1986), 80–9.

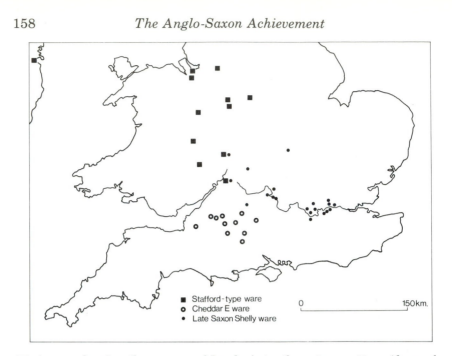

47. A map showing the sources of London's tenth-century pottery (drawn by Barry Vincent, after Alan Vince).

The towns of Wessex and the towns of the Danelaw differ in one respect, however. In Wessex, middle-ranking and lower-order market-places supported towns like Winchester, whereas in the Danelaw the regional depth of the market hierarchy was slower to form. In Wessex and southern Mercia, middle-ranking markets like Bath, Cricklade, Wareham and Wallingford were laid out soon after 878, though none of them was developed as fully as Winchester or York before the later tenth century. In the Danelaw territories, by contrast, only a few markets of this size served the expanses between the major centres. Places like Cambridge, Durham and Northampton served larger sub-regions than their West Saxon counterparts. The difference appears clearly in the map of mints operating in Edgar's time.[19] Southern England seems to have been swamped by moneyers operating not only in high- and middle-order markets, but in lower-order places as well. The excavations at South Cadbury (Somerset), an early eleventh-century refuge during the short period of the second wave of Viking attacks, reveal a lower-order market with a moneyer, a church and strong defences. During its short turbulent period as a refuge, South

19. M. Dolley & D.M. Metcalf, 'The reform of the English coinage under Edger', in R.H.M. Dolley (ed.), *Anglo-Saxon Coins* (London, 1961), 136–68.

48. An assemblage of tenth-century pottery from recent excavations in London (courtesy of the Museum of London).

Cadbury maintained the regulated market functions of the otherwise vulnerable market at Ilchester.[20] The Danelaw territories, on the other hand, apart from the main towns of Chester, Lincoln and York, where many moneyers were concentrated, seem to have been poorly served by mints.

It is tempting to seek a parallel for these contrasting circumstances in eleventh-century Denmark, where a ranked market structure existed in the west while a few large towns (notably Lund and Roskilde) emerged in the east. In a persuasive study of urban development in Denmark, Anders Andrén offers two explanations to account for these differences.[21] First, the kings of Denmark possessed an extensive patrimony in the west and were in a position to develop towns as political and ideological *points d'appui* more or less where they wished, whereas in the east the crown had comparatively little land. Secondly,

20. Leslie Alcock, *By South Cadbury is that Camelot. . .* (London, 1972), 194–201.
21. Anders Andrén, *Den urbana scenen. Städeroch samhälle i det medeltida Danmark* (Lund, 1985).

it was not until the late eleventh century that these new Danish towns became the markets for urban crafts and rural produce. Until this time their distribution across the landscape reflects their primary purpose as centres serving the new state.

Although the political and ideological significance of the new Alfredian towns should not be underestimated, the pre-eminent feature of the large burhs is the great range of craft production. Excavations in almost every Late Saxon and Anglo-Scandinavian town have uncovered workshops of some kind or other. Leatherworkers' shops have been excavated at Gloucester and Durham; wood-working has been identified in York and glass-making at Hereford and Lincoln; and potter's workshops have been found in nearly every large urban excavation.[22] The innovation of single-flue kilns and the kick-wheel for making pottery illustrate the technical changes that evolved to meet the new demand. Another example is the warp-weighted loom reintroduced at this time to enable increased textile production.[23] The introduction of carbonised steel blades in place of damascene swords, and the substitution of iron alloys and pewters for precious metals in jewellery, are further instances of techniques developed to meet the demands of an enlarged market.[24] The will to contrive underpinned the revolution everywhere. The new technology can in most cases be traced back to the Carolingians, who had either 'reinvented' a Roman technique or developed industries that had persisted in isolated places since later Roman times (see p. 120). A striking aspect of this revolution was the will to challenge tradition by deploying new technology. Experimentation among older craftsmen as well as apprentices may account for the large amounts of wasted, spoilt products that are a feature of Late Saxon archaeology. Similar developments occurred in industries as diverse as woollen production, stone quarrying and salt extraction.

But a massive leap in output is not the only characteristic of production in this period. Controlling costs by reducing the amount of labour and materials used was equally important as traditional craftsmen responded to the challenge and presumably trained apprentices to cope with new demand. The pottery industry gives the clearest illustration of the new decision-making that was needed to cope with increased demand.

An interesting contrast separates the Late Saxon pottery industries

22. The evidence now exists from countless excavations: for general essays see D.M. Wilson, 'Craft and industry', in D.M. Wilson (ed.), *The Archaeology of Anglo-Saxon England*, (London, 1976), 253–82; A. MacGregor, *Bone, Antler, Horn and Ivory. The technology of skeletal material* (London, 1985).

23. John W. Hedges, 'The textiles and textile equipment', in C. Heighway et al., 'Excavations at 1 Westgate Street, Gloucester', *Medieval Archaeology* 23 (1979), 190–3.

24. David A. Hinton, 'Late Saxon treasure and bullion', in D. Hill (ed.), *Ethelred the Unready* (Oxford, 1978), 135–58.

of Wessex and southern Mercia from the Anglo-Scandinavian industries of the Danelaw. Pottery production in Middle Saxon Wessex and
Kent evolved out of an indigenous tradition. No attempt was made in
the ninth century, for example, to imitate the technology or forms of
wheel-thrown Carolingian wares. Then, in about 900, the potter's
wheel was introduced into Wessex. The first results with this new tool
were fairly crude, and wares were frequently finished off by hand. By
the mid-tenth century, however, wheel-thrown pots were being fired
in single-flue kilns rather than in the uncontrollable clamp-kilns
typical of the Middle Saxon period. The range of forms increased
during the century with bowls, dishes, amphorae, decorated pitchers
and eventually lamps being added to the initial repertoire of cooking
vessels. Following this expansion was the emergence of lead-glazed
fine-wares (imitating similar Carolingian wares) which were traded
over much longer distances. By 1066 the potters of Wessex could claim
to have inherited a tradition stemming back to the seventh century.

In the Danelaw the history of pottery production is more complex.
Middle Saxon Ipswich-ware potters, unlike their West Saxon neighbours, had tried to imitate a limited range of Continental forms. After
about 800 the potters of the East Midlands tempered their wares
with crushed shelly limestone and introduced a moulding technique
to expand their production and range (see p. 141). Urban expansion
brought new developments in many of these areas. In Ipswich,
Norwich (Fig. 49), Thetford, Northampton, Derby, Leicester, Stamford,
Lincoln and York the wheel-thrown wares of the late ninth century
were being produced to standards that the West Saxon potters must
have envied. These wares, however, owe their typological genesis to
northern French pottery of the period and not to the indigenous Middle
Saxon pots. Stamford red-painted wares of the early tenth century
closely resemble pots made at Beauvais and in the region of Tours.
Only the shelly wares of the East Midlands preserved a native
tradition, though in this case too the repertoire of forms broke decis-
ively with the past.[25]

These developments in pottery manufacture, one of England's lowl-
iest industries, find an interesting corollary in coin-production, the
preserve of the moneyers, arguably the country's most highly regarded
craftsmen. The volume of coinage evidently increased dramatically
between about 890 and 920, with the result that coins of this period
commonly occur in archaeological contexts. The increased silver
content of Alfred's heavy penny, modelled upon Charlemagne's reform

25. I am indebted to Terry Pearson for information on the East Midlands shelly
wares; see his section in Glenn Foard & Terry Pearson, 'The Raunds Area Project: First
Interim Report', *Northamptonshire Archaeology* 20 (1985), 3–21. On Stamford ware see
Katherine Kilmurry, *The Pottery Industry of Stamford, Lincs., AD c. 850–1250* (Oxford,
1980).

denier, acted as an inducement to use coins more often in exchange. The clear, simple promotion of the authority of the issuing king also guaranteed the coin. The innovation of cash called for stiff regulations, as the laws of almost all the Late Saxon kings confirm, and simultaneously increased the temptation of forgery.[26]

In Wessex the tradition of using silver to strengthen the currency can be traced back to the late eighth century (see Chapter Five). But the Danes had no such tradition to draw upon. The copper-based stycas of mid-ninth-century Northumbria and the scarce series of East Anglian pennies show that few moneyers provided pennies that could compare with Alfred's strong currency. The Danes seem to have managed this problem, much as they had pottery production, by imitating northern French deniers (in the case of York), and copying some of Alfred's issues (in East Anglia). Were moneyers brought to England to support the few surviving in East Anglia, just as Canute later took English moneyers to Denmark in the eleventh century? Recent essays by Veronica Smart suggest that this was indeed the case.[27] A fifth of the moneyers making coins in early tenth-century East Anglia had Continental names. At York in the early years of Anglo-Scandinavian government, moneyers with Continental names outnumbered Scandinavian, and Smart points to a similar pattern elsewhere within the Danelaw territories. Scandinavian kings not only brought in Franks to help accelerate their economic expansion, but compelled them to teach Scandinavians the craft as well. Anglian production was organised to maximum effect, almost as if some textbook existed. The blueprint for this programme existed, of course, in Wessex. But where was the bullion obtained from to facilitate the shift from a copper to a silver currency in the Danelaw? Any answer to this question is little more than speculation at present, though the payments made to the Danes in 871, 876 and 877, as well as the plunder from many monasteries, may have provided enough silver to form the basis of the new currency.

Trade and commerce

New attitudes to trade and commerce are also apparent in the archaeological record. The widespread presence of coins at all classes of sites is a prominent illustration of market forces in this period. The

26. Cf. Richard Hodges & John F. Cherry, 'Cost-control and coinage: an archaeological approach to economic change in Anglo-Saxon England', *Research in Economic Anthropology* 5 (1983), 131–84; Grierson & Blackburn, op. cit. (n. 8), 303–16.

27. Veronica Smart, 'The moneyers of St. Edmund', *Hikuin* 11 (1985), 83–90; 'Scandinavians, Celts, and Germans in Anglo-Saxon England: the evidence of moneyers' names', in M.A.S. Blackburn (ed.), *Anglo-Saxon Monetary History* (Leicester, 1986), 171–84; see also Michael Dolley, 'The Anglo-Danish and the Anglo-Norse coinage in York', in R.A. Hall (ed.), *The Viking Age in the North* (London, 1978), 26–31.

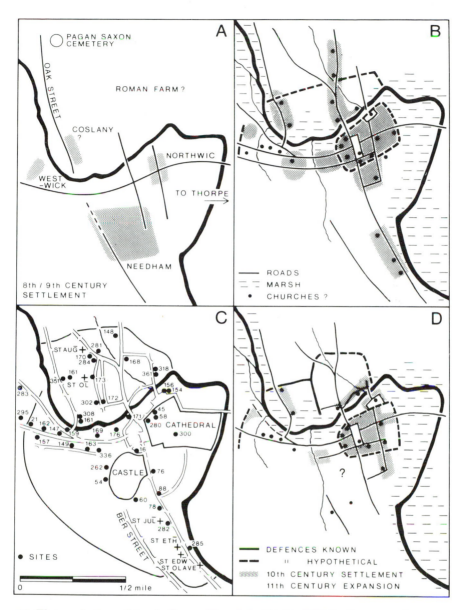

A

PAGAN SAXON
CEMETERY

ROMAN FARM?

OAK STREET

COSLANY
?

NORTHWIC

WEST
-WICK

TO THORPE

NEEDHAM

8th / 9th CENTURY
SETTLEMENT

B

ROADS
MARSH
• CHURCHES ?

C

148
ST AUG +
281
170
284
168
318
361
161
351
ST OL +
173
156
154
283
302
172
45
308
58
295
161
21 162
171
147
159
169
280 CATHEDRAL
176
300
157 149 163
336
16
262
CASTLE
76
54
88
60
78
BER STREET
ST JUL +
282
ST ETH +
285
ST EDW +
ST OLAVE +

• SITES

0   1/2 mile

D

?

DEFENCES KNOWN
"   HYPOTHETICAL
10th CENTURY SETTLEMENT
11th CENTURY EXPANSION

49. The evolution of Anglo-Saxon Norwich: (A) the Middle Saxon settlement;
(B) the tenth-century settlement; (C) the archaeological investigations; (D)
the town in the age of the Norman Conquest (drawn by Barry Vincent, after
Alan Carter).

discovery of several early tenth-century pennies in the workshops at Coppergate in York and Petergate in Lincoln, as well as at rural sites like Goltho (Lincolnshire) and High Gauber (North Yorkshire) reflects a phase in which the loss of coinage was acceptable.[28] From these losses we might deduce that the new currency was being minted in large quantities in an attempt to convince the community of its merits as the economic axes of society were irrevocably altered. Equally the coin loss might reflect the velocity of coin circulation, possibly as prices adapted turbulently to the new social and economic circumstances. The value of coinage may thus have altered as society came to terms with its new configurations.

A more vivid archaeological expression of the incipient commodity trade can be found in the remarkable quantities of pottery on all classes of sites in this period. Most Late Saxon pottery industries commanded sub-regional marketing spheres, but Stamford lead-glazed pitchers were distributed throughout central England. This example bears out the existence of some kind of ranked commerce, with prestigious commodities being marketed across regional boundaries.

Perhaps the most striking feature of Late Saxon material assemblages is the high proportion of locally made goods compared with the number of imports. At the Coppergate excavations at York, a silk cap, a fibula from the Low Countries and sherds of a Badorf-type relief-band amphora made in the Rhineland are practically the only imported tenth-century finds.[29] This paltry assemblage must be contrasted with literally tons of local pottery found in the excavations. Imports are equally rare in tenth-century Norwich, London, Winchester and Southampton. This absence may at first seem curious, coming as it does after a phase of considerable importation between the sixth and early ninth centuries. It seems to reflect the diminished role of international trade in the period. Certainly in Late Saxon times Southampton and Ipswich were but shadows of their great Middle Saxon phases. London, it seems, only began to prosper as a port late in the tenth century. Its wharfs were probably constructed in the later part of King Ethelred's reign, or even in Canute's, and were designed for mooring and loading the newly evolved deep-draughted boats with keels which are a feature of the new millennium.[30] Here it is worth reflecting that England's wealth during this epoch has often been attributed to its wool exports. The archaeological evidence, however, raises doubts about this interpretation, for foreign trade seems to

28. Henry Marbach, 'The balanced economic growth of Carolingian Europe: suggestions for a new interpretation', *Journal of Interdisciplinary History* 3 (1972), 261–73.

29. Richard Hall, op. cit. (n. 17), 88–91.

30. Richard Hodges, *Dark Age Economics* (London, 1982), 98–100; on London's Late Saxon trade see Alan Vince, 'New light on Saxon pottery from the London area', *The London Archaeologist* 16 (1984), 431–9.

50. A map showing mints operating in King Edgar's reign (after D.M. Metcalf and R.H.M. Dolley).

have been insignificant until after the second Viking raids and the formation of the North Sea Empire encompassing England and Denmark. Only then, after about 1025, were links with Germany and the French kingdoms revived. The historical implications of this evidence are intriguing. It supports the impression that Alfred inspired scant interest on the Continent. Nevertheless the absence of imported Scandinavian objects in Jorvik implies that its Viking connections have been exaggerated. Similarly, while the descendants of Edward the Elder married into the royal houses of western Europe, little direct commerce was generated by these alliances. Lastly, even though England's great clerics sought blueprints for change in the monasteries of Cluny and Gorze, the general pattern of Late Saxon behaviour seems to have been vehemently insular.[31]

31. Peter Sawyer, 'Anglo-Scandinavian trade in the Viking Age and after', in M.A.S. Blackburn (ed.), *Anglo-Saxon Monetary History* (Leicester, 1986), 185–200.

One last point arising from this urban revival needs to be stressed. The most striking feature of the new towns is not their existence – urban revolutions of similar character were beginning in many parts of tenth- and eleventh-century Europe, just as they did in the ninteenth century. It is the integrated, rational quality of the spatial planning that takes one by surprise. The monopolistic market systems and periodic fairs of Middle Saxon England were largely replaced by a hierarchy of ranked, competitive market-places. During the course of the tenth century most of greater Wessex came to be served by production-distribution facilities which processed bulk foods and daily commodities. In this part of England, at least, it appears almost as though an economic geographer has implemented Walter Christaller's central-place thesis, defining an optimal, least-cost organisational structure within a network of related sites.[32] Christaller's theory depends upon two central assumptions: first, the population, and thus its purchasing power, is distributed over an undifferentiated and unbounded surface; secondly, maximisation of profits and minimisation of costs (supply and demand) are regulated within this space through the market system. More detailed analysis is needed to substantiate this description of Late Saxon England, but at the moment the evidence appears almost too remarkable to be true. It is not so true, of course, for the Danelaw territories, as we have seen. Here perhaps traditional administrative loci exerted greater influence over the emergence of the market system.

Settlement expansion and the rise of the manor

As in the eighteenth century, the corollary of the industrial revolution was a revolution in agricultural practice. This was facilitated in the later ninth and tenth centuries by a climatic change: shorter, milder winters and longer, warmer summers distinguished the tenth century from the previous period.[33] Marginal upland grazing could now be brought back into use, for sufficient fodder could be grown in the longer summers to keep livestock through the winter. Andrew Fleming has detected traces of Late Saxon farming high up on Holne Moor, Dartmoor, while David Austin and his collaborators have attributed the beginnings of settlement in Okehampton Park, Dartmoor to this period. In the Danelaw the expansion was particularly dynamic. Fieldwork sponsored by the Fenland Research Committee has shown that the colonisation of the Cambridgeshire Fens first took place in

32. Walter Christaller, *Central Places in Southern Germany* (Englewood Cliffs, N.J., 1966).

33. H.H. Lamb, 'Climate from 1000 BC to 1000 AD', in M. Jones & G. Dimbleby (eds.), *The Environment of Man* (Oxford, 1981), 53–65.

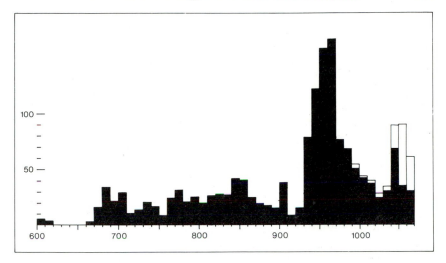

51. Anglo-Saxon charters and writs arranged by decades (writs are shown in outline). Note the huge growth in these land documents in the mid to later tenth century (drawn by Barry Vincent, after David Hill).

the tenth or eleventh century.[34] At the same time, following six centuries of virtual abandonment, the Peak District and the Yorkshire Dales were recolonised. At High Gauber, up in the Yorkshire Dales, a single Anglo-Scandinavian farmstead has been excavated. Further north, pollen cores taken from from Fellend Moss and Steng Moss attest vigorous clearance activity beginning in the mid to later tenth century.[35] Lowland England was also the scene of new colonisation: for example Della Hooke has reconstructed the extensive clearances of woodlands that took place in Late Saxon Warwickshire.[36] There are two important aspects of this sporadic picture of settlement expansion: first, the increase in peasant mobility, which should not be under-emphasised; and secondly, the search for new ground in marginal zones often deserted since Roman times, which reflects a considerable spirit of enterprise. The propensity to move and colonise new ground is a basic feature of this era, and one which I shall discuss further in Chapter Seven.

These pioneers, however, were not the only peasants to reformulate

34. Andrew Fleming & Nicholas Ralph, 'Medieval settlement and land use on Holne Moor, Dartmoor: the landscape evidence', *Medieval Archaeology* 26 (1982), 101–37; D. Austin et al., 'Farms and fields in Okehampton Park, Devon', *Landscape History* 2 (1980), 39–58; David Hall, 'Fieldwork and documentary evidence for the layout and organisation of early medieval estates in the English Midlands', in K. Biddick (ed.), *Archaeological Approaches to Medieval Europe* (Kalamazoo, 1984), 43–68.
35. Nick Higham, *The Northern Counties to AD 1000* (London, 1986), 313–15.
36. Della Hooke, *The Anglo-Saxon Landscape: the kingdom of the Hwicce* (Manchester, 1985).

the patterns of their daily lives. Surveys in the Danelaw counties of Lincolnshire, Norfolk, Northamptonshire and Suffolk show a good deal of local settlement mobility.[37] In particular, the polyfocal pattern of small Middle Saxon settlements was commonly abandoned either for one old homestead which became a nucleated village or for an entirely new site. In Northamptonshire, Glenn Foard has shown that this reshuffling of the residential lay-out was not restricted to a few settlements but encompassed most parts of the shire.[38] In contrast, a field survey of central Hampshire led by Stephen Shennan demonstrates that the settlement pattern established during the seventh century remained unaltered.[39] This difference may be a further illustration of the long and stable character of West Saxon rural life following the creation of the kingdom in the seventh century. As far as the Danelaw is concerned, though, the difference reaffirms the conjecture made above (p. 154) that new administrative apparatus was implemented in this period, leading to the use of new place-names as nucleated villages were created and as the Anglo-Scandinavian taxation authorities concocted their own formulae to describe traditional localities.

The nucleation of villages cannot itself be ascribed to the collective zeal of the peasantry. This was surely the work of a manorial class who sought affinity with the aristocracy, and even the Carolingian aristocracy, by constructing fortified manor-houses and their own parish churches. This subject, it has to be admitted, is a historical minefield. Not so long ago, for instance, R.A. Brown chastised archaeologists for their cavalier belief that the concept or principle of private fortification existed in pre-Conquest England.[40] Shortly afterwards, examples of small fortified pre-Conquest manors were excavated at Sulgrave (Northamptonshire) and Portchester Castle (Hampshire).[41] More recently still, the publication of Guy Beresford's impressive excavations of the manor at Goltho, attached to a clayland village 14

37. See, for example, Hayes, op. cit. (n. 14); Peter Wade-Martins, *Village Sites in Launditch Hundred* (East Anglian Archaeology, Norwich, 1980). David Hall, op. cit. (n. 34); Glenn Foard, 'The administrative organisation of Northamptonshire in the Saxon period', in S.C. Hawkes, J. Campbell & D. Brown (eds.), *Anglo-Saxon Studies in Archaeology and History* (Oxford, 1985), 185–222; I am indebted to Keith Wade for information about the survey of the Sandlings district of Suffolk.

38. Foard, op. cit. (n. 37); see also Foard & Pearson, op. cit. (n. 25).

39. Stephen Shennan, *Experiments in the Collection of Archaeological Survey Data: The East Hampshire Survey* (Sheffield, 1985); see also Michael Hughes, 'Rural settlement and landscape in Late Saxon Hampshire', in M.L. Faull (ed.), *Studies in Late Anglo-Saxon Settlement* (Oxford, 1984), 65–79. For a general essay see Christopher Taylor, *Village and Farmstead. A history of rural settlement in England* (London, 1983), 116–24.

40. R. Allen Brown, 'An historian's approach to the origins of the castle in England', *Archaeological Journal* 126 (1969), 131–48.

41. B.K. Davison, 'Excavations at Sulgrave, Northamptonshire', *Archaeological Journal* 134 (1977), 105–14; Barry Cunliffe, *Excavations at Portchester Castle*, vol. 2: *The Saxon* (London, 1975).

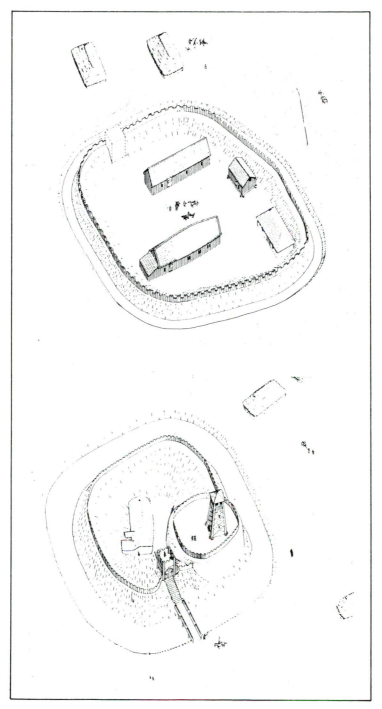

52. Reconstructions of the Late Saxon fortified manor (top) and subsequent Early Norman castle at Goltho (Lincolnshire) (after Guy Beresford).

kilometres east of Lincoln, has pushed the origins of private fortification back into the ninth century. At Goltho Beresford found that
the early ninth-century village was superseded by a small ringwork
inside which lay a cluster of buildings, including a fine bow-sided hall.
He dates this ringwork on historical grounds to c. 850–950, and charts
its substantial reconstruction during the period c. 950–1000, and again
in the period c. 1000–1080 (Fig. 52).[42] But Beresford dates the first
fortification using the sources in precisely the cavalier fashion that
would earn R.A. Brown's enmity. He gives three historical reasons for
ascribing a date to the fortification prior to the Viking raids and
settlement: first, the hall resembles a ninth-century royal hall from
Cheddar, implying that it is of Anglo-Saxon as opposed to Danish
construction; secondly, in this phase there was a dearth of artefacts
of Scandinavian origin; thirdly, Goltho is an Old English as opposed
to an Anglo-Scandinavian name. However, the pottery associated with
the phase 3 fortified manor consists precisely of those types dated to
the early to mid-tenth century in Lincoln.[43] Such a date would be far
more consistent with the emergence of manors discovered not only at
Sulgrave and Portchester, but also at Raunds (Northamptonshire). It
is clear, however, that the discoveries at Goltho are of enormous
significance in illustrating the rise of the local elite in Late Saxon
England. Goltho was not a special place in any sense, yet its village
merited an early fortified manor, which with each new phase became
a grander establishment. It must have been modelled on manors of
still grander style elsewhere in Lincolnshire, which in turn owed their
genesis to Carolingian private fortifications.[44]

The evolution of the manor as an institution in pre-Conquest
England and its early structural history may be illuminated by the
other new feature of the English landscape, the parish church. Several
excavations confirm the picture of church development first identified
at Wharram Percy (North Yorkshire) (Fig. 53). In the period before
the Conquest, the small timber church at Wharram Percy was followed
first by a stone variant, then by one with a nave and chancel, and
finally by an enlarged version of this third phase.[45] At Raunds
(Northamptonshire) a similar history has been unearthed, though in
this case a manor-house seems to have been built on a plot adjacent
to the new church.[46]

42. Guy Beresford, *Goltho* (London, 1987).
43. Coppack in ibid., 164–69.
44. Cunliffe, op. cit. (n. 41); Davison, op. cit. (n. 41); Foard & Pearson, op. cit. (n. 25); H.A.
Heidinga, *Medieval Settlement and Economy North of the Lower Rhine*, Assen 1987, 203–5.
45. R.D. Bell, M.W. Beresford et al., *Wharram Percy: The Church of St. Martin*
(London, 1987).
46. Graham Cadman, 'Raunds 1977–83: an excavation summary', *Medieval Archaeology*
27 (1983), 107–22; David Parsons, *Sacrarium*: absolution drains in early medieval
churches, in Butler & Morris (eds.), *The Anglo-Saxon Church* (London, 1986), 106.

53. View of the excavations inside St. Martin's, Wharram Percy (North York-shire) showing the outline of the tenth-century nave marked by rubble foundations (scales = 2m) (courtesy of John Hurst and the Medieval Settlement Research Group).

Raunds and Wharram Percy illustrate a process which led to the building of as many as 4,000 stone churches before the Conquest. Almost 500 of these still survive in some form or other, giving rise to what Richard Morris has described as the 'big bang' theory, referring to the construction of churches by lay lords in most villages in the space of a few decades.[47] Morris offers an interesting interpretation of this explosion in church-building: 'If we are to believe in the detonation of a big bang around 1000, then we must also believe in the existence of craft organisation which could provide sufficient manpower to erect, say, 200 churches in a decade by proposing that in this figure allowance has been made for the pre-existence of minsters, and for the likelihood that an appreciable number of the new foundations began as wooden buildings which might be constructable without calling upon more than local resources. It may well be that the appearance of the local stone church as an architectural type owes as much, if not more, to the emergence of a class of skilled technicians and a quarry industry, as to the downward diffusion of church-building habits from kings and aristocrats to local lords.'[48] Morris himself comes to no final conclusion on the matter, and proposes that the first churches were simple *ecclesiae propriae* alongside the residences of local lords.

A significant accompaniment of the new churches is their cemeteries. Community cemeteries, as I have noted in previous chapters, are a common feature of Early Saxon England but disappear after about 650 when control of burial was often exercised by minsters. Evidently centralised control of mortuary practice ended in the tenth century. This was bound to have implications for all sectors of the social spectrum, as we shall see.

Andrew Boddington has traced the short history of the cemetery at Raunds in remarkable detail (Fig. 54): 'The graveyard developed in a series of successive zones, each remaining in use as others were added. The primary zone of burial comprised a series of well-ordered rows centred on the church (Zone 1); these graves avoided a strip 2.5 metres wide adjacent to the church walls. At the east end of the area a 35- to 45-year-old man lay beneath a decorated cover set centrally within an area 1.5 by 1.5 metres within which only two infant burials were present; this may represent an exclusive burial plot. After an undetermined period, as the zone became full, burials overspilled haphazardly beyond its periphery (Zones 2 and 3); females were preferentially displaced to the west of the church into Zone 3. Encroachment toward the church walls also occurred (Zone 1A). Later the north-east corner was filled with curving rows adapted to the almost triangular shaped

47. Morris, op. cit. (n. 13), 49.
48. ibid., 53.

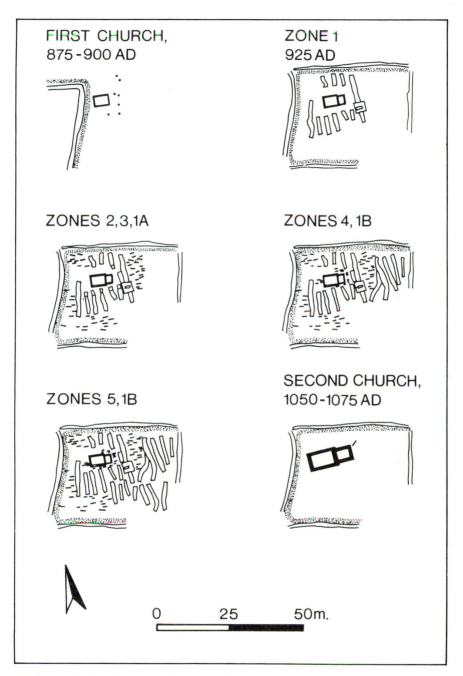

FIRST CHURCH,
875-900 AD

ZONE 1
925 AD

ZONES 2,3,1A

ZONES 4,1B

ZONES 5,1B

SECOND CHURCH,
1050-1075 AD

0   25   50m.

54. Raunds, Northamptonshire: the development of a tenth- and eleventh-century graveyard (after Andrew Boddington).

area (Zone 4), followed by the final phase of expansion which saw the infilling of the south-east corner (Zone 5).'[49] Beside the evidence for the exclusive plot, six stone coffins were found, presumably relating to the local elite. Boddington draws attention to the marking of graves, perhaps with pieces of wood, as well as the 23 zones within the cemetery. Finally, he notes the presence of infant burials around the eavesdrips of the church during the use of Zone 1B. Clearly, as he acknowledges, had this cemetery not been abandoned in about 1050/ 70, after little over a century of use, later burials would have masked this initial patterning.

This cemetery sequence reveals that burial hierarchies were still a feature of Anglo-Saxon England. Yet, in contrast to Early Anglo-Saxon cemeteries, the elite are modestly differentiated from the peasantry by having stone rather than wooden coffins. At the same time, the zoning and the evidence for marking graves shows that identity was considered important. Furthermore, in contrast to most cemeteries of earlier date, it was considered proper to bury infants within the graveyard rather than in less propitious circumstances. In the previous phase of community cemeteries during the Early Anglo-Saxon period infant burials are notably uncommon.[50]

The church and cemetery at Raunds, like the 'big bang' in church building, appear to be an index of an increasingly Christian society. Yet such a conclusion may be mistaken. Morris, for example, draws attention to a number of coin-hoards found in cemeteries.[51] These may be either Christian ritual deposits made by a lord offering up the burial ground or, as feasibly, an expression of gifts-to-gods practice made by an individual or individuals distrustful of the new mortuary rites. The large number of riverine deposits attributed to this period may be an interesting variation on this theme. Fine swords, seaxes, axes and stirrups (Fig. 55) found in rivers are traditionally attributed to careless Vikings. At Skerne on the Humber, however, John Dent has discovered a place where such depositions occurred regularly.[52] As many of these weapons are in fact of Anglo-Saxon manufacture, and as riverine deposits occur also in the heart of Wessex, it seems more likely that this was a widespread phenomenon in Late Saxon England. Military equipment of this type must have belonged to lords rather than peasants. Indeed, by the eleventh century a small amount of documentary evidence indicates that this kind of warrior equipment

---

49. A. Boddington, 'Raunds, Northamptonshire: analysis of a country churchyard', *World Archaeology* 18 (1986), 411–25 at 412.

50. Boddington, op. cit., 423; Vera I. Evison, *Dover: Buckland Anglo-Saxon cemetery* (London, 1987), 150.

51. Morris, op. cit. (n. 13), 50–1.

52. John Dent, 'Skerne', *Current Archaeology* 91 (1984), 251–3.

55. Tenth-century stirrup from the river Witham (Lincolnshire) (courtesy of the British Museum).

was being paid as death duties – a hereot – to the king.[53] It is also worth noting that in the Middle to Late Bronze Age similar finds are

53. H.R. Loyn, *The Governance of Anglo-Saxon England 500–1087* (London, 1984), 166; N.P. Brooks, 'Arms, status and warfare in Late Saxon England', in D. Hill (ed.), *Ethelred the Unready* (Oxford, 1978), 81–103.

described as ritual rather than haphazard losses. Richard Bradley, following the work of C.A. Gregory on conspicuous consumption, has postulated that these offerings reflected a phase of intense competition and stress within southern Britain.[54] Moveable wealth was being deliberately removed from circulation in gifts-to-gods ceremonies. It is likely, however, that the Late Saxon depositions relate to more complex conditions: not only the changing mortuary patterns, but also, as implied by the eleventh-century payment of hereots in warrior equipment, the changing military organisation imposed by the king. Weapons, after all, were the traditional accoutrements of the warrior-farmer in Middle Saxon England. They were symbols of an ethos which had passed by Late Saxon times, as the poet of *The Battle of Maldon* reminds us:

> . . .it could be understood that the young man had no intention of flinching at the fray when he took up weapons. Besides him, Adric too had a desire to serve his chief and lord in the conflict, so he proceeded to carry his spear forward into battle. He was possessed of a doughty will – as long as he was able to hold with his hands shield and broad sword: he was fulfilling a pledge when he was called on to fight in front of his lord.[55]

Significantly, King Alfred reformulated military service in order to combat the Danes. The power of the dynasty was now secured by a standing army, and the taxation obligations of the community as a whole were much more exacting than those recorded for pre-Viking times.[56] With the birth of the nation-state, the old order passed away, but not without registering their feelings to age-old gods, perhaps also with some Christian hope of salvation in the afterlife.

Despite these indications of stress in the seigneurial ranks during the formation of the Late Saxon state, it would be misleading to underemphasise the power of manorial families. Seigneurial authority was probably the driving force responsible for the creation of a new system of fields in the Danelaw in this period. David Hall believes that the medieval open-field system was introduced in Cambridgeshire and Lincolnshire during the ninth or tenth century. Since this development is likely to have been a corollary of the creation of nucleated villages, the later date seems more likely. Certainly in Northamptonshire the medieval field systems began in the tenth century, as they appear to have done in the Yorkshire Wolds. The model for the pattern

54. Richard Bradley, *The Social Foundations of Prehistoric Britain* (London, 1984), 96–127; C.A. Gregory, 'Gifts to men and gifts to god: gift exchange and capital accumulation in contemporary Papua', *Man* 15 (1980), 628–52.

55. S.A.J. Bradley (ed.), *Anglo-Saxon Poetry* (London, 1982), 520, lines 11–16.

56. N.P. Brooks, 'The development of military obligations in eighth- and ninth-century England', in P. Clemoes and K. Hughes (eds.), *England before the Conquest* (Cambridge, 1971), 69–84.

discovered in the Wolds has been traced by John Hurst to the eastern Frankish colonies settled during the ninth century,[57] an open-field system may be a further example of the Carolingian connection discussed in Chapter Five. In Wessex, though, the configurations of the medieval field system, like the pattern of villages, may have been formulated well before the age of Alfred.

The archaeology attests the bold evolution of local lords in the Danish territories, perhaps in emulation of the lordly authority which had a long tradition in Wessex. By contrast the archaeology of the peasantry is still comparatively impoverished. Little archaeological evidence exists at present for the arrangement of the houses in the Late Saxon village.[58] It remains unclear, for instance, whether the form of the Middle Saxon farm persisted unaltered into this period. If so, when did the Anglo-Saxon hall-house give way to its more compact thirteenth-century counterpart (see p. 184)?

Population expansion

Yet one obvious point regarding the peasantry appears fairly clear from the rural evidence: the population of England grew enormously after about 900. Survey data such as that from the East Midlands and from East Anglia suggest that the population virtually doubled between Alfred's time and the Domesday survey of 1086. If there was a population of about one to two million in 1066–86, it had been no more than between a half and one million in about 900. Put another way, while the Domesday population was smaller than that in Roman Britain at its zenith,[59] the Middle Saxon community was far smaller than the pre-Roman Iron Age one encountered by Julius Caesar. The precision necessary to detail demographic growth in this period is still lacking, but current archaeological surveys are certain to provide an impression of the orders of magnitude. Any explanation of this sudden population growth could only be speculative at the moment, but an instructive parallel for the Late Saxon circumstances might be found in the late eighteenth and nineteenth centuries when the population virtually quadrupled over a similar period. The Late Saxon evidence, like that from the nineteenth century, implies that a rising population was one of the features of the take-off, even if it was not a critical factor. There is no reason to regard population pressure as a causal factor triggering intensification of production in Late Saxon England.

The demographic evidence, vague as it is, seems to support the view

57. Hurst, op. cit. (n. 14), 87.
58. For example: B.K. Roberts, 'Village patterns and forms: some models for discussion', in D. Hooke (ed.), *Medieval Villages* (Oxford, 1985), 7–26.
59. P.J. Fowler, 'The countryside in Roman Britain: a study in failure or a failure in study', *Landscape History* 5 (1983), 8–9.

that reproductive strategies altered to take account of the needs of the fast-developing society. Several authors have shown that the legal rights of women improved in the tenth and eleventh centuries.[60] Yet a little evidence points to a generalised drop in their life-expectancy and stature.[61] Neither point is surprising. Women were needed to produce children, particularly in the towns. Greater personal freedoms encouraged mobility, and must have led at the same time to the relaxation of existing attitudes to the age of marriage and intra-kin marriage. These changes in child-bearing and perhaps in nutrition may have contributed to worse conditions for women.

The cultural dimension

Finally, did this economic and social revolution manifest itself in any cultural form? How did the shaping of a new society affect Anglo-Saxon art and taste? In this context we need to explore two interwoven issues: the evolution of an ethnic identity from a material standpoint, and the implications of the monastic reform movement for Late Saxon society.

A strong case can be made for an explicitly English cultural medium, established in the eighth century, given a distinctive national form in the ninth century, and widely recognised during the tenth and eleventh centuries. It could be said that England forged its own identity in these centuries much as Early Christian Ireland did. Yet such a generalisation fails to account for the adoption of Carolingian idioms by Anglo-Saxon artists in particular, naturalistic figures and the use of florid foliage decoration – just as it fails to account for artistic differences between the kingdoms of Wessex, Mercia and Northumbria. Each kingdom interpreted the Carolingian movement in its own fashion in the time of Coenwulf and Egbert. The wholesale assimilation of Carolingian ideas in Mercia (see p. 133), for instance, contrasts with the more tempered stance adopted in Wessex. Carolingian ideas clearly abounded before Alfred's time, while Scandinavian ones did not. The moulded jewellery of tenth-century Wessex owes its origin largely to Carolingian technology in the previous century. The Alfred jewel, therefore, should not be seen as the symbolic horizon of change leading towards a great cultural renaissance. Middle Saxon art in Wessex was well developed in fact by Aethelwulf's time, and no doubt these new artistic designs were generally accessible in

60. Margaret Clunies Ross, 'Concubinage in Anglo-Saxon England', *Past and Present* 108 (1985), 3–34 and references therein; W.G. Runciman, 'Acclerating social mobility: the case of Anglo-Saxon England', *Past and Present* 104 (1984), 23.

61. Andrew Nelson, *A study of stature, sex and age ratios and average age at death from the Romano-British to the Late Anglo-Saxon period* (unpublished M.A. thesis, University of Sheffield, 1985).

cheaper, more widely available artefacts. Tenth-century art was thus modified but not invented to meet the needs of the enlarged community.[62]

Ninth-century Northumbria, by contrast, was a distinctive region in which the concepts of the Carolingian age were poorly nurtured. This may have compelled the Danish conquerors to introduce alien coin, pottery, and perhaps to some extent artistic ideas as part of the greater package of the revolution outlined above. For this reason Viking art in north-eastern England has to be interpreted with caution, as do the red-painted pots made in Stamford and modelled on a northern French design. The elite were seeking their own idiom, but was it really Viking as such?

In Northumbria the so-called Scandinavian art, new to the Anglian territories, had to be developed to serve the same needs as the 'cheaper' jewellery identified in Wessex. Not surprisingly, workshops making jewellery and other ornamented materials are found in Lincoln and York just as they are in Winchester, serving not just sectional interests, as the Carolingian craftsmen did, but all levels of society. The Viking component, however, like the Carolingian, may have been exaggerated.[63]

With the aggressive confrontation of Wessex and the Danelaw, both regions searched for symbols of ethnic identity perhaps in part to compensate for the increase in social mobility, the eclipse of kinship and the rise of the state. By the mid-tenth century, we may conclude, England had a vibrant cultural identity, split between two traditions. This was the context for the monastic reform movement.

The monastic reform movement is generally identified as the process by which many Carolingian ideas were introduced by bishops Aethelwold, Dunstan and Oswald, when through the medium of the *regularis concordia* the state and Church reached a close accord.[64] Later hagiographers undoubtedly served these three bishops well, though it would be wrong to overlook the achievements in the arts and architecture that arose out of their efforts. Nevertheless, as was noted in Chapter Five, Carolingian liturgical ideas were being embodied in Anglo-Saxon churches throughout the Carolingian age. The new buildings were simply grander variations on a long tradition. Although this grandeur has been ascribed to the influence of Cluniac reform upon the English, it is worth noting that, apart from connections between the royal family and the Continent, England was

62. David Wilson, *Anglo-Saxon Art* (London, 1984).
63. A useful introduction is Rosemary Cramp, 'The Anglian tradition in the ninth century', in J. Lang (ed.), *Anglo-Saxon and Viking Age Sculpture and its Context* (Oxford, 1978), 1–32; see also James Lang, 'The Hogback: a Viking colonial monument', in D. Brown et al. (eds.), *Anglo-Saxon Studies in Archaeology and History* 3 (Oxford, 1984), 83–176.
64. Fleming, op. cit. (n. 7).

passing through one of the most insular phases in its history (see p. 164). Lastly, whereas Middle Saxon England, like Carolingian Europe, was the age of the monastery, Late Saxon England was the age of the parish church. Numerous excavations have confirmed that the first parish churches were constructed in timber or stone in the course of the tenth century, and around these evolved communal cemeteries. There was, as Richard Morris put it, a 'big bang' in church building, sponsored not by the bishoprics but by the local lords. As Harold Taylor, the doyen of Anglo-Saxon architecture, has remarked: 'the majority [of these churches]. . .give a clear impression of simplicity and veneration for the past; there seems to have been an unwillingness. . .to make way for modern innovations.'[65] These chapels possessed none of the liturgical features of the great Carolingian churches: they were simple buildings without crypt or narthex whose purpose was to symbolise the Christian authority of lords over their land. The parish church must have helped to shape the cultural life of Anglo-Saxon rural communities, not least because in mortuary matters it had usurped the traditional rights of the monastery.

By reasserting Carolingian imagery and liturgy the leading churchmen must have hoped not only to regain political status but also to focus secular attention on the Church's economic needs. It is no coincidence that Archbishop Aethelwold's great monastic achievements at Ely, for instance, go hand in hand with his systematic development of the abbey's properties. Yet, according to Robin Fleming, there was more than an economic motive for the accumulation of these great estates. King Edgar allocated great blocks of land in the newly conquered Danelaw to the Benedictine reform monasteries, much as the Carolingians had done, in the expectation of loyalty to the crown. Fleming also points out that for this reason the reform attracted an anti-monastic reaction after Edgar's death, as many aristocratic families suffered an erosion of jurisdictional and fiscal privileges.[66] As a result the artistic achievement of the reform movement may be judged as a device to regain support from a small section of society. Since the mid-ninth century the Anglo-Saxon Church, in common with its later Carolingian counterpart, had suffered a grave attrition of status. Its revival coincided with the apogee of West Saxon royal power, by which time the cultural and political configurations of the English had been largely mapped out.

In sum, the first industrial revolution transformed Anglo-Saxon England. The development of towns with rows of workshops and heaps of industrial waste, like the emergence of the medieval village and its distinctive culture, eclipsed many traditional values, compelling the

65. H.M. Taylor, 'Tenth-century church building in England and the Continent', in D. Parsons (ed.), *Tenth-Century Studies* (Chichester, 1975), 167.
66. Fleming, op. cit. (n. 7).

old aristocratic order and the Church to come to terms with the change. In these circumstances we need to determine the fate of the peasantry.

The origins of medieval society

You know that no man can reveal any talent or rule and steer any dominion without tools and material. That without which one cannot carry on that craft is the material of every craft. This, then, is a king's material and his tools for ruling with, that he have his land fully manned. He must have men who pray, and soldiers and workmen. Lo, you know that without these tools no king can reveal his skill. Also, this is his material, which he must have for those tools – sustenance for those three orders; and their sustenance consists in land to live on, and gifts, and weapons, and food, and ale, and clothes and whatever else those three orders require. And without these things he cannot hold those tools, nor without these tools do any of the things that he is charged to do. For that reason I desired material to rule that dominion with, that my powers and dominion would not be forgotten and concealed. (King Alfred's translation of Boethius, *Consolations of Philosophy*, ch. 17)[67]

The Carolingian age was a paradox in one fundamental aspect. As Jacques Le Goff has shown, it embodied 'a genuine ideology of productive effort, an energeticism which can be detected on the economic, political and cultural planes'.[68] The management of labour was recognised as an important variable in the evolution of the political system. Yet labour was immobilised by a network of obligations ranging over the whole sphere of the sacred and profane. The driving spirits of this age appreciated the significance of labour, possibly from their study of ancient texts, but they failed to liberate society from the bonds of kinship.[69] By the eleventh century, nevertheless, a tripartite society composed of *oratores, bellatores* and *laboratores* had begun to take shape and is first described as such by Adalberon of Laon in about 1025. The division of labour on which European society is founded must have occurred in the intervening two centuries. Le Goff is quite explicit about the first reference to this social configuration: the late ninth-century commentary to King Alfred's Anglo-Saxon version of Boethius' *Consolations of Philosophy* refers to a new schema in society. Alfred plainly acknowledges that a class of labourers had emerged. Precisely who these labourers were is not known, but it is likely that they were the elite group of land-clearing pioneers and the new urban craftsmen. So in this moment of change and mobility there

---

67. D. Whitelock (ed.), *English Historical Documents*, vol. 1 (2nd ed., London, 1979), 919.
68. Jacques Le Goff, *Time, Work, and Culture in the Middle Ages* (Chicago, 1980), 86.
69. ibid.

was recognition of the concept of individuality which is an essential feature of the new nation-states.[70]

Historians have been understandably captivated by the first real flowering of this individuality in the twelfth-century renaissance. They associate it with the slower economic changes that took place in the post-Carolingian regions. Yet, as Le Goff hinted, the English were in the forefront of this social revolution. Here I shall comment on the circumstances of the labourers in England, leaving any explanation of the early evolution of labour to the final chapter.

The beginnings of this new schema in society are most readily detected in the towns. Townsfolk now lived in tenements and prayed at small urban parish churches; they worked in small backrooms and traded at street markets or at large periodic fairs outside the town gate. The seeds of this lifestyle were sown at Hamwic in the day of King Ine, though urbanism and marketing were now no longer restricted to the aristocracy in Late Saxon times and attitudes to property were probably different. Craftsmen from Alfred's age onwards presumably had a stake in urban expansion. But what was the attraction of specialisation and the volatile hurly-burly of commerce as opposed to the stability of agrarian life?

It seems that the social freedoms and material advantages offered by town-life induced peasants to set up shops in otherwise rather filthy conditions. Late Saxon governmental planners understood the incentives and, to judge from the archaeological evidence, skilfully exploited the situation. The Danes did just the same and thus represented a considerable threat to the West Saxons.

The preconditions for urban expansion and social change were rooted in Middle Saxon society on the eve of the Viking attacks. But in what form? The altered shape of rural settlements in the age of Offa and afterwards may furnish a clue. Greater emphasis upon storage and signs of 'planned' communities imply that agricultural output was being managed and increased (p. 139). Not only were agrarian products being stored in advance of circulation and exchange, but it seems likely that per capita productivity was increasing. For whatever reason, attitudes to agriculture were under review in the ninth century, as they were all over western Europe.[71] But how was increased productivity created? Was it simply imposed?

70. See, for example, Peter Brown, 'Society and the supernatural: a medieval change', *Daedalus* 104 (1975), 133–51; Colin Morris, *The Discovery of the Individual* (London, 1972); Charles M. Radding, 'Evolution of medieval mentalities: a cognitive-structural approach', *American History Review* 83 (1978), 577–97; Lynn White jr., 'Science and the sense of self: the medieval background of a modern confrontation', *Daedalus* 107 (1978), 47–59.

71. See, for example, Georges Duby, *The Early Growth of the European Economy* (London, 1974), and Massimo Montanari, *L'alimentazione contadina nell'alto Medioevo* (Naples, 1979).

No evidence exists to suggest that lords were imposing new working regimes; indeed, it is only in the tenth century that the rural settlement hierarchy begins to include the lord's manor. Instead we must suppose that the impulse to satisfy demand outweighed the drudgery of the labour.[72] New tools may have permitted this transition to proceed smoothly, although the evidence for the widespread use of such tools as the mould-board plough, for instance, in Late Anglo-Saxon England remains slight and controversial. Increased production, however, might be achieved by re-arranging properties and dividing the landscape into individually owned plots. This awesome task must have started in the ninth or tenth century, when the pattern of medieval fields took shape. Productivity was thus generated by direct involvement in one's patrimony. Such an extensive reorganisation is hard to imagine – even if it was to recur as a feature of the agricultural revolution in the eighteenth century. As in the eighteenth century, it was probably based on social change, in this instance 'the replacement of kinship by service as a criterion of status'.[73]

In these circumstances it may be no coincidence, as Margaret Clunies Ross has argued, that resource polygyny became less common.[74] Was this a victory for the Church, which had repeatedly attacked polygyny? In Jack Goody's opinion, the Church wished to limit heirship since about 40 per cent of families would then be left with with no male heir, and their land would thereby pass to abbeys or monasteries.[75] However, the prominence of Late Saxon widows and daughters as inheritors suggests that attitudes to inheritance and women altered to the disadvantage of the Church as social mobility intensified. Respect for the inheritance rights of elite women in Late Saxon England is consistent with their changing status throughout Europe. More significantly, though, reproductive strategies altered, causing substantial demographic increases in Late Saxon times. Preliminary palaeopathological analyses show that women died earlier than in Middle and Early Saxon times and had shrunk to statures commonly found in Roman Britain. There seems to be a paradox here. Women's rights may have improved, but women as a whole suffered as a result. The parallel with the conditions of Victorian women is too extreme, but should be kept in mind none the less. Finally, we should note the incidence of the infant burials at Raunds, nearly all close to the church itself, and belonging to the late tenth

72. E. Paul Durrenberger (ed.), *Chayanov, Peasants and Economic Anthropology* (New York, 1984). This aspect of Chayanov's work is discussed further in Chapter Seven.

73. Runciman, op. cit. (n. 60).

74. Ross, op. cit. (n. 60).

75. Jack Goody, *The Development of the Family and Marriage in Europe* (Cambridge, 1983), 102–56.

or early eleventh century. The statistics of infant mortality may provide some insight into the demography of the village, but the discovery of these burials is more significant in revealing that the salvation of children now merited consideration in adult terms.

These impressions of Late Saxon England support Le Goff's conclusion. A new schema was taking shape. But does this mean that old values and traditions were irrevocably eclipsed? Are we to conclude that the Victorian belief in the long evolution of Anglo-Saxon democracy is a myth; that Late Saxon England was no more than a regional variant of the feudalism being conceived across post-Carolingian Europe?

The status of kingship, the inception of the manor alongside the parish church, even the monastic reform movement, would suggest that this was the case. Yet eminent historians like Marc Bloch have refused to believe in Late Saxon feudalism.[76] Bloch noted that social mobility in Late Saxon England was surprisingly easy and that new criteria for status in society were swiftly conceived as the state began to exert itself upon the nation. On the other hand, Bloch's perspective has been tempered by the unexpected archaeology of the English castle. Private fortification, the supreme expression of post-Carolingian feudalism, first occurs in late ninth-century Germany and had evidently reached England by the mid-tenth century.[77] The power of the minor aristocracy and local lords may then have been reduced by the centralising powers of the monarchy and the powerful aspirations of the Benedictine reformers in the late tenth century. Old values had certainly passed, yet by the turn of the millennium fine manorial buildings at Goltho, Porchester Castle and Sulgrave were in their own way as impressive and European in their character as the royal palace at Cheddar.[78]

Such a picture might lead us to to conclude that it was the peasants who were truly disadvantaged at this time. Yet, if so, how are we to account for the new opportunities to cultivate marginal, high-risk ground, or even to migrate to the new towns? Ideally, of course, we need to know much more about the peasant households themselves. At present it is not clear whether it was during the tenth and eleventh centuries that the size of peasant dwellings began to shrink from floor areas of 50 square metres or more to a later medieval norm of just over 40 square metres. Yet even in late medieval times the English peasant possessed much more space than his counterparts in Provence, or indeed in twentieth-century India. In fact the floor-space of the

76. Bloch, *Feudal Society* (n. 3), 183.

77. Walter Janssen, 'Some major aspects of Frankish and medieval settlement in the Rhineland', in P.H. Sawyer (ed.), *Medieval Settlement* (London, 1976), 56.

78. Beresford, op. cit. (n. 42); Cunliffe, op. cit. (n. 41); Davison, op. cit. (n. 41); Philip Rahtz, *The Palaces at Cheddar* (Oxford, 1979).

peasantry from Anglo-Saxon to medieval times was on a par with that of the urban working-class in the ninteenth century (42–59 square metres).[79]

*

We are left with a dilemma. In archaeological terms Late Saxon England was altogether different from the previous age. Hamwic was forgotten – amazing as it seems – and might be regarded as a symbol of a lost age. In this it shares much in common with the Old Minster at Winchester, which Barbara Yorke describes as an image of pre-Alfredian times superseded by the great New Minster commissioned in Alfred's life.[80] But are we to conclude that the individuality of the English is the creation of a virtuous prince who could adapt policy to fortune? Clearly King Alfred's part in these circumstances should not be underestimated. It was he, after all, who began the process of English unity. Nevertheless the Anglo-Scandinavian kings also merit an important place in this history. Bearing in mind the material with which they had to work, their achievements were, if anything, more impressive than those of the West Saxons. Evidently Wessex and the Danelaw were the real beneficiaries of the Carolingian experiment. Marc Bloch appreciated this to some extent. But to explain the causes and roots of the revolution, we cannot turn to the deeds of Great Men; instead we must discover the reasons for the reception and development of these alien ideas. In the absence of an Adam Smith, we must turn to the archaeology of the millennium.

79. On Anglo-Saxon building sizes see S. James, A. Marshall & M. Millett, 'An early medieval building tradition', *Archaeological Journal* 141 (1984), 182–215, esp. 186–91; for the Middle Ages: Christopher Dyer, 'English peasant buildings in the later Middle Ages', *Medieval Archaeology* 30 (1986), 19–45.

80. Barbara A.E. Yorke, 'The Bishops of Winchester, the Kings of Wessex and the development of Winchester in the ninth and early tenth centuries', *Proceedings of the Hampshire Field Club and Archaeological Society* 40 (1984), 61–70.

7

The Genesis of a Nation

England, like all European nations, was founded in a 'Dark Age'; we shall never quite understand how. The main objection to belief in the inevitability of English unification is that it is all too easy. It is virtually incredible that what did not happen until long afterwards in countries that were initially subjected to a single political authority should have happened automatically in a country that was not.   (Patrick Wormald)[1]

The Anglo-Saxon achievement was not the result of some inevitable progression, a juggernaut that simply propelled itself onwards until the eighteenth century. Nor can it simply be attributed to its great men, some of whose footprints have been scrutinised in the foregoing pages. If any single explanation is to be found for the unexpected success of the Anglo-Saxons, it might be in the potentially conflicting desire for a European context, on the one hand, and the competition between the patchwork of insular territories on the other. In the search for the Dark Age origins of English individuality we must take a long-run, wide-angle vision – an anthropological vision – of the millennium.

The first illustration of this critical mediation between the wider world and the complex insular configurations occurred even before the Roman administration left Britain. Only the brief and eccentric prosperity of some southern British villas in the early fourth century punctuates the inexorable path towards dereliction which began in the late third century. These villas reflect no more than a temporary exploitative phase by the colonial administration on the eve of collapse. Complete collapse before the final Roman withdrawal is, however, now well attested by numerous excavations. The social implications of these are currently a matter for speculation, but without doubt a tribute-based society was reduced to one composed of atomistic kin-based groups. Such a momentous change was bound to be significant in the subsequent evolution of the Anglo-Saxon peoples.

As a result, Britain was not an obvious destination for displaced

1. Patrick Wormald, 'Bede, the *Bretwaldas* and the origins of the *Gens Anglorum*', in P. Wormald (ed.), *Ideal and Reality in Frankish and Anglo-Saxon Society* (Oxford, 1983), 128.

Germanic communities. On the Continent the Germanic migrations were made by tribesmen suffering from the wider Roman economic malaise. They were hoping to raise the quality of their lives by discovering prosperous niches within the Empire. Fifth-century Britain, as we have seen, hardly stands comparison with the world of villas and towns (albeit mostly in decline) in the rest of the western Roman Empire or even the complex societies now being documented by archaeologists in north Germany and Jutland.[2] In fact, bearing in mind the aboriginal political conditions, the attractions of Britain were few.

After the Roman withdrawal small farming communities occupied ecological niches like the Lark Valley in Suffolk or parts of old villa-estates such as Barton Court Farm in Oxfordshire. It is safe to conclude that these people maintained some Roman traditions. Their jewellery, for example, bears the stylistic hallmarks of the late Roman age. These objects can readily be distinguished from the small number of grave assemblages which betray a north German or Scandinavian origin. These latter assemblages, found in Kent, the Thames Estuary, East Anglia and Humberside, are all that record the arrival of any aliens. If Mucking (Essex) was one of their encampments, and this must remain speculative, the migrants were comparatively few in number. Perhaps Gildas was correct and the pioneers were in fact a small number of fifth-century Germans hired by the warring factions of sub-Roman Britain.

One important factor in this age was bound to be the geo-politics of the mosaic of tribal territories. Nearly thirty tribes are described in the seventh-century Tribal Hidage, and it is likely that many more existed in the wake of the Roman withdrawal. The impact of exogenous groups on such fragmented political units is uncertain. Some insight into this impact may be provided by Marshall Sahlins in his description of James Cook's fateful encounter in 1778 with the Hawaiians. Cook's logs vividly describe how the Hawaiians provided Cook's ships with foodstuffs in return for iron goods. But there was more to this exchange than the goods themselves. Of course, the iron goods were avidly prized by the Pacific Islanders. But in the long term it was Cook's impact upon Hawaiian culture and its chiefs that was perhaps most significant. Thereafter 'the chiefs distinguished themselves from their own people in the manner that Europeans were different from Hawaiians in general. . .from which ensued an order of political economy. The chiefs self-consciously appropriated the personages of the European great alongside an appropriate European style of the sumptuary life. The famous Kanzehameha, conqueror of islands

2. Lotte Hedeager, 'Empire, frontier and the barbarian hinterland: Rome and northern Europe AD 1 – 400', in M. Rowlands, M. Larsen & K. Kristansen (eds.), *Centre and Periphery in the Ancient World* (Cambridge, 1987), 125–40.

between 1795 and 1810, never tired of asking passing European visitors if he did not live "just like King George". Already by 1793 three of the dominant Hawaiian chiefs had named their sons and heirs "King George".[3]

There is a tendency to treat this kind of Pacific history as *anthropology* and therefore quite separate from our western experience. However, the parallel between Cook's experiences in the Pacific and Frankish connections with the Kentishmen late in the fifth century may not be entirely fanciful. Ian Wood's proposal (see p. 31) that the Kentish king was drawn into the Frankish orbit of political and economic influence as early as the 480s would explain many sweeping changes in Britain.[4] At this time the political, economic and ideological foundations of Gaul were being transformed, almost certainly triggering a phase of important exchange relations across the North Sea. If Wood is correct, one attraction for the Kentishmen in joining Clovis' political hegemony was the dynamic ideological current emanating from the Frankish court, supported by material goods (textiles, glasses, jewellery, pots, etc.) of a kind that had been unavailable in Britain for a century.

One consequence of the rise of the North Sea interaction zone was that some sub-British kingdoms could form close connections with southern Scandinavia. Once again they may have been seeking mercenaries, offering land as payment at a time when social competition in Denmark was intense. This period seems to have coincided with a short-lived connection between several Late Celtic territories in western Britain and Byzantium. It is probably no coincidence that the *Anglo-Saxon Chronicle* records the arrival of Aelle in Sussex and Cerdic in Wessex in this period. Likewise Gildas, writing several generations later, attributes the legendary battle of Mons Badonicus to this time. The final decades of the fifth century, it seems, marked the point when the virtual isolation of sub-Britain came to an end.

From then on the material culture of Britain altered dramatically. Anglo-Saxon objects assigned on stylistic grounds to this period begin to occur in significant numbers in cremation and inhumation cemeteries. Concurrently, the fortifications enclosing the sub-Roman 'palace' at South Cadbury were refurbished. We must remember, in the light of James Cook's impact upon the Hawaiians, how readily and unpredictably social process may be altered. Frankish supremacy over the Kentishmen, for example, would have been interpreted differently by each of the neighbouring sub-Roman territories. With the inevitable rivalry between the patchwork of territories, primitive political regimes were bound to be affected by the introduction of new

3. Marshall Sahlins, *Islands of History* (Chicago, 1985), 140.
4. Ian Wood, 'The end of Roman Britain: continental evidence and parallels', in M. Lapidge & D. Dumville (eds.), *Gildas: new approaches* (Woodbridge, 1984), 23–24.

(Continental) resources and the attendant competition for them. New relations with Franks, Scandinavians or Byzantines probably stimulated the need to project an identity. As rivalries and competition intensified, these identities would have been accentuated.[5]

An outcome of this peer polity interaction may be illustrated once more by the Hawaiian experience. Here, Sahlins shows, there was a fascination with British and American names among the elite. For example, at one assembly in 1812 an American trader noted chiefs named Billy Pitts, George Washington, Billy Cobbett, Charley Fox, Thomas Jefferson, Bonapart and Tom Paine.[6] Even though the leaders of Hawaiian society were on the periphery of the Industrial Revolution, they were powerfully manipulated by the prevailing world system, and in particular by those ruling its leading societies. In a more ramified way we may project a similar use of status in Early Saxon England, modestly manipulated by forces beyond the shores of the island. The ranking of dead within the cemeteries of this period provides some rough-and-ready expression of this.

The ranking of graves as though the dead expressed their roles in life is no longer favoured by archaeologists, since too many assumptions are made in analyses of this kind. However, the method has more to commend it if the burials are studied as part of the archaeological record as a whole. As noted in Chapter Two, the sudden growth in the number of cemeteries containing grave-goods must be set beside the seemingly egalitarian structure of the known settlements. Farmers, it appears, held a status in death that was not visibly apparent in their lifetimes.

A notable feature of the richest burials, however, is the strident use of Germanic ornamentation on the grave-goods. It is as though those at the apex of the social pyramid sought to use material culture to recall a north European tradition. Are these the graves of migrants of the fifth century, or, like the Gallo-Romans buried in the row-graves, are they peoples converted to a new ideology and keen to express their connection with an epic past? Settlements like West Stow continued from Late Roman to Middle Saxon times with minimal changes to the vernacular architecture, and it is tempting to interpret their rich grave assemblages as the property of individuals sharing a perception of a culture rooted in a Continental background. It is doubtful, in other words, whether many were genuinely Germanic in origin.

The dwellings offer an important clue to the social structure of these peoples. It is tentatively proposed that the farmhouses of the period bear witness to the survival of a household unit which had been

5. This theme is discussed in various settings in Colin Renfrew & John F. Cherry (eds.), *Peer-polity Interaction and Socio-political Change* (Cambridge, 1986).
6. Sahlins, op. cit. (n. 3), 141.

shaped during the Roman occupation of Britain. That is, in these parts of Britain Celtic household units were not revived. The surviving unit was not the same as that which existed outside the Empire – in Denmark, for example. It also differed significantly from household units in the rest of the old Western Roman Empire. Jack Goody has persuasively argued that from the later fourth century the Church began to alter traditional reproductive strategies in the old Western Roman Empire by fostering restrictive attitudes to marriage from which it profited by inheriting large tracts of land.[7] Recent archaeological surveys and excavations suggest that the Church was as powerful a force in the Late Roman countryside as it was in the cities.[8] As a result, the Late Roman peasantry adopted a family structure that conformed to the strictures of the Church. However, the Church failed to convert the Britons to this code. It was on the point of establishing itself in the towns and at certain villas when the province was abandoned. As a result, a social unit forged from Iron Age stock during the great demographic expansion of the second century, when the Empire was at its zenith, outlived the momentous events which enveloped the political superstructure in the later fourth century. St Augustine's mission in the late sixth century was therefore able to introduce to the British (or Anglo-Saxons as they had become) Late Roman notions whose infrastructure had evolved slowly over many generations.

In short, as prehistorians have now dismissed the notion of invasions in the Neolithic, Bronze and Iron Ages, we are left in our history with only one real invasion – that by the Romans. This landmark in the island's history appears to be matched by the traumatic departure of the Roman administration, leaving conditions which were both aboriginal and highly sensitive to alien concepts. During the following two centuries unusual social configurations were established which proved fertile ground for St Augustine's late classical ideas.

Kingship as a social category had been on the point of emerging as kingdoms like Kent forged alliances with the Merovingians, but was made manifest with the arrival of the missions. The Church provided the apparatus by which tribal leaders could mobilise labour for public works and military duties. It is, therefore, no coincidence that small pre-Christian communities like Cowdery's Down and Yeavering assumed a palatial character at this time. Among the package of ideas introduced by the Church was the notion of time itself, writing and the invention of languages. These were implements for the storage of

7. Jack Goody, *The Development of the Family and Marriage in Europe* (Cambridge, 1983).
8. Charles Pietri, 'Chiesa e comunità locali nell' occidente cristano (IV–VI D.C.): l'esempio della Gallia', in A. Giardina (ed.), *Societa Romana e Impero Tardoantico III; Le Merci gli Insediamenti* (Rome, 1986), 761–86.

concepts and objects of distinction, provoking competition between the numerous Anglo-Saxon tribes. Language, in particular, was a powerful tool as communications between the territories were undoubtedly increased by the Church, and as dynasties sought to prove their epic origins. The introduction, survival and diffusion of English dialects, supplanting Celtic and Latin, could well be a consequence of the aboriginal circumstances of the fifth century, the cultural homogeneity of the community, and the powerful need to create a past for political purposes after about 600. Place-name evidence, mostly relating to the enormous changes in land management in the seventh century, may have little to do with ethnicity in the traditional sense. The English, it can be argued, were a race who made use of the epic past of a small minority to contrive social change. To argue the reverse – that the migrants were many – requires the unequivocal identification in the archaeology of the migration.

Of course, England was by no means unified. Until the Viking invasions of the 860s there were many territories that owed their origins to post-colonial days. The Tribal Hidage, dating from the seventh century and attributed to a Mercian king, illustrates this vividly. Anglo-Saxon England consisted of thirty or more kingdoms and groupings at this time; far more than the large regional kingdoms within Gaul and Italy, for example. Peer-polity interaction – political competition and emulation between these territories – was indisputably a mechanism for unequal change and development between 600 and 900. The Church, to start with, actually used this competition to its advantage. Monks like St Cuthbert were able to accumulate great tracts of land during this period. Yet despite political competition and the aggressive missionary role of the Church it had to grow up 'in the interstices of local aristocratic lordship'. Moreover, the Church was regionalised, with each bishopric holding land only within its kingdom. This restricted the authority of the Church, and helps to explain why kings began to treat its representatives no differently from other powerful laymen.

Yet change was not limited to one small section of society. The construction of fences around the farms of this age, as well as the shuffling of the settlement pattern, confirms the historical impression that property was no longer considered in tribal terms but designated as belonging to individuals. Interestingly, the definition of property in life appears to have followed the definition of cemetery plots, as though circumstances considered appropriate for the dead were emulated by the living. At the same time in some villages (e.g. Catholme, Raunds) the Roman and sub-Roman dwellings were superseded by large bow-sided halls. This suggests, though it is improper to place much emphasis on the observation, that the the household unit itself altered with the advent of the Church. The scope of the changes to the form of seventh-century settlements certainly reflects the integrated nature of Anglo-Saxon society.

It appears that all sections of the community responded to the changes in political structure and resource management, within one or two generations, much as they responded to the change in ideology. But it would be a mistake to believe that old values were simply extinguished. As historians have shown, the seventh-century laws of Kent and Wessex reveal very different values placed upon ceorls. In Wessex the equivalent rank of a *gesithcund man* carried a wergild six times as large as that of a ceorl, a freeman, but in Kent the ceorl's wergild was much larger in proportion, so that the eorl's wergild was only three times as large. In short, the gap between these two ranks was much wider in Wessex than Kent. These differences have previously been attributed to the tribal laws introduced during the migrations. However, if we discount the migrations as a powerful cause of change, we must seek an explanation in the aboriginal circumstances of the fifth century, and perhaps in the manner in which these differences developed once there was access to prestige goods after about 480. In particular, the prominence of imported objects in most cemeteries in Kent contrasts with their paucity in Wessex. It is possible that the West Saxon elite was able to regulate the flow of prestige goods, whereas in Kent free access to imports was a factor in shaping the social stratigraphy.

Archaeology has shed new light on the advanced political evolution of late seventh-century Wessex and one of its most outstanding leaders, King Ine. At Hamwic Ine almost certainly founded a 45-hectare planned town which for the first time in post-Roman Britain embodied the concept of administered production and marketing. Here the long-established practice of prestige goods exchange was significantly developed in political and economic terms. Here a range of craftsmen possibly working for noble families were able to produce commodities. A key point about this new form of productive specialisation is that it necessitated some social interdependence. The concept reveals a far-reaching level of political and economic originality which, like the gridded street plan itself, must owe its origins to Ine's mentors in the Church. Most importantly, the notion of individualism, fostered by long-distance exchange over the previous century, was extended and amplified in society as craftsmen in the town recognised an interdependence in their labouring circumstances and (unwittingly?) initiated the atrophy of kinship in favour of service.

In building Hamwic Ine was probably the first king to use royal power to create public works which involved mobilising labour from the whole territory. It is likely, of course, that Ine was helped by a tribal constitution in which the king and his nobles found mutual advantage in the maximisation of their economic efforts. The apparent absence of similar emporia in the other kingdoms during this period, along with indications of their trade connections with Frisian free-lance merchants, suggests that the highly centralised political character of Wessex remained unique for some time.

After Ine, however, Wessex was unable to capitalise on its new tribal constitution. And although Hamwic survived, presumably in tradition if not in law, it simply served as a motive for neighbouring kingdoms to change their constitutions. In East Anglia, Mercia and Northumbria, however, there may have been some attrition of royal power as well as of the authority of the Church. Bede, to his dismay, experienced these conditions in later life. Moreover, trade competition had almost certainly generated a phase of inflation. In this instance the parallel with Hawaii may once more be instructive: ' "Billy Pitt" Kalaimoku and "John Adams" Kuakini, leaders of nineteenth-century Hawaiian society, soon tired of their Chinese silk dressing-gowns and European waistcoats. Inflation and a surfeit of particular prestige items generated shifting patterns of commerce which became increasingly divorced from the commoners.'[9] In Middle Saxon England, inflation may have accelerated conspicuous consumption – in ceremonies connected with the living rather than the dead – as wealth was disposed of in alliance-making gestures. Faunal assemblages, the prominence of women in this period and the significance of imported objects such as wine pitchers give us glimpses of the unstable quasi-Christian world on which the author of *Beowulf* reflected.[10]

The fame of King Offa almost certainly rests on his desire to formulate a Mercian political constitution like that which existed in Wessex, and conceivably by about 760 in East Anglia and Northumbria too. His opportunity to do this arose after a long life, as the Carolingian renaissance first began to flower and after about 780 provided the circumstances in which the machinery for dynastic kingship could be devised. The renaissance is better known for the innovation of a new spiritualism and the revival of classical aspirations. Yet the Roman past was remote to the Anglo-Saxons. Furthermore, because of the geographical disposition of the Church, the innovation of a *klosterpolitik* such as Charlemagne fostered in his Empire was not possible. Nevertheless, the small-scale Anglo-Saxon political systems afforded their ambitious kings the opportunity to experiment with Carolingian ideas more effectively than the Carolingians themselves. Offa successfully imitated aspects of Charlemagne's political ideology. He also cultivated the Church, but cautiously prevented it from either amassing political power or developing its productive capacity. The

9. Sahlins, op. cit. (n. 3).

10. J.M. Wallace-Hadrill, *Early Germanic Kingship in England and on the Continent* (Oxford, 1971), 72–97.

other kingdoms seem to have followed suit. The archaeology of the emporia at Hamwic, London, Ipswich and York, and a possible second tier of inland market-places, shows that the economy was expanding. There were monetary reforms and technical advances, as well as a new emphasis upon storage instead of conspicuous consumption. The pre-conditions for take-off were laid, but the ability to articulate this revolution was essentially as restricted in England as it was within the Carolingian territories. One striking result, however, was the acceleration of Anglo-Saxon ethnicity, a spirit best reflected in the forging of a distinctive artistic style during this era – a style which incidentally appealed to the eclectic Carolingians. There is an overall impression that the Anglo-Saxons were as integrated a society as they had been in the seventh century and, despite the expansion of the economy and the inexorable eclipse of kinship, quite unlike the Carolingians.

Such changes must have affected English society in other ways. The third or fourth generation of craftsmen at Hamwic, like those in London, Ipswich and York, must have been forging a separate identity beyond the bounds of traditional tribal customs. Similarly the ninth-century farm buildings at Catholme and Raunds suggest that the long halls had been replaced by smaller dwellings, as though once again the household unit was adopting a new arrangement. Interpretation of the evidence is of course highly speculative, but the family structure of the English may well have been a variable of some real significance in this unfolding history. Certainly the formation of the cnicht's guild at Canterbury in 838 reveals the increasing role of the individual in England.

This was Alfred's inheritance. Unlike the Carolingian kingdoms, the Anglo-Saxon Church had not usurped the pool of individual skills, immobilising them as far as the development of the state was concerned. The constitution of Wessex not only favoured a strong warrior king, but allowed the development of crafts and the perpetuation of the process of individualisation. Alfred's version of Boethius' *Consolations of Philosophy*, in which he describes the existence of three orders, including labourers, reveals that he was well aware that the artisanal energy (as Le Goff describes it[11]) of the Carolingian age could be manipulated to political advantage. Alfred, unlike Charlemagne, was successful in implementing his ideas because his authority was not vested in the Church but in the nobles and people whom he valiantly led against the Vikings. His success endured because he used the Viking threat to the advantage of his dynasty, persuading the West Saxons that it was their duty to eliminate Danish conquerors from East Anglia, Mercia and Northumbria. In Wallace-Hadrill's view,

11. Jacques Le Goff, *Time, Work and Culture in the Middle Ages* (Chicago, 1980), 86.

Alfred emphasised the Carolingian belief that 'Christians are really God's war-band under Christ's kingship and that of Christ's deputy, the earthly king'.[12] Such propaganda became increasingly important as the Danish kings emulated his industrial achievements in territories where the material for economic and social development was less advanced than in Wessex. Alfred's place in history as the architect of the first English Industrial Revolution may thus have been partly contrived by the need to compete successfully with the Danelaw.

Yet the real enigma is how Alfred successfully fostered the evolution of a labouring class to the political advantage of his dynasty. What gave ordinary villagers the incentive to co-operate in dismantling the old tribal order and replacing it with a more complex set of rules? This question lies at the heart of our enquiry into the origins of English individualism. The evolution of an ordinary Middle Saxon farm at Goltho (Lincolnshire) into a private fortified manor certainly seems to indicate the eclipse of peasant rights to the advantage of the local nobility. In the past historians such as Rodney Hilton have certainly argued this way. In his view 'the manor was the institution through which a man's power as a landowner, and as a lord, was exercised in order to realise economic, social and political ends'.[13] Manors like Goltho thus mark not only the inception of a feudal order, but also the beginnings of the English peasantry in the anthropological and historical sense.

Here we need to remind ourselves of what peasants are, and of the primitive societies from which they evolved. The best-known definition of a peasantry in these circumstances is that of Eric R. Wolf: 'The peasant . . . does not operate an enterprise in the economic sense; he runs a household . . . In primitive society, surpluses are exchanged directly among groups; peasants, however, are rural cultivators whose surpluses are transferred to a dominant group of rulers . . . A peasantry always exists within a larger system . . . There exist in more complex societies social relations which are not symmetrical, but are based, in some form, upon the exercise of power . . . Where someone exercises an effective superior power . . . over a cultivator, the cultivator must produce a fund of rent. It is this production of a fund of rent which critically distinguishes the peasant from the primitive cultivator . . . The term peasant denotes no more than an asymmetrical relationship between producers of surpluses and controllers.'[14]

A critical feature in the eclipse of primitive societies and the evolution of peasantries is the question of incentive. In this connection

---

12. Wallace-Hadrill, op. cit. (n. 10), 140.
13. Rodney Hilton, 'The manor', *Journal of Peasant Studies* 1 (1973), 109.
14. Eric R. Wolf, *Peasants* (Englewood Cliffs, N.J., 1966), 2–10; see also Sydel Silverman, 'The peasant concept in anthropology', *Journal of Peasant Studies* 4 (1978), 49–69.

the Russian economist A.V. Chayanov, researching during the era of the Russian revolution, has been a prevailing influence on the analysis of the asymmetrical relationship between producers and controllers. His most celebrated conclusion was that the degree to which peasants exert themselves is determined by the equilibrium of family demand satisfaction and the drudgery of labour. He believed that for a peasant each additional unit of value produced is more desirable than the last, whereas each additional unit of labour is more burdensome and loathed.[15] But we need also to take note of Chayanov's less commonly quoted view that peasants will make decisions so as to maximise 'gains' and minimise 'costs'. As he put it: 'Our critics are free to understand the labour-consumer balance theory as a sweet little picture of the Russian peasantry in the likeness of the rural French peasants, satisfied with everything and living like birds of the air. We, ourselves, do not have such a conception and are inclined to believe that no peasant would refuse either good roast beef, or a gramophone, or even a block of Shell Oil company shares, if the chance occurred. Unfortunately, such chances do not present themselves in large numbers, and the peasant family wins every kopek by hard, intensive toil. And in these circumstances, they are obliged not only to do without shares and a gramophone but sometimes without beef as well.'[16]

Drawing upon this, we may surmise that in Late Anglo-Saxon England the additional units of labour expended were rewarded sufficiently to remove any sense of drudgery. This was obviously facilitated by the fact that the population was small and able to lay claim to attractive environmental resources in the process of expansion. But it was also facilitated by the access which peasants had to commodities. Alfred appears to have appreciated this. In the critical passage of his version of Boethius, he not only describes the tools needed to sustain a king, but accepts that the three orders of society depend upon land, gifts, weapons, food, ale and other material necessities. The need for demand satisfaction was not lost on Alfred.

The speed with which commodity production was developed in tenth-century England differs markedly from the circumstances prevailing in the old Carolingian regions at that time, or a little later in Denmark. The clear distinction between commodities produced in Wessex and those produced in the Danelaw should alert us to the great significance of what Keith Hart has called 'commoditisation'. Material culture, it seems, was being used as a mode of non-verbal communication. As Shanks and Tilley have observed, material culture

15. E. Paul Durrenberger, 'Introduction', in idem. (ed.), *Chayanov, Peasants and Economic Anthropology* (New York, 1984), 9–10.
16. Cited by Donald L. Donham, 'Beyond the domestic mode of production', *Man* 16 (1981), 515–41 at 518.

56. King Edgar adoring Christ: the New Minster Charter, BM Cotton Vespa-
sian A. viii, folio 2v (courtesy of the British Museum).

can play a particularly powerful role in those societies where communication exists almost exclusively at a verbal level and writing is poorly developed.[17] The codes embedded in the material culture may not be understood, but may nevertheless help to make consensus appear natural. Commoditisation, in short, may have been a powerful instrument in the development of West Saxon autonomy, as it was in the Danelaw, producing an ethnic identity and a sense of the state.

Commoditisation, however, begs many questions. The commodity is associated with the rise of capitalist markets. It is human labour embodied in a product or service offered to society rather than consumed directly by its producer. Yet the direct commerce of modern times 'is only one of the ways people have found to make their labour social through the circulation of its products'.[18] As such, Keith Hart has asserted, 'commoditisation may be defined as the progressive abstraction of social labour'.[19] To document this abstraction, Hart has defined a sequence of ten steps in the progressive abstraction of social labour:

The commodity is:

(1) *A thing produced for use.* The first stage in the abstraction of labour is its embodiment in an object standing outside the producer.

(2) *Alienated.* It is made social by being produced for the use of another, someone foreign to the unit of production and reproduction.

(3) *The product of divided labour.* Productive specialisation requires and enhances social interdependence: an interlocking system for the provision of individual and social needs necessitates organisation of mutual rights and obligations.

(4) *Circulated by means of exchange.* Two-sided reciprocal transfers are a common, but not the only, way of circulating the products of divided labour.

(5) *Exchanged through the market mechanism.* A giant step in the abstraction of social labour occurs when people make an immediate determination of quantitative equivalence or exchange value, often in a routinised setting.

(6) *Crystallised as pure exchange value, i.e. money.* Money is a commodity whose only use is a means of exchange.

(7) *Used as capital to make profit.* When money is used to make more money, it constitutes a new active principle in social life.

(8) *Deployed as industrial capital*, to purchase means of production – both produced (machines, raw materials) and non-produced (labour, land). The wage form is a crucial step in the abstraction of social labour since human beings now buy and sell their own productive capacities.

17. Michael Shanks and Christopher Tilley, *Reconstructing Archaeology: theory and practice* (Cambridge, 1987), 133.
18. Keith Hart, 'On commoditisation', in Esther N. Goody (ed.), *From Craft to Industry* (Cambridge, 1983), 38–49 at 40.
19. ibid.

(9) *Predominantly human labour itself*, when services come to outweigh goods in the sphere of commoditisation production.

(10) *An abstract cipher*. Social labour is measured directly, without material transfer, as computerised transactions which represent human subjects as numbers in information-processing machines.[20]

Hart argues that each step in this sequence generates a residual category which tends to negate development. He lists these as follows:

(1) Something which is not the product of human labour; something produced which is not useful; an aspect of human interaction (e.g. a service) which is not objectified.

(2) Something produced for one's own use or for the use of a unit with which one is identified. The concept of alienation, depending as it does on an insider/outsider distinction, is clearly relative to the boundary defining the other.

(3) A thing given in the absence of a division of labour, for the sake of sociability and even reproduction; for example, certain marriage transactions in primitive homogeneous societies.

(4) One-sided transfers in which direct reciprocity is denied and asymmetry is emphasised: tribute, extortion, public finance, sacrifice, redistribution, charity.

(5) Transfers in which there is no determination of value by reciprocal exchange of equivalents, e.g. some systems of delayed gift return.

(6) Commodities that have some use in addition to serving as a form of currency and all items which are sold merely for use.

(7) Money spent passively on consumption, rather than being invested to accumulate more money.

(8) Earlier forms of capital – merchant's capital (buying and selling products) and usurer's capital (making money with money alone).

(9) The first phase of industrial capitalism, when primary and secondary production predominate and much labour is still not sold for wages.

(10) When commodity relations still involve material things more than computerised abstractions.[21]

Hart's scheme 'is a selective paraphrase of Marx, omitting most of what he had to say on the subject of surplus value and class struggle'.[22] But Marx defined a commodity as an object produced for others having both use value and exchange value. As Hart observes, 'Exchange value can only be determined where products enter routinely into immediate exchange with each other. So, for Marx, the commodity is synonymous with markets, and his definition embraces all of steps 1–5 above, leaving the emergence of money capital and the commoditisation of labour as the distinctive features of the modern age.' He saw commoditisation where a market was dominant (5–8), but he lost sight of the origins of the commodity (1–4), and its possible evolution (9,10).

20. ibid., 40–1.
21. ibid., 42–3.
22. ibid., 44.

Such a definition, as Hart asserts, obscures the manifest similarities between all the societies which have achieved an advanced division of labour.[23] This definition has, however, been either explicitly or implicitly commonplace in medieval history, where there has been a dependence upon written sources describing commoditisation as opposed to physical evidence of the process itself.

Using Hart's steps, it is apparent that steps 1 and 2 existed by the time the Church arrived in England. In Wessex, however, commoditisation evolved to step 3 when Ine created the conditions for social interdependence at Hamwic. A century later, encouraged by Carolingian idealism, commodities were beginning to be circulated by means of exchange (step 4). The 'giant step', as Hart puts it, was 5. This was set in motion during the late ninth century, and must be based both upon the long tradition of social interdependence and upon the widely perceived benefits of increased materialism. By Edgar's reign the pattern of mints and the management of coinage indicate that these twin forces had been fused in a highly integrated relationship between towns and the countryside. In this relationship lay the roots of what Peter Sawyer described as 'the wealth of Late Saxon England'.[24]

The wide-scale distribution of coarse and fine pottery, quernstones, honestones and minor metalwork throughout England endorses Sawyer's view that English markets were patronised by most levels of society. The peasantry was not, as a group, prevented from participation. Equally, *contra* Hilton,[25] archaeological evidence from the Norman and Angevin epoch until the crucial late Middle Ages attests that the relationship between town and country embraced most levels of society. As Sawyer contended, the town played a more or less constant demographic role in English society between AD 1000 and the fourteenth century. During this period the pre-conditions of capitalism, as Marx defined it, were established with the first steps to separate man from the land.

From the tenth century, therefore, English peasants bore the exaction of lordly demands, but they were able to mitigate the drudgery of their lot by maintaining and managing their resources in ways that the more recent peasantries scrutinised by Chayanov, for example, have often found impossible. The reasons for this successful economic integration are obviously complex, but in some rooted in the unusual social heritage of the English. The English identity was born in the peculiar circumstances of the fifth and sixth centuries, and in the

23. ibid.

24. Peter Sawyer, 'The wealth of England in the eleventh century', *Transactions of the Royal Historical Society* 15 (1965), 145–64.

25. Rodney Hilton, 'Reasons for inequality among medieval peasants', *Journal of Peasant Studies* 4 (1978), 271–84 at 271–2 & 277; for a contrary view, largely in support of the thesis presented in this chapter, see Kathleen Biddick, 'Medieval English peasants and market involvement', *Journal of Economic History* 45 (1985), 823–31.

absence of the Church. Thereafter the *gens Anglorum* and the *ecclesia Anglorum* were twin ideas that were never fused in the coherent manner witnessed on the Continent. The competition between these forces fuelled the evolution of both, building upon fundamental social attributes originating in the fifth century. In particular, it fostered the centralisation of political power witnessed in the construction and maintenance of Hamwic. Here, as early as the late seventh century, the process of commoditisation created a degree of social interdependence in which the concept of individual specialisation was embedded. This powerful meshing of political and tribal aspirations must have stimulated the competition between the great kingdoms of England over the following century. From then on the Carolingian renaissance nurtured the peculiar social order of the Anglo-Saxons, and it comes as no surprise to discover a confederation of individuals forming a guild as early as the ninth century. England was well advanced in the evolution of individual rights. The division of labour favoured by Alfred and his Danish counterparts in the late ninth century must have triggered a transformation not only of daily life, but also in people's conception of the world. In describing this transformation John F. Benton draws special attention to 'a shift from a culture in which shame and worth accorded by peers predominated to one in which a sense of both guilt and self-esteem became far more common, which profoundly affected the way in which individuals perceived themselves'.[26] The mechanisms of this momentous change, Benton believes, lay in the hands of the Church and of mothers educating their children. Such mechanisms lie within the archaeologist's grasp. The proliferation of Late Saxon parish churches, each with its own cemetery, and perhaps too the incidence of infant burials at Raunds may illustrate how the eleventh-century reforming concepts of self-awareness and self-examination in the hope of salvation were disseminated. But was this new English personality to be transformed completely by the Norman and Angevin kings?

Historians are now stressing the existence of basic administrative and social growth from Late Saxon through into Norman times. In Professor Loyn's opinion, the full power of the monarchy 'had already moulded the English community into governable shape' when the Normans took over.[27] Central power was fully exercised in conjunction with local freedoms through shire courts. Representation was granted to those who held landed wealth, and the basic rights were preserved throughout the Middle Ages. Taking a longer perspective of English government, one might conclude that a constantly evolving form of

26. John F. Benton, 'Consciousness of self and perceptions of individuality', in R.L. Benson & G. Constable (eds.), *Renaissance and Renewal in the Twelfth Century* (Oxford, 1982), 263–95 at 294.
27. H.R. Loyn, *The Governance of Anglo-Saxon England* (London, 1984), 171.

government can be traced from King Ine's time up to the later Middle Ages.

It would be far-fetched to describe Anglo-Norman society as proto-capitalist. Instead we might conclude as follows: that the class structure was rooted in an agrarian system that evolved slowly, if at times unevenly, adopting and blending insular and Continental influences. This evolutionary process was sufficiently advanced on the eve of the Black Death to ensure that the great fourteenth-century recession did not result in the same traumatic decline as had occurred during the third century. With its roots spanning a millennium, the English peasantry survived the Black Death and continued to prosper. Thereafter we witness a new step on the ladder of commoditisation, as peasant attitudes to surplus, reflected by the barns and sheds in their farmsteads, become more pronounced. This was, perhaps, the beginning of a proto-capitalist age.

Index

Aachen, palace, 118
Abbasid Empire, 119, 136
Abingdon, monastery, 52
Adalberon of Laon, 181
Adric, 176
Aelle, 32, 188
Aethelbald, King of Mercia, 69, 88, 96, 97; burial, 126; reign, 142; morals, 109–10
Aethelbehrt, King of Kent, 135; laws, 58; tributes to, 63
Aethelwold, Bishop of Winchester, 4, 179–80
Aethelwulf, King of Wessex, 105, 148, 178; endowments by, 122; supremacy, 126
Aetius, 22
Aghlabids, 119
agricultural tools, 183
Alamanni, trade, 54
Alcock, L., excavations by, 32
Alcuin, 4, 102, 103, 115, 121, 123, 135, 136, 157
Aldwyck on the Strand, emporium at, 94
Alfred Jewel, 178
Alfred, King of Wessex, 85, 105, 122–3, 152, 178, 181, 182, 194, 195, 196; role in English origins, 4; victory over the Danes, 7, 50; monastic lands, 52; reign, 84, 156; age of, 126, 177, 185; dynasty of, 127; Asser's biography of, 132; church building, 148; treaty, 154; laws, 160; coins, 161–2; trade, 165; reforms military service, 176; defeat of Danes, 201
Alps, 17, 45, 84
America, migration to, 23
Andrén, A., 159
Andrews, P., 74
Angles, 50–2, 65, 91, 96; settlement, 10; in Britain, 17; Bede on, 25
Anglo-Saxon Attitudes (by Angus Wilson), 46–8, 53

Anglo-Saxon Chronicle: authors of, 7; on migration period, 22, 23; on Anglo-Saxon royal homes, 32; payments to kingdoms, 77; on reign of Ine, 90; on Cynewulf, 91; on Repton, 153; on invasions, 188
Annales School of history, 8
Aquitaine: trade, 72; conquest by Charlemagne, 117
Arabs, trade, 119
Arbor Low (Derbyshire) barrow, 64
Arnold, C.J., 27, 28, 32, 38–9, 62
Arthur, King of the Britons (see also Ambrosius), 4, 7, 23, 32, 33, 34
artistic movements: Northumberland, 77, 102, 105; Carolingia, 116, 118, 136; Wessex, 126; Mercia, 129; manuscript illumination, 129; Anglo-Saxon, 145–6, 178; Hiberno-Saxon, 178–9
Ashton, T.H., 150
Asser, biographer of Alfred, 123, 132, 152
Augustus, Emperor, 117
Austin, D., work, 166
Austrasia, 72; burials from, 53; courts, 54; contact, 56; trade, 76–95
Avars, 143

Baldwin-Brown, G., 123
Baltic Sea, trade, 119, 136
Barberini Gospels, 146
Barham (Suffolk): coins from, 77–8; excavations, 98–9
Barton Court Farm (Oxfordshire), 185; villa at, 17; desertion, 25–6, 27; excavations, 36; estate, 52
Bassa, founder of Reculver, 107
Bassett, S., 128
Bath: Roman, 16, 17; foundation, 158
Battle of Maldon, The, poem, 176
Bavaria, 117
Bede, 136, 193; age of, 1, 68, 102–3, 110; impact of, 4; writings of, 7; description of invasions, 10; on settlements, 12; in

theological debate, 19; on Roman withdrawal, 22; history of invasion period, 23, 25; invasions, 28; family structures, 36; on polygyny, 40; on life and history of the Church, 43–4, 56; inheritance, 46; on Paulinus, 58; on Ine and merchants, 92; on reform, 105; ideals, 106, 108, 115; on church building, 123
Bedford, 143
Behrtwulf, King of Wessex, coins, 133
Benedictines, 180, 184
Benevento, S. Sophia, 104
Beneventum, 142–3; trade, 119; agriculture, 120–1; coins, 133; war, 147
Bensington, battle of, 134, 143
Benton, J.F., 201
Benty Grange (Derbyshire), barrow, 64
Beonna, King of East Anglia, Fig. 32, 101, 106, 142; coins, 74, 133; trade, 91
Beowulf (poem), 143, 145; heroic king in, 5; on heathen values, 43; on kingship, 58; on king's works, 88–9; halls, 112
Beresford, G., 168–72
Bertha, marriage to Aethelbehrt, 31, 40, 42, 54, 55
Biddick, K., 13
Biddle, M., 49–50, 86, 87, 94, 124–8, 132, 147–8, 153–4
Bishophill, York, 135; colonia and monastery, 104
Bishopstone (Sussex), 62
Bismarck, Germany of, 116
Blackburn, M., on coins, 71–2, 74
Black Death, 202
Bloch, M., 184; on feudalism, 4, 151–2
Bloomfield (Barrow), 46
Blunt, C., 135
boats: flat-bottomed, 80; tolls, 96; deep draft, 164; keels, 187
Boddington, A., 172, 173, 174
Boethius, *Consolations*, 181, 194, 196
bone-working, 83, 84, 87, 146
Boniface, 40, 105, 115, 123
botanical studies, 36–7, 38; Hamwic, 84–5
Bourdillon, J., 137
bracteates: distribution of, 31; from Denmark, 32
Bradley, R., 176
Brandon Staunch Meadow (Suffolk), 71, 106, Fig. 35, 109
Braudel, F., 6, 8, 12
Breedon-on-the-Hill (Leicestershire), sculpture, 129–30, Fig. 39

Britford Church (Wiltshire), 148
British Empire, 7
Brixworth Church (Northamptonshire), 128
brooches, from cemeteries, 28
Brooks, N.P., 60, 88, 122, 124
Brook Street excavations (Winchester), 49, 50, 132, 156
Brown, R.A., 168
Brühl, C-R., 49, 50
Buckland (Dover), 32, 39, 136; cemeteries, 28
Buckland, P., 144
buckles, gilded, 146
Budny, M., on manuscript illumination, 129, 146
building technology, 120, 132, 142
Burgundia, trade, 54
burhs, 86, 143–4, 160
Burrow Hill (Suffolk): excavations, 71, 98–9, 106; coins, 77–8
Byzantium, 188, 189; rise of, 24, 29; merchants, 32; wars with, 54

Caedwalla, King of Wessex, 76–7, 85, 90
calendars, Latin, 44
Cambridge, excavations, 143, 158
Campbell, J., 8
Cannadine, D., 3
Cannington (Somerset), 33
Canterbury, 148; Roman, 20, 49, 50, 53; emporia, 55; excavations, 71; bishopric, 94; archbishop of, 121–2; church building, 123–4; art, 129; monasteries, 133; pottery, 135; pottery production, 141; *cnicht*'s guild, 147, 194; tenth century, 156
Canute, King of England: impact of, 4; coins, 162; reign, 164
capitalism, 3, 4, 41, 200–1; modern, 2; origins of, 9
Carolingian Empire, 72, 155, 177, 178, 180, 195, 196, 200, 201; dynasty of, 74, 91; pots, 61, 84; economy, 97, 120; coins, 101; trade, 35, 36, 104, 119; aristocracy, 105, 128, 168; political change, 114; Renaissance, 115, 116, 117, 118, 121; churches, 122, 123, 124, 126, 128, 133, 179; art, 129, 178–9; building, 132–3; reforms, 134; pottery production, 141; craft production, 142; ideology, 143–4; courts, 145; architecture, 146, 148; collapse, 149; age of, 151, 181; technology, 160; forts, 170; Europe, 184, 185, 193–4
carpenters, 60

Cassington (Oxfordshire), 10, 11, Fig. 2, 62
Cassiodorus, 23
catastrophe theory, 6, 7
Catholme (Staffordshire), 26, 34, 61, 112, 190–2, 194
cemeteries, 110, 128, 136, 153–4, 174, 191, 193; sub-Roman, 10; Anglo-Saxon, 12, 32–3, 40–1, 53–4, 68, 172, 188–9; peasant populations in, 16; excavations, 25–8; Merovingian, 30; pottery from, 37–8; Frankish, 39; Christian, 46–9, 69, 180, 183, 184, 201; Winchester, 50; Kent, 55, 56–7; barrows, 64; coins, 78; Southampton, 80; coffins, 81; minsters, 105–6; pagan, 108; nineteenth century, 151; Viking, 153–4; mausolea, 126
central place theory, 7, 166
Cenwalh, King of Wessex: founds Old Minster, Winchester, 49; church building, 124, 148; age of, 126
Cerdic of Wessex, 32, 34, 188
cereal production: corn, 16; Hamwic, 84–5
Chalton (Hampshire): enclosures, 61; desertion, 62; excavations, 81
Charlemagne, 117, 145, 148, 194; coins, 73, 91; government, 115; age of, 116; dynasty, 118, 121, 144, 152; court, 122–3; reforms, 133; trade with Offa of Mercia, 136; reign, 142; war, 143
Charles Martel, 72–3, 105
Chayanov, A.V., 196, 200
Cheddar, 185; Anglo-Saxon palace, 132; hall, 170
Chedworth, Roman villa, 16
Chelsea, Council of (786), 121, 134
Chelsea, mint, 134
Chester, 159
Chichester, 156
Childeric, King of the Franks, conversion, 30
China: trade with, 119; silk, 193
Chrodegang of Metz, 105, 122
Churchill, Winston: historian, 1; biography of, 7
Cirencester: Roman, 16; cemeteries, 40; churches, 128
Cissa, Unider-King of Wessex, 52
Claudius, Emperor, invasion of Britain, 13, 22
Clausentum, *see* Hamwic
climate, 67; effect on history, 6; change, 166
clothing: from cemeteries, 30; Frankish, 40, 41; wool cloaks, 136; silk cap, 64; exchange, 193
Clovis, King of the Franks, 54; conquests, 30; reign of, 31, 34, 40; court, 188
Clunies Ross, M., on polygyny, 183
Cluny: monastery, 165; Cluniac reforms, 179
cnicht's guild, 147, 194
Coelwulf, King of Mercia, 122
Coenwulf, King of Mercia, 105, 122, 178; ritual, 133; dispute, 144; death, 146
coffins, 106, 174; coffin burials, 81
coinage, 179, 200; pennies, 46, 72, 76, 91, 105, 106, 122, 129, 136, 139–42, 161, 162, 164; sceattas, 46, 71–4, Fig. 21, 77–8, 79, 83, 87–8, 90, 93–4, Fig. 30, 101–3, 105–7, 129, 136, 146; deniers, 73, 76, 101, 120, 133, 161; gold and silver, 57, 71, 74, 76, 77, 91, 92, 94; Carolingian, 118–20, 155; tremisses, 71; Frankish, 55; distribution, 98–9; solidi, 72; analysis, 76; clusters, 78; production, 141–2; stycas, 149, 155; forgery, 162; hoards, 174
Collingbourne Ducis (Wiltshire), 32; cemetery, 28
Consolations of Philosophy (by Boethius), 181, 194
Constantine, 118
Constantinople, 16, 23
Cook, James, explorer, 187–9
Cooper, J. Fennimore, on Indians, 4
Coppergate excavations, York, 109, 148, 157, 164–5
Cowdery's Down (Hampshire): houses from, 35; excavations, 60, 89, 110, 133, 190
Cox Lane, Ipswich, excavations, 134
Cramp, R., 102, 104
Crawford, O.G.S., 12–13
Cristaller, W., 166
Crondall Hoard, 57
Crowland, 52, 108
cults (pagan), 25, 43–4, 46, 68
Cunliffe, B.W., excavations in Bath, 16, 17
Cymric, 3
Cynewulf, King of Wessex, 91

Danelaw, 52, 150, 152, 162, 164, 180, 195–6, 198; towns, 154–5, 157, 159; industry, 161; territories, 166; field systems, 176–7; warfare, 179
Danes, 142–3, 150–5, 185
Danevirke (Denmark), 73, 144

Dar es Salaam, Anglo-Saxon trade with, 9
Dartmoor, 166
Davies, W., on Tribal Hidage, 57–8
Deerhurst (Gloucestershire), 128
Denmark, 126, 165, 188; settlements, 25–6; graveyards, 32; tenth-century circumstances, 56, 67, 68; coins from, 73, 163; emporia, 83; king of, 88–9; trade, 119; political instability, 147; treaty, 154; eleventh-century circumstances, 159; houses, 190
Derby, pottery, 161
Devon/Cornwall: annexation, 90; conquest, 147
Dickinson, T., cemetery studies, 27–8
Dixon, P., 34
Domburg (Walcharen), emporia, 72, 73
Domesday Book, 64, 177; population estimates in, 13, 15
Dorchester-on-Thames (Oxfordshire), 20–1
Dorestad: emporia, 72; foundation, 86; trade, 95, 119
Dover, cemetery, 28, 32
Droxford (Hampshire), cemetery, 32
Duby, G., 118, 119, 120
Dunstan, Archbishop of Canterbury, 179
Dunstan's Clump (Nottinghamshire), homestead, 34
Durham, 158, 160

Eadberht, King of Northumbria, 104; coins, 102; age of, 103
Ecgberht, King of Kent, 134
Ecgfrith, son of Offa, 121
Edgar, King of England, 156, 158, 165, Fig. 50, 200; gifts, 180
Edward the Elder, King of England, 156, 165; towns, 154
Edwin, King of Northumbria, palace, 58
East Anglia, kingdom of, 98–101, 135, 162; adopts Christianity, 46; dynasty, 56, 77, 78; coins, 30
Egbert, King of Wessex, 105, 134, 148, 178; exile, 122; supremacy, 126
Ely, 108, 180
emporia (see also ports and towns), 55, 121, 132, 135, 136–7, 141, 142, 143, 144, 146–7, 149, 161–4, 156–7, 160, 165, 192–3, 194; Anglo-Saxon, 58, 134; excavations, 70, 72, 73, 76, 77, 78, 92, 94, 95, 97, 99, 101, 102, 112–13; Hamwic, 116; Carolingian, 119; Ipswich, 154
enclosures and boundaries, Fig. 24, 88–9,

106; Mucking, 26; Hamwic, 80–1, 85; Ipswich, 99; villages, 110, 189–91; Anglo-Saxon towns, 147; towns, 155
English Channel, 55, 92
environmental studies, 8, 30
Ethelflaeda, Queen of Mercia, 129
Ethelred the Unready, 164
Evison, V., 28, 38, 39
Eyrar, 89
Exeter, 49, Fig. 15; tenth century, 156

fairs, periodic, 76, 89, 96, 99, 166; Quentovic, 55
farms, 12, 37, 38, 39, 112, 167, 177, 189, 195; in Roman Britain, 13, 20, 26, 36; marginal, 15; Anglo-Saxon, 13, 34, 36, 86, 110, 191; in Italy, 29; medieval, 52; at Windsor, 94; buildings, 137–9; nineteenth century, 151; Anglo-Scandinavian, 154–5
faunal studies, 193; Anglo-Saxon Portchester, 13; Hamwic, 84–5, 137
Feddersen Wierde, 24
Fellend Moss (Co. Durham), pollen cores from, 167
fenland archaeology, 106, 108, 154, 166–7; Lincolnshire, 8, 13; Roman, 15; sub-Roman, 19; population decline, 20–1; monasteries, 52; settlements, 64
Fenland Research Committee, 64, 166–7
Fernie, E., 45–6
feudalism, 151–2, 183–4
field systems, 176–7; Anglo-Saxon walls, 13; in eastern/Frankish lands, 120; open field systems, 154
Finberg, H.P.R., 52
fishing, 108
Fleming, R., 180; on land, 152
Fletton, sculpture from, 129
Foard, G., 168
Fordwich (Kent), 55, 92, 93
fortifications/defences, 188; Danevirke, 73; towns, 86, 155, 156–7, 159, 182; Offa's Dyke, 88, 144; walls, 135, 147–8; burhs, 143; Repton, 153–4; South Cadbury, 158–9; manors, 168–73, 182
Fosse river, 103, 148
Fowler, P.J., 13, 15
Frankish Annals, 117, 118
Frankish Kingdom: kings, 30–1, 54, 72; grave goods, 32, 33, 38; funerary attire, 40; pottery, 41, 84; ecclesiastical architecture, 45; jewellery, 46; towns, 49–50; trade, 55–6, 87–9, 91, 121, 135–6, 189; place-names, 67; warfare, 73; coins, 74; cemeteries, 108; dynasty,

115; annals, 117; church/churches, 123, 126; artists, 129; crafts, 164; colonies, 177; court, 188
Fridugis, pupil of Alcuin, 121
Frisia, 56, 72–3, 74, 77, 78, 91, 94, 96–7, 103, 119, 135, 193
Fuller Brooch, 129, 145, Fig. 45

Gandesheim Casket, 136, 146
Garton-on-the-Wolds (Humberside), 46
Gasar (Iceland), 89
Gatcombe (Somerset): villa, 16; buildings from, Fig. 10
Gaul, 30, 67, 84, 191, 196; peasants of, 15; decline, 17, 29; Provence, 17; history of, 20, 23; offshore forts, 24; cemeteries, 28; towns, 50; trade, 54; society, 56; excavations, 131; pottery, 161; trade, 165, 188; coins, 162
Gem, R., 122, 123, 124
Germany, 30–1, 117, 118, 119, 165; imports from, 16; people, 25; villages, 26; pottery, 78; Danevirke, 73; territories, 105; Bismarck, 116; archaeology, 187; excavations, 131; fortified manors, 184
Giddens, A., 66
gift exchange, 40, 41, 52, 55, 56, 57, 61, 104, 106, 110, 119, 181
Gildas, 23, 34; on Anglo-Saxon settlements, 12; on Roman withdrawal, 22; on Battle of Mount Badon, 188; on invasions, 25, 28; history, 42
glassware, 41, 87, 148; Roman imported, 16; Frankish beakers, 32; vessel, 49; Roman production, 50; trade in, 55; production of, 120; window glass, 128; Anglo-Saxon, 160; Frankish, 188
Gloucester, 160; St Oswald's Priory, 128–9; tenth century, 156
gold: trade in, 56; bullion, 57, 72, 90; coins, 92; Frankish, 136; jewellery, 160
Goltho (Lincolnshire), 164, 168–72, Fig. 52, 170, 184, 195
Goody, J., 21, 43, 69, 183, 190
Gorze, monastery, 165
Goths, raids by, 17
grave goods (*see also* cemeteries), 10, 27, 28, 30, 37, 38; Anglo-Saxon, 32, 33; pottery, 39; Sutton Hoo, 39; lack of, 46; rich, 48; Winchester, 49; disposal of, 53; Kent, 55; barrows, 64; accompanying St Cuthbert, 68, 108;

York, 109; wealthy, 136; late Roman, 187–8; Germanic, 187
Gregory, C.A., 41, 176
Gregory of Tours, 23
Grierson, P., 57, 71, 72, 74
Grimoald, King of Benevento, 120
Grubenhäuser, 11, 26, 82
Grundrisse (by Karl Marx), 9
Guthlac, monastery, 52

Hadrian, Pope, 121
Hadrian's Wall, 144
Haithabu, 82, 120
Hall, D., 176
Hall, R., 157
Hamwic, 71, 74, 142; excavations, 77–8, 80–92, 106, 134–7, 147, 149, 182, 192–4, 200–1; coins, 77, 99; emporia, 94–6, 104; crafts at, 112; foundations, 116; merchants, 121; administration, 132; pottery/pottery making, 141, 164; streets, 156; development, 185
Hart, K., 196–200
Harvey, M., 154
Haslam, J., 143
Hawaiians, 187–9, 193
Haverfield, F., 20
Hayes, P., fieldwork, 108
Heabehrt, King of Kent, 134
Hedda Stone, 146
Hedeager, L., 24
Heighway, C., 128–9
Hereford, 143, 160
hereot, 88–9, 175–6
Herlihy, D.L.: on Anglo-Saxon houses, 36; on women, 40
Heybridge (Essex), 25
Hiberno-Saxon ornament, 129, 146
High Gauber (West Yorkshire), 167; village, 164
Hill, D., 88; on Offa's Dyke, 144
hill forts, Fig. 9, 34; sub-Roman, 32–3
Hilton, R., 195, 200
Hlothere, King of Kent, 76
hoards: ritual destruction, 41; coins, 71, 72, Fig. 21, 103; silver, 96
Holne Moor (Dartmoor), 166
honestones, 200; imports, 84
Hooke, D., 167
Hope Taylor, B.: Yeavering excavations, 58, 60; Old Windsor excavations, 112, 113
Hrothgar, King of the Danes, 88–9
Huitarvellir (Iceland), 89
Humber river, 174
Huns, raids by, 17

Hurst, J.G., 177
Hwicce, Kingdom of, 74; coins, 78
Hygebehrt, Archbishop of Mercia, 121–2

Iceland, 89
Ilchester, excavations, 159
illuminated manuscripts, 102, 108, 129, 144–6
India, dwellings, 184
Ine, King of Wessex, 69, 115; grants to, 52; law codes, 63; coins, 76–7; reign of, 90, 182, 202; laws, 92, 112; abdication, 91; Bede on, 92; building, 113; conquests, 147; founds Hamwic, 85–6, 88, 94, 192–3
inheritance customs, 40, 53, 57, 183; Bede on, 46; J. Goody on, 69
invasion/migration theory, 28, 38, 42; Normans, 1; Anglo-Saxon, 4, 7, 12, 22, 23, 24, 32, 152, 187, 192; theory of, 5; in prehistory, 11, 190; Barbarian, 17; Europe and Mediterranean, 25; migration theory, 67; Danes, 153–5; Vikings, 191; archaeology, 191
Ipswich, 148, 154, 156, 194; emporia, 55, 56, 92, 97–101, 104, 142–3; excavations, 58, 71, 134–5, 137; coins, 77–8; crafts, 88; pottery, 95, 134–5, 141, 161; trade, 77–8, 121, 164; metalwork from, 46
Ipswich ware, 135, 161
Ireland: raids, 17; Early Christian, 178
iron industry, 17
Isle of Wight, annexation, 85
Italy, 56; Roman, 15, 17; history from, 23; Ostrogoths, 29; conquests, 30; towns, 50; trade, 54; social transformation, 67; farming, 120; excavations, 131; sculpture, 148; kingdoms, 191
Itchen river, 80

Jaenbehrt, Archbishop of Canterbury, 121–2
James, E.: on cemeteries, 30; on place-names, 67
Jarrow: monastery, 71, 107, Fig. 34; excavations, 106, 108
jewellery, 39; Anglo-Saxon, 9; chip-carved, 14; cemeteries, 28; brooches, 46, 106; styles of ornament, 66; production, 160; fibula, 164; tenth century, 178; late Roman, 187–8
Julius Caesar, 34, 177
Jutes, 25; settlement, 10, 17; in England, 65
Jutland, 25, 117, 187; Danevirke, 73

Kanzehameha, Hawaiian chief, 187–8
Kemble, J.M., 10, 12; on Anglo-Saxon invasions, 42
Kent, Kingdom of, 86, 102, 143, 154, 187, 188, 190, 192; imported pottery, 31, 32; tribes, 33; ranking, 39; cemeteries, 40; missions, 42–3; churches, 45–6, 93; court, 49; alliance/trade, 54–5; king, 58, 74; coin exchange, 76–7, 98; trade, 91, 92, 95, 96, Fig. 29, 97–8; emporia, 94; settlements, 99; elites, 103; architecture, 104; monasteries, 107; bishoprics, 121–2; aristocracy, 124

labour/labourers, 183, 194, 196, 198–9; waged, 2; mobilisation, 32, 88, 153, 190; Roman Britain, 36; in monasteries, 119; on labour, 120–1; division, 181, 201
Lankhills Cemetery (Winchester), 40
Lark Valley (Suffolk): farms in, 26; settlements, 38, 187
laws, 117, 178; seventh century, 39, 192; Anglo-Saxon, 53, 58; Ine's, 88, 92, 112–13
Leach, E., on pagan religions, 43
leatherworking: book covers, 108; in towns, 160
Leeds, E.T., Fig. 2, 12; work on Anglo-Saxon archaeology, 10
Le Goff, J., 181, 182; on Carolingia, 120–1
Leicester: town, 49; pottery, 161
Leo III, Pope: anoints Charlemagne, 117; coins, 133
Levison, W., 115–16, 142
Levi-Strauss, C., 43; on women, 40–1
Lichfield, see at, 121–2
Lincoln excavations, 154, 157, 159, 160, 161, 164, 169, 170; workshops, 179
Lindisfarne Gospels, 102, 108
linguistic studies, 12
literacy, 43; emergence, 66; writing, 66–8; Carolingian, 144–5; Anglo-Saxon, 144–5, 149; development, 190–1
liturgical objects, 134, 180; St Cuthbert's cross, 46–8; reliquaries, 108; Anglo-Saxon, 136
livestock farming, 166; West Stow, 36; Hamwic, 84–5, 137; fens, 108
Lombards, 118; towns, 50; cemeteries, 53; trade with, 54
London (Lundenwic), 51, Fig. 15, 54, 77, 193; Roman, 49; royal court, 50; palace at, 53; excavations, 71, 94; trade, 76, 121; emporia, 86–7, 92, 95–6, 101, 104, 136–7, 143, 147–8; coins, 97–8; mint,

134; pottery, 135; pottery industry, 156; tenth century, 164
looms, Anglo-Saxon, 160
Loyn, H.R., 201
Lucca, 86
Lund (Sweden), excavations at, 159
Lyminge, cemetery, 28

Maaseik *casula*, 136, 146
Macfarlane, A., 2, 4, 9, 152; definition of capitalism, 3
Manchester, W. (biographer of Churchill), 7
manors: records from, 6; Anglo-Saxon, 152, 183, 184; fortified, 168, 173, 176
Maori chiefs, 4
market economy/market places, 50, 54, 76, 86, 143, 155–9, 166, 182, 193, 198, 200; Roman Britain, 13, 15
marriage, 40, 42, 54, 55, 115, 165, 178, 183; laws, 21; alliance, 190
Marx, Karl, 200; origins of capitalism, 2; *Grundrisse*, 9; on exchange, 41, 55; on capitalism, 76; on markets, 119
mausolea: Anglo-Saxon, 126–8; Repton, 153–4
Mauss, M., on theory of exchange, 41
meat production sites, Anglo-Saxon, 137
Medehamstede Abbey (Peterborough), 108, 129
Melpham, fictional tomb at, 46
mercenaries, 187, 188; Saxon, 22–3; Roman, 24; Gildas on, 25; fifth century, 42
Mercia, Kingdom of, 52, 114, 129, 150, 152, 153, 154, 155; trade, 57, 58, 96, 161; tributes, 58, 64; supremacy, 69; coins, 74, 77, 91, Fig. 30; kings, 88, 105, 142, 191; conflict, 90; political relations, 97, 98; towns, 101, 158; elites, 103, 104; villas, 110; eighth century, 115; supremacy, 116; see at, 121–2, 125–6; aristocracy, 124; architecture, 130; churches, 133; war, 143–4; craft production, 148; art, 178; politics, 193, 194
Merovingia, 72; alliances, 23; cemeteries, 30; dynasty, 40, 42; kingdom, 54; kings, 56; monasteries, 119
metal working, 87, 120; Anglo-Saxon, 46; Hamwic, 83, 84; Whitby, 106; jewellery, 129, 136; iron workshops, 141; Anglo-Saxon ornament, 145–6; production, 160
metal analyses, coins, 74
Metcalf, D.M., 71–2, 74, 77, 78

Middle Anglia, 64, 74, 77, 103, 110, 142–4, 148, 150, 153, 154, 155, 177, 187, 193, 194
Miles, D., 52
millstones, 16
Millet, M., 60
mineral production, 13
minster churches, 122–4, 126, 138–9, 143–4, 148, 153, 154, 155, 156, 158; cemeteries of, 69; Hamwic, 83; land belonging to, 94; York, 102; Winchester, 108; burial, 105–6; Reculver, 107; wealth, 109
Minster-by-Thanet (Kent), 92, 93, 149
mints, 73, Fig. 23, 134, 135, 156–9, 161–2, 164–5, Fig. 50, 200; Wessex, 57; Carolingia, 72; Frisian, 78–9, Fig. 22; Offa's, 94; Kent, 122; Anglo-Saxon, 139–41
Misbach, H., 90
missionaries, 4, 9, 42–4, 46, 49, 53, 56, 58, 61, 72, 115; Anglo-Saxon, 190–1; Victorian, 7; churches of, 109
monasteries/abbeys, 157, 180, 183, 191; cemeteries, 46; Crowland, 52; walls, 61; excavations, 71; coins from, 78; Anglo-Saxon, 86, 117, 133; Kent, 92–3, 122; Northumbria, 102; economy, 104; reforms, 105, 106–8, 123, 179, 184; decadence in, 110; Carolingian, 118–19, 136; lands of, 152; French, 165
Monk, M., 84, 85
Montesquieu, 115
Montreuil-sur-Mer, 55
Morris, R., 172, 174, 180; on Anglo-Saxon churches, 44; on York, 157
mortar mixers, 120, 131, Fig. 41, 132, 133
Moulden, J., 104
Mount Badon (*Mons Badonicus*), battle of, 23, 33–4; Gildas on, 188
Mucking, 26, 187
Mul, King of Kent, death of, 77
Myres, J.N.L., 10, 25, 38

Napoleon, Emperor, 115, 117
Nasman, U., 31
Nazeingbury monastery (Essex), 107
Nees, L., 116
Neidermendig lava querns, 136
Nelson, A., 40
Nelson, J., 50–2, 152
Neustria, 72, 84, 85, 95; burials, 53; courts, 54; king of, 55; trade, 90
New Forest pottery industry, 17
New Guinea, 56
New Minster (Winchester), 155–6, 185

Normans, 1–3; conquest, 10; population, 15; cathedrals, 124; era, 200–2
North Elmham Minster (Norfolk), 138, Fig. 49, 139
Northampton, 129–32, 143, Fig. 40, 158, 161; palace excavations, 149
Northumbria, 64, 74, 77, 78, 102–6, 110, 134, 136, 150, 154, 162, 178, 179, 193, 194; kingdom, 52, 58; coins, 91
Norwich, excavations at, Fig. 1, 148, 156–7, 161, 163, 164, Fig. 49

Offa, King of Mercia, 4, 69, 95, 101, 105, 114, 116, 121–2, 133–6, 193–4; mints, 94; reign, 97, 139–46; marriage, 115; coins, 129
Offa's Dyke, 88, 144
Okehampton Park, 116
Old Minster (Winchester), 46, 49, 108, 124, 125–6, Fig. 37, 185; excavations, 148
Old Windsor, mill at, 86, 112–13
On the Fall of Britain (by Gildas), 22
Origins of English Individualism (by A. Macfarlane), 2, 3
Ormside Bowl, 146
Orwell river, 99
Ostrogoths, 54; control of Italy by, 29
Oswald, Bishop of Worcester, 179
Ouse river, 148; settlements, 103
Oxford, 10; coins, 77; pottery, 134; tenth century, 156

Pactus Legis Salicae, 31
"Pada' on coins, 71
palaces/royal sites, 117–18, 149, 184, 188, 190; Anglo-Saxon, 50, 58, 60, 61, 71, 72, 132, 135, 137; Southampton, 85; London, 88, 94; Ipswich, 99; York, 100–2; halls, 112–13; Northampton, 129; estates, 141–2
palaeopathological studies, 172, 174, 178, 183–4, 193; Anglo-Saxon cemeteries, 32, 40; Hamwic, 83; cemeteries, 107–8
parishes, 28, 168, 170, 172, 180, 182, 184; creation of, 36; boundaries, 63
Paul the Deacon, 118
Paulinus, mission of, 58
Pavia, 86
Pecsaetan tribe, 46, Fig. 20; burials, 64, 65
Penda, King of Mercia, 57, 69
Pepin of Herstal, 86; coins/coinage, 72–3, 76; death of, 90; expansion, 92; coin reforms, 91, 97

Pepin III: coins, 74; coin reforms, 101; conquests, 117
Pepin, son of Charlemagne, 121
Petersfinger cemetery, 28
Picts, 17
Pirenne, H., 121
plough, 183
Po valley: church, 45; agriculture in, 120
Pocock, J.C.A., 3
pollen analysis, 167; from Rhineland, 30
Porlaksson, H., 89
Portchester Castle, 26, 81, 132, 137, 168, 170, 184
pottery, 15, 16, 17, 20, 26, 28, 29, 32, 33, 37, 38, 41, 50, 55, 56, 83, 84, 87, 90, 95, 96, 99, 101, 102, 106, 120, 134, 135, 141, 142, 156, 157, 159, 161, 164, 170, 179, 188, 193, 200
Procopius, 23
Provence, 54, 56, 72, 84

quarrying industry, 160, 172
Quentovic, 55, 72, 84, 86
quernstones, 84, 85, 136, 200
Quirk, R., 124, 126

Ramsbury (Wiltshire), smithy, 141–2
Raunds (Northamptonshire), 26, 61, 71, 109, 111, 112, 139, 170–4, 183–4, 194, 201
Ravenna, 45
Reculver (Kent), 92, 101, 122
Redwald, King of East Anglia, 56
Reece, R., 20, 22
Regulus Concordia, 179
Renfrew, A.C., 6, 7, 8
Repton (Derbyshire), 126–8, 149, 153–4
Rhine/Rhineland, 16, 24, 30, 72–3, 120, 134, 164
Rhone valley, 54
Richborough (Kent), 92
Rigold, S., 7
Rivenhall villa (Essex), 16, 17, 25–6
Rochester, Bishop of, 96
Rodwell, K. and W., 16–17
Roffe, D., 154
Roskilde, 159
Roystone Grange (Derbyshire), 3
Ruin, The, Anglo-Saxon poem, 49, 132
Runciman, W.G., 139
runes, on coins, 77
Russia: Roman trade with, 9, 119, 136; revolution, 196

Sabine Hills, 117
Sahlins, M., 4, 187–9

St Albans, 20, 32, 49
St Augustine, 91; missions, 4, 43, 49, 92, 190; age, 53
St Cuthbert, 102, 191; grave, 46–8; gifts to, 52; coffin, 108
St Gall Plan, 119
St Swithun, Bishop of Winchester, 122; tomb, 126; church, 148
St Wilfred, 102
Salin Style I, 28
Salisbury, 148
Sancton cemetery, 78, 102
Sandwich: trading site, 92; church, 93
salt extraction: Fens, 108; industry, 160
Sandings (Suffolk), 8, 99
Santa Sofia Benevento, 104
Saracen raids, 147
Sarre (Kent), 55, 92, 93
Sawyer, P., 200
Scots raids, 17
sculpture, 129, 148
Sellwood Forest (Somerset), 32
Service, E., 4, 12, 71
Severn Valley, 78
Shanks, M., 196
Shennan, S., 168
Shore Forts (Saxon), 24, 26
shroud burials, 106
Sicily, churches from, 45
Sigebehrt, King of Wessex, 91
Silchester, 16
Sims-Williams, P., 4, 23
Skerne (North Yorkshire), 174
slaves: theft of, 31; trade, 33; ranking, 39; gifts of, 41
Smart, V., 162
Smith, Adam, 150–1, 185
Smith, R., 3, 18
soapstone, 120
social stratification, 1, 2, 38–40, 41, 56, 57, 67, 69, 70, 112
Solent, 85
South Cadbury, 32–3, 34, Fig. 9, 158–9, 188
Speyer, 46
Spong Farm (Norfolk), cemetery, Fig. 8
Sri Lanka, Roman trade with, 9
Stamford, 164; excavations, 154; pottery/ pottery production, 161, 179
steam engines, 150
Steng Moss (Co. Durham), pollen cores, 167
Stenton, Sir Frank, 116; on Mercian kings, 69
stirrups, 174–6
Stonea (Cambridgeshire), 17, Fig. 5

strap ends and tags, 24, 25, 136, 137, Fig. 49, 146
Stuckert, C.M., on cemeteries, 32
Sulgrave (Northamptonshire), 168, 170, 184
Sutton Hoo, Figs 13 and 14; ship burial at, 39, 46–7, 48; Redwald, 56; and Yeavering, 58; metalwork, 60; survey, 99; burial, 106, 108
Sweden, barrows, 48
Synod of Whitby, 44

Tamworth watermill, Fig. 44, 140
Taplow barrow, 46
Tassilo Chalice, 136
taxation systems, 176; Roman Britain, 13; collection, 16; Northumbria, 64; food rents, 89, 112; Carolingia, 117; Danelaw, 154–5, 168
Taylor, H.M., 180
temples, 29; Yeavering, 58
textiles: trade, 55; Brandon (Suffolk), 106; production of, 160; Frankish, 188; Chinese, 193
Thames valley: settlements, 20, 26; cemeteries, 28, 187; district, 77; farms along, 94; coins, 95–6; mills on, 113; capture, 134, 143; boundary, 144; mints, 156
Thanet, Isle of (Kent), 92, 96
Thetford (Norfolk), 157, 161
Thirlings (Northumberland), 62
tile production, 120
Tilley, C., 196–8
Tours, 161
Trent valley, 20, 128, 153
Tribal Hidage, 25, 57, 58, 59, Fig. 16, 64–5, 66, 95, 187, 191
tribute, 63, 73, 186
Tunisia: African Red Slipware from, 32; churches, 45
Tweddle, D., 104

Valsgärde-Vendel, barrows, 48
Vandals, raids, 17
"Vanimundus', on coins, 71
Verona, 86
Vierck, H., 31, 64
Vince, A., 134; on London, 94–5

Wales, 66, 144; in sub-Roman period, 36
Wallace-Hadrill, J.M., 92, 194–5; on East Anglian dynasty, 56; on legislation, 58
Wallingford (Oxfordshire): coin distribution, 77; market, 158
wall plaster, 126

Wantsum Channel (Kent), 55, 92, 97, 122
Wareham (Dorset), 158
watermills, 86, 112–13, 140, Fig. 44
Wealdon iron industry, 17
Wealth of Nations (by Adam Smith), 151
weapons, 174, 176, 181; in graves, 30, 39; helmet at York, 109; production, 141; swords, 143, 160
Wearmouth, monastery, 71
Weber, Max, 150
wergild, 192
Wessex, Kingdom of, 155, 162, 166, 168, 177, 178, 179, 185, 194, 195, 196, 198, 200; royal house, 32, 33; ranking, 39–40; Church in Dorset, 46; bishoprics, 49, 50; monasteries, 52; mints, 57; coins, 74, 90–1, 93; kings, 76–7, 101; road systems, 80; trade, 86, 87, 88, 89, 96; laws, 92, 192; emporia, 94; social change, 97; under Alfred, 123–4; supremacy, 126; warfare, 142–3; towns, 147, 158; church, 148; rivalry with Danes, 150, 153–4; villas, 154; settlements, 182; Cerdic, 188
West Stow (Suffolk), 26, 34, 36, Fig. 11, 37, 38, 62, Fig. 18, 189, 190
wharfs, in London, 164
Wharram Percy (North Yorkshire), 154, 170–2, Fig. 53
Wheeler, R.E.M., 8
Whitby: monastery, 71; coins, 78; excavations, 102, 106
Wicken Bonhunt (Essex), 132–3, 135, 137, 139, 146
Wigber Low (Derbyshire), 64, 65, Fig. 20
Wiglaf, King of Mercia, 126–8
Wijster (Netherlands), 24
Willibord, 115
wills, as documentary sources, 6
Wilson, A., 46, 48, 53
Winchcombe (Gloucestershire) 128

Winchester, 20, Fig. 26, 108, 124, Fig. 37, 179, 185; continuity at, 17; Roman, 25, 32; excavations, 46, 49–50, 71; streets, 86–7; bishopric, 94; buildings, 132; Roman walls, 147; Old Minster, 48; New Minster, 155–6; market, 158; pottery production, 164
Windsor (Berkshire), 94
Wing (Buckinghamshire), 128
Witham Pins, 129, 146
Withington (Gloucestershire), villa estate, 52
Witton (Norfolk), 62
Wood, I., 31, 188
Wood, M., 1
wool production, 84, 136, 160, 164
Worcester: cathedral, 128; excavations, 143
Worcester, Bishop of, 96
Wormald, P.: on York, 102; on Bede, 105; on royal halls, 112; on Offa's Dyke, 144
Wrigley, E.A., 151
Wroxeter, 20
Wulfhere, King of Mercia, 57, 58, 69
Wulfred, Archbishop of Canterbury, 122, 124
Wystan, King of Mercia, 126

Yeavering (*Ad Gefrin*), 60, Fig. 17, 61, 190; palaces, 10, 58; theatre, 86; excavations, 110, 113; halls, 129; era of, 132
York (Eoforwic and Jorvik), 20, 49, 51, Fig. 15, 53, 71, 78, 92, 148, 153–4, 157–9, 160, 161, 162–5, 179, 194; bishopric, 94; excavations, 102–4, 109, 135–7
Yorke., B., 49, 50, 132, 185